Maria Parloa

Miss Parloa's Young Housekeeper

Designed Especially to Aid Beginners; Economical Receipts for those ...

Maria Parloa

Miss Parloa's Young Housekeeper
Designed Especially to Aid Beginners; Economical Receipts for those ...

ISBN/EAN: 9783744786348

Printed in Europe, USA, Canada, Australia, Japan

Cover: Foto ©Andreas Hilbeck / pixelio.de

More available books at **www.hansebooks.com**

MISS PARLOA'S
YOUNG HOUSEKEEPER

Designed Especially to aid Beginners

ECONOMICAL RECEIPTS FOR THOSE WHO ARE COOKING
FOR TWO OR THREE

BY

MARIA PARLOA

FOUNDER OF TWO SCHOOLS OF COOKERY AND AUTHOR OF "THE
APPLEDORE COOK BOOK," "MISS PARLOA'S KITCHEN COM-
PANION," "MISS PARLOA'S NEW COOK BOOK AND
MARKETING GUIDE," "FIRST PRINCIPLES OF
HOUSEHOLD MANAGEMENT," ETC.

ILLUSTRATED

BOSTON
DANA ESTES AND CO.

PREFACE.

WHEREVER I have gone in the last fifteen years in following my calling as a teacher of cooking, earnest appeals have been made to me to plan my next book for the especial benefit of those who have just begun, or who are about to begin, to keep house for two or three. The young wives want to know how to buy supplies for a small family; how to cook economically and well; what to do with food that is left over from any meal; and numerous other things pertaining to their daily work. At last I have set about telling them. They will find that it is not necessary to have an immense income in order to live well. Strict adherence to careful instructions will, with a little good sense thrown in, enable a young housekeeper to accomplish wonders. She can practise economy and at the same time have a table that is attractively and wholesomely spread,—something for which most housekeepers strive without knowing the best way to reach the goal. Of course, not all who begin to build a home are obliged to count every dollar they expend. For the benefit of those who can start in their married life with a servant to aid them and money enough to indulge in luxuries, some special information and advice are given. But, after all, the aim has been particularly to lend a hand to those whose incomes are moderate; to make the book a simple one, — one that even a girl may take interest in studying. If it prove of value to those young women who are establishing homes for themselves, its chief mission will be accomplished.

M. P.

ROXBURY, MASS., 1893.

CONTENTS.

	PAGE
A Word with the Young Housewife	1
About Furnishing the House	4
Division of the Household Work	22
Some Things to be Learned Early	31
Work on Washing Day	44
In the Dining-Room	52
Buying Food and Caring for It	60
Soups	80
Fish	96
How to Cook Meat	112
Sauces for Meat and Fish	164
Salads	172
Vegetables	177
Miscellaneous Dishes	200
Bread in Various Forms	217
Cake	241
Pastry	253
Puddings	260
Sweets	289
Beverages	300
Preserves and Pickles	307

CONTENTS.

	PAGE
For Those who Live on Farms	324
Care of the Sick	338
When Cleaning House	352
Odd Bits of Useful Knowledge	361

Index	391

MISS PARLOA'S
YOUNG HOUSEKEEPER.

CHAPTER I.

A WORD WITH THE YOUNG HOUSEWIFE.

IF one were to get a hundred reputed good housekeepers to come together and give their ideas of what constitutes good housekeeping, no two would agree upon all points. There are essentials which every one recognizes, but there are many things which one housekeeper considers of the greatest importance, whereas another may think the same things of minor consequence or of no consequence whatever. It is a sad fact that some good housekeepers are not good home-makers. The young housekeeper should bear in mind that, while it is essential that the home should be clean and orderly, and the food well cooked and regularly served, this does not make the home. One can get all these comforts in a well conducted hotel or boarding-house, but the man or woman is to be pitied who has no higher ideal of a home than what is furnished by a hotel or boarding-house, no matter how sumptuous. A selfish woman can make a good housekeeper, so far as the keeping of the house in perfect running order is concerned, but it is difficult for a selfish or lazy woman to make a home. A young woman who would create an ideal home must possess some judgment, and a heart in which charity and sympathy have a large place.

My idea of good housekeeping is where a woman keeps her home sweet and orderly; provides simple, well cooked food; makes her home so restful and cheerful that all who come into it shall be better for breathing the atmosphere of kindness and cheerfulness that pervades the place; and where the household machinery always runs smoothly because of the constant thoughtfulness of the mistress of the house. A place like this is truly a home, and the woman at the head of it deserves the respect and admiration of everybody. I have seen such homes among the rich and among the poor, for neither wealth nor poverty prevents the right person from filling with the atmosphere of comfort and happiness the house of which she is the mistress.

A housekeeper's duties are many, and, to one nervous and fretful, they are exhausting. What seems to the woman of good digestion and steady nerves a mere trifle, to be laughed at and forgotten, may appear to the delicate, nervous woman a calamity to be wept over. Much of the irritability from which women suffer is due to their expectation of too much of themselves and others. If women would be reconciled to the inevitable, they might make everybody about them much happier. A choice bit of china may be broken. Is it worth the while to make the whole household miserable for what cannot be helped? A dish may be spoiled in the cooking. It will not help your digestion or that of the family to fret over it. You may be naturally very orderly, but some members of the family may not. Wil' it pay to make them and yourself uncomfortable by worrying over the matter? If your servant or any other member of the household should not come up to your standard, throw the mantle of charity over the faults that you cannot remedy, and pray that others may be equally charitable to you.

The good housekeeper will certainly look well to the ways of her household, but her eyes will be those of the kind, just woman. She will not look for miracles; she will not expect to get the best supplies and service when paying only the lowest price; she will not hope to make something out of nothing; she will be brave enough to live within her means, even if they be small; she will not be afraid to do her work honestly and well; and, finally, she will be so true to herself at all times, and so adjust and simplify her domestic duties that she will not exhaust body and mind in trying to do two persons' work for the sake of "keeping up appearances." How many families lose all the comforts of home life in this senseless effort! If you stop to consider what this "keeping up appearances" means it puts the people in a very unenviable light, for it simply means that people want to give you a false impression of their possessions. No member of the family is so much injured by this deceptive life as the housekeeper. All her power of body and mind is bent to the task of making the best possible appearance with the smallest amount of expenditure. Intellect is cramped in the battle and all repose is gone from home life. No matter how good the housekeeping, the spirit of the home-maker is not there. No young woman has a right to dwarf her life for such a purpose. Let her make the most of the means at her command, but let her never sacrifice her physical, moral, and mental well-being to a desire to make a display disproportionate to her circumstances, for that is not good housekeeping.

CHAPTER II.

ABOUT FURNISHING THE HOUSE.

IN these days of lavish ornamentation and bric-à-brac, the young housekeeper must be on guard against filling her house with such furnishings as would make it stuffy and cause it to lack individuality. The home should be an index to the character of the family. Do not furnish your house fully until you have lived in it a while. Buy at first only such furniture as you need for comfort. When you are settled you can study the needs of each part of the house, and, after you have fully determined exactly what you want, buy it whenever you see an advantageous chance.

Never decide hastily upon a piece of furniture; purchase for the future as much as for the present. It is true fashions change in furniture from year to year, but it is only people of large means who can follow a fashion of this kind. The plain, elegant styles are quite expensive as compared with the ordinary pieces which are turned out of factories by the thousand, and which are covered with ornamentation to catch the popular fancy. One quickly wearies of such furniture; besides, it is not so well made as the plainer styles, and therefore gets out of order very easily.

Get the things necessary for kitchen, bedroom, dining-room, and sitting-room before doing anything about the parlor, and let every article be of good quality, no matter how plain. Make an estimate of what you can spend on each room; then get the best things possible.

What to Buy for the Chambers.

One can get a chamber set for as low a sum as twenty-five dollars; but the prices run up rapidly until the hundreds are reached. Handsome, well made sets, with little or no ornamentation (the quality of the wood, and the finish, giving them a simple elegance not found in more showy pieces) cost from forty to seventy-five dollars. The set includes bedstead, dressing-case, wash-stand, towel-rack, a small table, two common chairs, and a rocker. The more expensive sets have the English wash-stand. No marble is used with the finest chamber furniture. The springs, mattresses, etc., must be purchased separately, as a rule. Have good ones. Have shades and plain muslin curtains for the windows. Stain the floors, if possible. If you prefer not to do that, use straw matting, with one rug beside the bed and another in front of the wash-stand. In buying the toilet set select one that has a plain, fine shape and simple decoration.

Dining-room Furniture.

There are two articles which one must have for this room: a table and some chairs. It often happens that the young housekeeper, not realizing the necessity for having these of generous size, and well made, chooses articles that appear good, but which, in a short time, become unstable. Oak is the most satisfactory wood for the dining-room. Have the table of good width, as a narrow one never looks well. The chairs should be strong, broad-seated, and with high backs.

Having the chairs and table, you can wait for the other things, although a sideboard table is a desirable thing, if one can afford it. If you cannot have exactly what you want, be patient. Sideboards, sideboard tables, and china closets of glass all come in such simple yet tasteful designs that one may be sure to like them all one's life. It will pay to wait for such a piece of furniture. Have a hard-wood floor, if you can; otherwise have the floor stained. Just enough of the floor may be stained to make a deep border, and a simple rug be placed in the centre of the room. Shades, without any draperies, answer very well for this room.

Comfort in the Sitting-room.

In the sitting-room, where the family gathers for the evening, and where some members of the household spend a good part of each day, put all the comfort you can. Let it be one of the largest and brightest rooms in the house. There should be a bookcase, a firm table of good size, several comfortable chairs, a couch with plenty of pillows, a good lamp, with a shade that will not try the eyes, some pictures, a few plants and shades and draperies that will soften, but not exclude, the light. If possible, have an open fireplace. Let this be a room that shall always be remembered as one of the pleasantest spots in the world. When possible, have a hard-wood or a stained floor, with a rug in the centre.

Selecting Carpets and Rugs.

In buying carpets remember that the best are always the cheapest. The more limited one's means are, the more essential it is that only a good article shall be purchased. The best quality of body Brussels will outwear two or more of the cheaper tapestry carpets. A finely woven smooth ingrain carpet may cost half a dollar more per yard than one of common texture, but it will be cheaper in the end. Nothing is more unsatisfactory than one of the loosely woven straw mattings. A fine matting, costing say from sixty to seventy cents a yard, will last a dozen years or more, with constant wear, too. It is so fine that but little dust sifts through, and the strands do not pull apart, as in coarser grades. Rugs for the centre of the room can be made from a body Brussels, with a border to match.

ABOUT FURNISHING THE HOUSE. 7

They should be tacked down. Japanese cotton rugs, pretty and durable, cost from three to six dollars. They are good for bedrooms, bath-rooms, and sitting-rooms. Buy handsome rugs whenever you can afford to. They are a good investment; for, unlike carpets, they do not wear out, and you can hand them down in the family the same as silver or diamonds. A beautiful Oriental rug is a joy forever. In selecting one be particular to see that the colors are rich, and have some brightness. In general, when choosing carpets, have the groundwork rather light, and the colors somewhat neutral. Such a carpet will always look clean, and you will not feel the need of shutting out the sunlight through fear of the carpet's fading.

Choosing a Dinner and Tea Set.

To the young housekeeper of limited means the choice of her table china is quite an important matter. One can get sets for seven and eight dollars, but I should not advise buying anything cheaper than a fifteen-dollar set. If a decorated set be wanted, take one having soft tints, because people soon get weary of seeing pronounced colors or patterns.

Very pretty English sets of one hundred and fifty pieces, decorated in blue, may be had for fifteen dollars. Minton sets of one hundred and thirty-six pieces, basket-pattern border, and decorated in a fine shade of blue, are offered as low as twenty-five dollars.

American china sets in colored decorations are sold at about the same price as the English. Plain white French china sets of one hundred and thirty pieces cost about thirty-five dollars. The quality and prices rise rapidly until sets costing hundreds of dollars are reached.

In making a choice from the great variety displayed there are several things to consider. For instance, what price can you afford to pay? Is the style one that will be lasting, and are the goods durable? It often happens that the decoration of a cheap set is much daintier than that of some of the more expensive kinds.

The English and American wares are thick, and do not chip or break easily; but when they do chip, the broken part soon becomes dark. The glaze on these wares cracks readily when exposed to a high temperature. In a dinner set one does not notice particularly that the ware is thick; but thickness in the cups and saucers is disagreeably noticeable, especially in the English wares. Then, too, unless one get a " stock pattern," it will often be difficult and expensive to replace a broken piece. The dealers intend to carry a pattern five years; after that one cannot feel sure of replacing a broken piece without much delay and expense. Plain white French china can always be replaced; the glaze does not crack when exposed to a high temperature; if chipped, the broken part does not become discolored; the ware is in good shapes; the cups and saucers are delicate and pretty, so that a full set of the china is desirable, which, to my mind, is not the case with the English or American wares.

In buying the French china it is wise to get plates with rolled edges. It seems to me, all things considered, that the French china is the most satisfactory, unless there is to be rather rough handling, when I would advise the purchase of the English or American productions. In that case I would further advise that only a dinner set be bought, and that something daintier be taken for the tea and breakfast table.

Odd cups and saucers are quite proper, and give variety and brightness to the table. Odd dessert and salad plates, also, are to be preferred to the regulation sets. The dessert plates and cups and saucers that may be picked up here and there in one's travels are constant reminders of pleasant experiences.

ABOUT FURNISHING THE HOUSE. 9

Dainty Things for the Table.

Glass has largely taken the place of silver on some of the most elegant tables, many housekeepers collecting and prizing cut-glass as they would jewels; but the woman of moderate means and good taste will find it possible to set her table with plain, clear glass of dainty and elegant shapes which will add brilliancy to the entire table service. Water bottles, or carafes, as they are commonly called, are much used, and are a great convenience. Individual salt-cellars are again used instead of the salt-shakers which were so popular for many years. These salt-cellars come in glass, dainty china, and silver. A small silver salt-spoon is placed by each one. The china and silver are by all odds the most effective on the table. Pepper bottles of odd designs are placed by the salt. Castors are not in favor.

Bread-and-butter plates may be used at all meals, but are particularly suited for breakfast, luncheon, and tea. They are placed at the left of the regular plate. When the butter and bread are passed, you put them on this plate, dispensing with the small butter plate. These little plates are a great help in keeping the table-cloth clean. They come in several sizes and tasteful patterns.

Fashions in Cutlery.

Table cutlery, as the designation was formerly understood, included all the knives and forks, nut-picks, etc. To-day, among well-to-do people, all the forks, except that which belongs to the carving set, are either sterling-silver or silver-plated. It is astonishing how the table appliances have multiplied in this luxurious age. For the fish course there are sterling-silver knives and forks of special shapes, and a broad silver knife and fork for serving the fish. Oyster forks of another shape are considered indispensable when raw oysters are served. Knives and forks of medium size are used for entrées, the forks being silver and the knives having silver, silver-plated, or steel blades. For the meat course the forks are silver and the blades of the knives steel. The dessert knives and forks are silver-plated; the butter knives that are placed by the little bread-and-butter plates are silver. So it will be seen that the cutlery of to-day does not mean for fine tables what it did formerly. Common knives and forks are made with flat tangs, to which pieces of wood or bone are joined for the handle. In fine knives the tang is made round, and is pressed into a round groove made in the handle. Sometimes this is fastened with a rivet, sometimes with a spring, and again with some cement.

The handles of the finest knives are weighted, unless made of a heavy material like silver. This is important, as it causes the knife to lie flat upon the table. Handles are made of sterling silver, mother-of-pearl, ivory, grained celluloid, plain celluloid, etc. Buckhorn and imitations of buckhorn are used a great deal for carving sets. Ivory has been used the most for the best class of knives and forks, but in furnace-heated houses the ivory is apt to split. Even the greatest care does not insure against it, and dealers find that this often happens while the goods are kept in their stores. As a substitute for ivory, celluloid, grained celluloid, and ivorine are coming into use. These substances neither crack, stain, nor turn yellow, as does the ivory; which, of course, is a great consideration. Mother-of-pearl handles cost about twice as much as ivory. With proper care one can keep them in good condition through a lifetime. Sterling-silver handles are very handsome and satisfactory. Knives and forks with metal handles, which are plated with the rest of the knife or fork, are the most commonly used, because they are so easily cared for and are not liable to get out of order. They are, however, not found upon elegant tables.

WHAT IS NEEDED IN THE KITCHEN.

The kitchen is so important a part of the home that the furnishing should be such as to make the work there both easy and successful. The following list may aid the young housekeeper when making her purchases. The woman with a limited purse may find that she will have to strike out many things from the list, while the woman with a large house and money in plenty will probably extend it.

The Range.

Upon no one article of household furniture do the comfort and well-being of the family depend so much as upon the kitchen range or stove. A poor range will spoil not only food, but also good temper and happiness; whereas the right sort of range, well treated, will be a source of the greatest comfort and economy. No matter what else you feel you must economize in, do not let it be in buying the kitchen range. Some ranges have reached such a degree of perfection that it is hard to see where they can be improved. The plainer the range the easier it will be to keep it clean, and of course the cost will be less than if it be trimmed very much. Before making a choice, examine every part thoroughly. Always try to get one that has a large oven in proportion to the size of the range. There should be plenty of dampers that can be used to hasten the fire or to check it, so that it will keep twelve hours, if necessary. Ranges are made that will do this. Learn all the characteristics of your range, and treat it well; then it will be an invaluable friend to you.

In the kitchen, as in every other part of the house, it is economy to furnish with good articles. Poor cooking utensils are never cheap. In buying iron utensils, be sure to get those that are thoroughly finished. The steel goods come higher than the cast-iron, but they are so smooth that they are four times as valuable in the kitchen as the rougher makes.

The granite or agate ware lightens the labors in the kitchen wonderfully. It is, however, very expensive, and is not so well made as formerly. When buying this ware, examine it closely to see that there is no defect in the enamel. A careful housekeeper who does her own work will find this ware a great comfort, it is so light, smooth, and clean; and with good treatment it will last well.

Mixing-bowls come in yellow and white ware. The white is stone china, and is more durable than the yellow; and although it costs more than the latter, it is cheaper in the end. A steamer of medium size is one of the most useful utensils. If it be light and simple, it will be used frequently for making puddings and for warming over food, etc. The cheapest kind is made of tin, and in two parts, the lower part being a deep saucepan, into which the water is put, and the upper part a round pan with a perforated bottom. Be particular to see that the cover and all other parts fit well.

Here is a list of articles with which all kitchens should be supplied : —

List of Articles most in Use.

Basins, of granite ware, — one three-pint, one two-quart, one one-gallon.
Bowls: yellow, — two two-quart, one three-quart, one one-gallon, two six-quart; white, — six, each holding about a pint; two smooth ones, each holding about a quart.
Bread board.
Bread pans, two, for small loaves.
Broilers, — one for fish, one for other uses.
Broom.
Bucket, or tin box, for sugar.

Cake pans, three, — one deep, two shallow.
Carving knife and fork.
Case knives and forks, six each.
Chairs, three, — one to be low and comfortable.
Chopping knife and bowl.
Coffee-pot.
Colander.
Cups and saucers, half a dozen.
Dipper, long-handled.
Dishcloths, two, — one being of wire.
Dishpans, two.
Dish rack.

Double boilers, two, — one holding one quart, the other two.
Dredgers for salt, pepper, and flour.
Dripping-pans, two, — large and small.
Duster.
Dustpan.
Egg-beater.
Flour scoop.
Flour sieve.
Frying-basket.
Frying-pans, — one, small, with short handle; four with long handles, Nos. 1, 2, 3, 5.
Glass jars for rice, etc.
Graters, — one for nutmegs; one coarse, for general use.
Griddle.
Lemon squeezer, glass.
Measuring cups, two.
Meat board.
Meat rack, small.
Moulding board.
Muffin pans, two, — each holding eight or twelve muffins.
Pitchers, four, for milk, etc.
Plates, one dozen.
Platters, two stone-china, for meat.
Pudding mould, melon, three-pint.
Quart measure.
Range.
Rolling-pin.
Roll-pans, French, holding six or eight rolls.
Scotch bowl, No. 4.
Skewers, set of steel.
Soap-shaker.
Spice boxes or jars.
Spoons, — six teaspoons, two table spoons, two wooden spoons, two large iron spoons.
Steamer.
Stewpans, — two one-quart, two two-quart, two three-quart, one six-quart.
Stone pots, several small ones, with covers, for various kinds of meal.
Stove-brush.
Strainers, two, small, — one for general use, the other for gravy; also one of fine wire.
Tables, two; if possible, have one covered with zinc or enamel cloth.
Teakettle.
Teapot.
Tin boxes for bread and cake.
Tin plates, four, deep.
Tin sheet.
Towels, — three kinds for dishes, and others for the hands.
Vegetable masher.

FURNISHING THE LINEN CLOSET.

In olden times the bride came to her new home with a generous supply of linen, the greater part of which was spun and woven by her own hands; in many cases, indeed, the flax was raised and prepared for the spinning-wheel by her. In some parts of Europe this custom still exists. The bride of to-day takes great pains and pride in providing her household linen, many months being given to dainty sewing and embroidery. Each article has stitched into it many bright hopes and day dreams. Nothing else in the furnishing of the home has blended with it so many tender, loving thoughts, and to the woman of sentiment it is more sacred than almost any other household possession. Once acquired, this love for fine household linen will cling to a woman all her life. Indeed, what material thing can she bring to her new home that will give more pleasure than a generous supply for her linen closet?

Imported Linens.

Irish, French, Scotch and English table linens cover many grades, from the coarsest to the finest weaving and the most elaborate patterns. All the new designs are large, but in some of the choicest damasks it is possible to get small patterns, if they be preferred. The damask sold by the yard rarely reaches a higher price than two dollars and a half. If one wish for especially pleasing designs and extremely fine quality, it will be necessary to buy the set, — table-cloth and one dozen napkins. The usual width of the best table damask is two yards and a half, but it may be three yards in width. The cloths come from two and a half to four yards in length. In these handsome cloths the border is deep, and the centre frequently perfectly plain.

Table-cloths and Napkins.

The range in quality and price of table linen is greater than that of almost any other fabric. It is a long step from the materials that are so coarse, so loosely woven that they might be used for sieves, to the double damask, so fine that even under a magnifying glass it is almost impossible to discern the threads. One can buy three or four yards of the coarse fabric for about a dollar, and it is possible to be asked one hundred times as much for a dozen napkins and a table-cloth, three or four yards long, of the finer quality.

ABOUT FURNISHING THE HOUSE. 15

But the average housekeeper does not go to these extremes. It does, however, often happen that a woman with a limited purse, and a thousand calls upon it, makes the mistake of buying table linen of too inferior a grade. It is not economy to purchase a mixture of cotton and linen. Better a coarse all-linen table cloth than a fine one with part cotton, which may look attractive in the store, but cannot be laundered well, whereas the pure linen will improve with age and wear. In purchasing table linen the questions that the housekeeper should ask herself are : Will it be subject to hard wear, and be laundered by inexperienced hands? Can I afford to replenish it frequently? Shall it be fine and beautiful, or shall it be durable, with as much beauty as possible under the circumstances?

The finest goods are of Irish and French manufacture ; but the German, while coarse, wear wonderfully well, and some of them have very handsome designs. Nothing in the way of linen lasts longer than the half-bleached damask, and if one live in the country, this may be bleached to a snowy whiteness in a few months. In purchasing these German goods it is wise to get a cloth that costs at least one dollar and a half or two dollars per yard. A cloth of this kind will outwear several of the cheaper grades that are mixed with cotton, and if properly laundered it will always look well. Of course, one can get in these goods a fair piece of table linen at seventy-five cents or a dollar per yard, but the better quality will be found to be the cheaper in the end. Dinner, luncheon, and tea sets may be had, the cloth costing no more than if bought by the yard, with the advantage of having a border all around it.

A piece of heavy felt or double-faced Canton flannel will be required under the table-cloth. It will cost about eighty cents a yard. It is a good plan to get one that will answer when the table is enlarged for guests. It can be folded double when the table is small.

Size and Quality of Napkins.

Fashion has decreed that a napkin shall not be put on the table a second time until it has been washed. Few housekeepers, however, have the means to provide themselves with such a supply of napkins, not to speak of the laundress to care for them; so the napkin ring is still a necessity in the average household. It is important, however, that the supply be large enough to admit of their being changed two or three times a week. For general use a dinner napkin is to be preferred, unless a separate set of table-cloths and napkins be desired for breakfast. In that case the napkins should be smaller than for dinner. All napkins are finished with a plain hem, or are hemstitched.

Fringe is rarely used, except on fancy doilies. The plain square napkin comes in all sizes, from twenty inches to the size of the dinner napkins, which measure twenty-seven inches; and the cost is anywhere from one dollar and a half to fifty dollars a dozen. At five or six dollars a dozen one can get napkins that are good enough for ordinary use. The cheaper and smaller ones are unsatisfactory. Whenever possible, the napkin should match the cloth. One cloth will outwear two sets of napkins; therefore it is well to get two dozen napkins to each cloth. One cannot err in laying in a generous stock of plain ones, but the style of the small fancy napkins is constantly changing, and one should not buy too many of them at a time.

A Word about Doilies.

Small square or round doilies are used a great deal under finger bowls, Roman punch, and sherbet glasses. These dainty bits of napery can be purchased in all the stores where embroidery and materials for needlework are sold; also in the linen stores. These doilies are either

ABOUT FURNISHING THE HOUSE. 17

hemstitched or fringed. The embroidery is usually in washable silks, fine flowers or Dresden patterns being the favorites. Doilies also come in Irish point, Mexican work, and various kinds of lace. Larger doilies for bread, cake, cheese, etc., are embroidered in white or colored silks, with appropriate mottoes. Ladies who wish to do this kind of work for themselves, or their friends, can send to a stamping and embroidery store for a sample doily, and the materials for a dozen or more. One should aim to get as much variety as possible in color and design in the dozen. A very fine linen is the material generally used.

At the Oriental stores there can be found a small doily, of a crêpe-like material, thickly embroidered with silk, or silver and gold thread. They come with and without a fringe, the fringed ones costing more than twice as much as those without. I prefer those without the fringe for table use. These doilies can be washed, but it must be with great care. If the housekeeper will be careful to wash and iron her doilies herself, they will always look fresh and dainty. Make a strong suds with hot water and white castile soap; wash the doilies in this, and rinse them in several warm waters. Squeeze them very dry, and spread them on a clean towel, and cover another towel over them. Roll up tight and iron immediately.

Tea, Carving, and Tray Cloths.

For the small tables that are set for five o'clock teas and card parties, etc., there are many pretty and inexpensive cloths. Plain linen, with a plain or double row of hemstitching, makes a satisfactory cloth. The cost is about one dollar for a cloth measuring a yard square; plain damask, with hemstitching, costs from one dollar and a half to two dollars a square yard, and one dollar more for a cloth measuring two square yards. Some long damask cloths, with open-work borders and a fringe, cost four or five dollars. Small hemstitched cloths of linen and damask come for carving cloths, tray cloths, and centre pieces. They cost all the way from twenty-five cents upward. These are useful in protecting the table, and they may be made decorative by embroidery.

Sheets and Pillow Cases.

Sheets should always be of generous length and width; never less than two yards and three quarters long, with the breadth, of course, depending upon the width of the bed. While linen sheets are desirable, they are not within the means of all housekeepers of even fair incomes. Cotton cloth makes a most satisfactory all-the-year-round sheet, and a good quality can be purchased at from twenty-five cents to seventy-five cents per yard, the cloth being from two yards to two and a half wide. Indeed, one can buy good sheets already made, two yards and a half wide, for one dollar and a quarter or one dollar and a half apiece. It is always more economical to buy the cloth and make them at home, for two hems do not mean much work. Unbleached sheeting may be made up, and bleached on the grass. Buy unbleached cotton for servants' sheets and pillow cases, but do not make them too small. If the bed linen be made of generous proportions it will protect the bedding, and be more comfortable for the sleepers. Linen sheets three yards long can be bought for from five to fourteen dollars per pair. Pillow cases to match sell from two to three dollars and a half per pair. The finest are hemstitched.

Bed Spreads and Blankets.

For many years the honeycomb and Marseilles spreads have been almost universally used. They are still sold in large quantities, and will always be popular, for they need only to be hemmed in order to be made ready for use.

ABOUT FURNISHING THE HOUSE. 19

They do not rumple readily, they keep clean a long time, and are, indeed, a most serviceable article. The Marseilles quilts cost from two to fifteen dollars. Some come in colors; but let no housekeeper be tempted by their beauty, for she will find it a difficult matter to make them harmonize with the other furnishings of her rooms. Dimity is being used again. It costs from two dollars and a half to four dollars and a half a spread. If one wish to make a bolster scarf to go with the dimity, it will be necessary to purchase a small spread and cut it in two. These spreads, being dainty and easily washed, are in great favor.

Materials for spreads come in all sorts of fabrics. Gobelin cloth and what is called basket cloth, both soft, pretty goods, are found two yards wide, and cost about one dollar and a half a yard. These materials are made into spreads and bolster scarfs; or, instead of the scarfs, a round bolster may be covered with the material. These spreads and scarfs are often embroidered in washable silks.

Next to bed linen and towels in plenty, one of the essentials for the health and comfort of the household is the stock of blankets. Cotton batting comforters are cheap and warm, but extremely debilitating to the sleeper; and since they cannot be washed, they are uncleanly, as compared with the woollen coverings. Use plenty of blankets instead, and have them washed frequently. For people of limited means, blankets that cost from five to six dollars a pair are serviceable. People are buying more blankets that are made of part wool and part cotton than of the all-wool patterns. This is because they can be washed frequently without shrinking. Select a smooth, soft blanket with white cotton binding. The simpler the border the longer it will please you. If possible, have a pair of summer blankets for each bed. These cost from three to ten dollars a pair. They can be washed as easily as a sheet, and are a source of the greatest comfort in hot weather. As they will last the greater part of a lifetime, get good ones. When blankets are not in use they should be folded smoothly, pinned in sheets, and placed on shelves in the linen closet.

Bath and Bedroom Towels.

In nothing relating to the supplies of her house does the average housekeeper make so many errors as in the matter of towels. It has not been wholly her fault in the past, but it certainly will be in the time to come, if bright borders and deep fringes decorate the towels with which she furnishes her chambers and bath-rooms. As in the past, so it is now: there is nothing so satisfactory for general use as the huckaback towels. They are excellent for absorbing water, and the slight friction is both pleasant and healthful. They are now hemstitched, and cost from twenty-five cents to a dollar and a half apiece, according to size and quality. The goods can be bought by the yard if one prefer to make her own towels. There are huckaback towels of fancy weaving, which, hemstitched, cost from fifty cents to on dollar and a quarter apiece. Some of these are fringed, at thirty-seven and a half cents apiece. Damask towels, which are really more for show than use, cost from twenty-five cents to two dollars and a half. For the bath-room there are really so many good things that it is a difficult matter to choose. There always should be soft coarse towels that will absorb water quickly, and at the same time cause a slight friction. The towels also should be of generous size. The huckaback is always good for drying off, but there should be a good friction towel after this. Among the good bath towels are crash towels, at twenty-five cents apiece. Oxford towels, something like huckaback, but very large — 26 × 50 inches — are one dollar apiece. Imperial bath towels, of a peculiar style of weaving, absorbing water like a sponge, cost a dollar apiece. Turkish towels make an excellent friction towel, and are within the means of all. They can be bought for even less than twenty-five cents; but I would not advise anything cheaper than twenty-five or fifty cents, as a towel of this kind should be large. An article which to me seems ideal as a friction towel is the kind made of linen tape, which costs one dollar.

For Kitchen and Pantry.

There should be a generous supply of kitchen and pantry towels. Nothing is more satisfactory for glassware than the plaid linen towels. These should be kept for silver, glass, and fine china. Goods of this same character come in stripes, and cost from twelve and a half to thirty-seven and a half cents per yard. Fine Russian crash, when softened by a little wear, makes the best kitchen dish towel. It grows finer and whiter with each week's use, whereas the very coarse fabric really never softens. Every kitchen should be supplied with half a dozen stove towels. Get twilled brown cotton crash; cut it into yard-and-a-half lengths and hem it. Keep but two of these towels in the kitchen, and have one washed each day. They are to use in handling the pots and pans about the stove and oven. There should be a generous allowance of crash towels in the kitchen, as every utensil should be carefully wiped with one that is clean and dry.

The hand towels in the kitchen should be soft and smooth. Frequent wiping on the rough Russian crash will soon make the hands red and rough, as this hard fabric scratches and does not wipe dry. A twilled crash of cotton and linen, which may be bought from twelve and a half to fifteen cents a yard, makes satisfactory hand towels. There are many varieties.

CHAPTER III.

DIVISION OF THE HOUSEHOLD WORK.

IT is a perplexing task for young housekeepers to divide properly the weekly work of the household. Even when I start to write on the subject, many difficulties present themselves, as no two houses are conducted on exactly the same plan. What would be the right thing for one home would be entirely impracticable in another. The woman who does her own work, or keeps but one servant, must, of course, plan her work quite differently from the woman who keeps two or more servants. Then, too, the place and mode of living will influence the arrangement of household work. For example, in the country the style of living is much simpler than in the city; the hours are more regular, there are fewer stairs to go over, less dirt and dust accumulate, and, in short, practically all the work is done on two floors. This makes the duties of mistress and maid lighter than in the city house. The pure air, quiet surroundings, and long, uninterrupted hours make it possible for a woman to accomplish a great deal of housework in a day, and yet have leisure for reading, sewing, and quiet thinking.

But, on the other hand, the city housekeeper has her advantages, such as the house fitted with all modern conveniences; stores and markets close at hand; and, if extra or heavy work is to be done, easy means of getting men and women to do it. The changing scenes in the city take woman out of herself and the narrowing cares of home life, and keep her interested and in touch with the world, thus making her duties less irksome than they might be in a regular and monotonous life.

DIVISION OF THE HOUSEHOLD WORK. 23

Yet, no matter where one resides, there are certain daily duties that must be attended to if people would live decently and in order. I will try to map out programmes of these duties, so that the inexperienced housekeeper will be able to outline her daily work by them. It is not to be expected that these programmes will be followed exactly; they are simply suggestions which each housekeeper may adapt to the exigencies of her own household.

Every-day Duties.

As there are many routine duties that must be performed every day, I will treat of them here. Special work will have a day assigned to it. It is almost appalling to look at the list of daily duties of the household, when one remembers that it frequently happens that there is but one pair of hands to do all the work; yet there are thousands of women who are well and happy in passing their lives that way, knowing that they contribute to the health and comfort of their families. If there be system in doing the work, the burden will be materially lightened. Each member of the family has his or her duties. Habits of order and punctuality should be cultivated. Being late at meals and leaving things out of place will increase the burdens of the housekeeper in a marked degree.

What to do in the Morning.

First, make the kitchen fire; take up and sift the ashes. After brushing all the dust from the range, wash off the surface with a cloth and soap and water; then polish it with stove blacking. Rinse out the teakettle, and after the water has been running from the cold-water pipes for about five minutes, fill the kettle and place it on the fire. Sweep and dust the kitchen. Put the breakfast dishes on to heat. Air the dining-room and set the table; then prepare and serve the breakfast. Clear the breakfast table assorting the dishes and freeing them from scraps of food. Soak in cold water any dishes that are soiled with mush, milk, or eggs; put the silver in a pitcher of warm water.

Go up stairs and open the chamber windows, if they were not opened the first thing in the morning. Take the clothes from the beds, one piece at a time, and spread over chairs or a low screen, so that the air shall pass through them freely. Beat the pillows and bolsters, and place them in a current of air. Turn the mattresses so that they shall be aired on all sides. Leave the rooms to air for an hour, or longer if possible.

Return to the kitchen and wash the dishes; then put them away at once. Wash the dish-towels in plenty of soap and water, and rinse thoroughly; when possible, dry them out of doors. Air, brush, and dust the dining-room; then draw the shades. Make the beds, empty the slops, and wash and wipe the bedroom toilet china. Put the rooms in order and dust them. Next wash the basins and the bath-tub, if necessary, and dust the bath-room.

Dust the halls and sitting-room, and any other rooms that may require it. Collect the lamps and trim them. Prepare the dinner or luncheon. If you live in the city, the vestibule and sidewalk must be swept, and perhaps washed. The earlier this work is done, the better, as there will be less annoyance from frequent passers early in the morning. If the home be in the country, the front and back steps and the piazzas should be swept at the hour most convenient for the housekeeper. In freezing weather do not, of course, attempt to wash the piazza, steps, or sidewalk, as the result would be an icy surface, dangerous to limb and life.

Special Work for Special Days.

On Monday, as soon as the water is warm, put the clothes to soak in strong suds. After the breakfast dishes have been washed, begin to wash the clothes. While one boilerful is being scalded and a second batch of clothes has been prepared for the boiler, put out the line. Now put the scalded clothes in the rinsing water. Take nearly all the hot suds from the boiler, and replace with clean cold water, putting the second batch of clothes to scald in this. Rinse the first lot and put on the lines to dry; continue the work until everything except the flannels and colored articles have been washed. While the coarse towels are being scalded, wash and hang out the flannels; next wash the colored things. When all the clothes have been hung out, empty the boiler and wash and wipe it until perfectly dry; also clean the laundry. Now take a luncheon. Do the chamber-work, and then prepare the family luncheon or dinner. The brushing up and dusting must be omitted to-day. After the noonday meal, wash the dishes and clean up the kitchen. Bathe, and change your clothes; and after resting, take the clothes from the lines and sprinkle and fold them. Flannels must be taken in while they are still slightly damp. Iron the flannels, and after that prepare the evening meal. In the short winter days it will be best to wash the flannels and colored clothes before the white articles, as the more rapidly a woollen or colored fabric dries the better it will look.

On Tuesday, directly after the breakfast dishes have been washed and the dining-room put in order, begin ironing, starting with the plain pieces, such as sheets and pillow-cases. As soon as the irons work smoothly, iron the starched clothes. In about two or three hours the fire must be replenished. When this is done, and while it is burning up, do the chamber work. If all the ironing cannot be done in the forenoon, finish it, if you can, in the afternoon. The meals for washing and ironing days should be as simple as possible.

Where one Servant is Kept.

If there be one servant in the house, the mistress can make these two days less burdensome, if she herself will wash the breakfast dishes, put the dining-room in order, and make the beds. If there be children in the family, they can be taught to do the lighter work. In suggesting that the chamber work be left until the fire is renewed, it is supposed that hard coal is used. If wood or soft coal be used, the fire will have to be replenished frequently; and since these substances burn much more readily, the time for chamber work will be limited unless the draughts be closed. Wednesday is often taken by housekeepers for a sort of off day; but if, as is the case in many Eastern towns, Thursday be the servant's day out, it will be better to sweep on Wednesday, and have the lighter work done on Thursday. Once in two weeks should be often enough for a thorough cleaning of most of the rooms in a well regulated house. A room properly cleaned will be in a better sanitary condition at the end of two weeks than one that is only half cleaned every week. If the floors be of natural wood, or be stained or painted, the dust and lint must be wiped off with a dry cloth every few days, but if the floors be carpeted the thorough sweeping once in two weeks should be sufficient, except in a sitting-room or dining-room. I will give the method of cleaning a room properly. These directions, slightly modified, apply to all rooms.

Cleaning a Room by System.

Remove the draperies, and dust and remove all small articles. Dust all the furniture, removing the lighter articles and covering the heavy pieces; dust and cover the pictures. Brush the walls and ceilings, being careful to remove all dust from the tops of the doors and windows. Brush all dust from the window frames, ledges, and blinds. If there be rugs on a bare floor, roll them up and put them out of doors to be beaten and aired; then sweep the floor with a soft brush. After all the dusting and washing of windows has been finished, rub the floor with a soft, dry cloth. If it be a stained or painted floor, wipe it a second time with a cloth slightly dampened with kerosene; or if it be polished, do the polishing at this time. If the room be carpeted, sweep it with a clean broom; if the carpet be very dusty, sprinkle over it, before sweeping, corn meal or sawdust, slightly dampened; or, if it be more convenient, take dry salt. Let the dust settle, then sweep the carpet a second time. Now dust the room, wash the windows, and remove the covers from the furniture and pictures. After this has been done, put two gallons of tepid water in a pail with four tablespoonfuls of household ammonia. Wring a cloth out of this and wipe the carpet, rubbing hard to remove any dust. Beat the rugs by spreading them face down on clean grass or a smooth board and beating with a switch or rattan beater. If it be impossible to lay them flat, hang them on a line and beat them. Place them on the floors, and put the furniture, ornaments, and draperies in place. Clean one or more rooms in this manner on Wednesday morning. Prepare the noonday meal, and after this has been served, and the dining-room and kitchen put in order, rest until it is time to attend to the evening meal.

The Last Half of the Week.

On Thursday, after the regular work is done, the morning should be devoted to various odd tasks, such as cleaning the refrigerator, and inspecting and cleaning the cellar. See that no decaying vegetation, damp paper, etc., is there. Wash the cellar stairs. Next clean the kitchen and prepare something for the evening meal; then serve the noonday meal.

The remainder of the weekly sweeping should be done on Friday morning. Every two weeks the silver should be cleaned in the afternoon. Many housekeepers clean silver every week, but if it be properly washed and wiped each day this will be unnecessary.

As there must be some extra cooking done on Saturday for Sunday, plan for that on Friday, making all the arrangements possible, so that this work may be done early Saturday morning, while the fire is at its best. All the materials for cooking should be in the house on Friday afternoon or early Saturday morning. If fruits are to be prepared for the next day's baking, get them ready some time on Friday. Saturday is usually a busy day. Extra cooking and cleaning must be done, that the work on Sunday may be light. Many housekeepers change the beds on Saturday, rather than on Sunday. If this be the practice, when the rooms are put to air, remove the soiled linen and spread out the fresh, that it may be well aired. If possible, rise early enough to clean the steps, piazza, and sidewalk before breakfast. As soon as the regular morning work is done, attend to the extra cooking. When this is finished, clean the kitchen and its closets, the china closets, and the back hall.

A Day of Rest.

Plan to have as little work as possible to do on Sunday, but do not fall into the error of wearing yourself out on Saturday and making all the family uncomfortable on Sunday, simply because you would not break the Sabbath. The woman who manages to keep her family comfortable and happy on this day, even if it be necessary to do a little extra work to attain that end, will have a better moral and spiritual influence than she who makes all the members dread the day as being one of the most uncomfortable in the whole week at home. In most families on this day the breakfast is late and the dinner served about two o'clock, the supper being light and informal. While there are many housekeepers who still cling to the old custom of having cold dinners, the majority have a hot one, as it often happens that this is the only meal throughout the week at which the whole family is sure to meet.

If but one servant be kept, she ought not to be required to perform any duties after the dinner dishes have been washed and put away. The remainder of the day and evening should belong to her. If there be no servant, the housekeeper surely is entitled to what little rest she can get after dinner, and the other members of the family should find it a pleasure to prepare whatever light refreshments may be required in the evening. Remember that there are heavy duties for Monday morning, and do not leave a lot of dishes in disorder to add to these burdens.

Two or More Servants in a Family.

The round of duties for the week having been thus outlined, I wish to make a few suggestions to the woman who keeps two or more servants. The duties must be so divided that each shall bear her proper proportion of the work. In the case where there are several servants, there is greater ceremony in the mode of living. Suppose there be two servants, and the family be fairly large. The second girl must do all the upstairs work, take care of the parlors, halls, dining-room, china closet, etc. It will be her duty to care for the silver, glass, and fine china. Every evening, after the dining-room work is finished, she will go to the chambers, empty all slops, refill the water pitchers, turn back the bed clothes, and lay the night garments on the bed. She will draw the shades and see that there is a stock of matches, towels, etc. In the morning she will attend to the dining-room, put the breakfast dishes on to heat, dust the lower halls and parlors, and sweep the steps and sidewalk. The cook will care for all the lower part of the house, her own room, the cellar, and the back steps and stoop. The washing and ironing must be divided between them. It is usual to have the cook do the plain washing and ironing, while the second girl takes the starched clothes. If, however, the second girl be required to do plain sewing, the cook does the heavier part of the washing.

In the matter of the duties of a servant each housekeeper must make her own laws, but the more servants there are, the more clearly must each one's responsibility be defined, and the mistress will save herself an immense amount of annoyance if she will take pains to divide the work of the household with good judgment and with justice, not allowing any dictation in the matter. She should not be hasty in reaching a conclusion, but should be firm in her decisions.

CHAPTER IV.

SOME THINGS TO BE LEARNED EARLY.

Proper Management of Fires.

ONE of the first things a young housekeeper must master is the science of managing fires. Now, a coal fire is like some people: it will stand a certain amount of nagging, pressure, and neglect, but it will make you suffer in some way for all your abuse. On the other hand, with uniformly fair treatment, it will repay a hundred-fold in comfort.

The demands upon the kitchen fire are varied. Sometimes we want a very hot oven or surface, and again we must have only a moderate amount of heat. The degrees of heat must be regulated by the various checks and draughts in the range, rather than by the use of a greater or less amount of coal. In the morning remove all the ashes and cinders. Put the shavings or paper on the grate loosely, and then put in the kindling wood, crossing the pieces, that there may be a free circulation of air. Open all the draughts and light the fire. As soon as the wood begins to burn, put on some coal. Let the fire burn for ten minutes; then shut all the dampers, but keep open the draught in front of the fire. When the coal begins to burn well, add enough fresh fuel to come nearly to the top of the lining of the fire-box. Keep the front draught open until all the coal has become ignited, but not until it becomes red-hot. Now close the front draughts, and the fire will be hot enough for anything you may want to do for hours to come. Should you want only a moderate heat, there are checks with all modern ranges which enable you to make the combustion very slow. If greater heat be wanted, open the draughts, and in ten minutes you will have a glowing fire.

These are the great secrets of always having a good fire when you want it: Do not let the coal burn to a white heat; when you do not require a hot fire, open all the checks; when you want a hot fire, close the checks and open the draughts; and, of course, the moment there is no further need of a hot fire, close the draughts and open the checks again. A fire built and managed in this manner can be used constantly for four or five hours.

Points about the Furnace Fire.

The furnace fire should be shaken down and raked perfectly clear in the morning. A few shovelfuls of coal should be put on, and all the draughts opened. The ashes should then be taken up. As soon as the coal begins to burn well and the fire looks clear at the bottom, put in enough coal to come almost to the top of the fire-pot. Keep the draughts open until all the gas has burned off; then close them, and later, if the fire be too hot, open the checks. Except in extremely cold weather, this is all the attention that ought to be necessary through the day. The fire must be raked down and fresh coal or cinders put on in the evening, but a small amount of coal will answer for the night, unless the draughts have been open the greater part of the day.

On an extremely cold day it may be necessary to have the draughts open a part of the time, and some coal put on at noon.

All the clinkers should be removed when the fire is raked down in the morning. The water pan should be replenished at least once a day. Some careless people leave the ashes for a day at a time at the bottom of the furnace, where they absorb the heat, robbing the house of its share.

If the furnace fire be allowed to burn to a white heat it

will be ruined for that day, unless more coal be put on a little later. The cold-air boxes must admit enough air to drive the hot air through the house, but not more than can be heated.

Heating stoves and open grates are to be managed as far as possible the same as a furnace. With the stove there is no trouble, there being plenty of checks and draughts. The open grate is not so well provided.

Keeping the Refrigerator Sweet.

Few duties are more important than that of keeping the refrigerator in perfect condition. If the lining be broken in any part, so that the water soaks into the wood, attend to the relining at once ; or, if the refrigerator be not worth that, discard it wholly. Never have the waste-pipe connected with the plumbing in the house.

Have the refrigerator placed where it can be flooded with air and light whenever necessary, but, of course, in as cool a place as possible. Once a week have everything removed from it. Take out the shelves and wash them in hot soap-suds; then pour boiling water over them. Place them in the sun ; or, if that fails, by the range, that they may be perfectly dried. Now take out the ice rack and wash and scald in the same way, except that, as there are grooves or wires in this, the greatest care must be used to get out every particle of dirt that may have lodged there. Next wash out the ice compartment, running a flexible wire rod down the waste-pipe, that nothing shall lodge there. Put two tablespoonfuls of washing soda into a quart of boiling water and set on the fire. When this boils, pour it into the ice compartment ; follow this with a kettleful of boiling water, and wipe dry. Now wash the other parts of the refrigerator with hot soap-suds, and wipe perfectly dry. Be careful to get the doors and ledges clean and dry. Leave the refrigerator open for an hour, and then return the ice and food to it.

Plan this work for a day when the iceman is due. The work should be done immediately after breakfast, so that the refrigerator shall be ready when the ice comes.

Should you, after this care, still have trouble, do not use the refrigerator. It will be far better to get along without the comfort it affords than to endanger health and life by using a contaminated article. Food never should be put in a refrigerator while warm, because it absorbs the flavors of other food and also heats the refrigerator.

Getting the Greatest Good out of Lamps.

In these days, when lamps are used so much, the care of them is quite an important matter. If the lamps be good and have proper attention, one cannot wish for a more satisfactory light; but if badly cared for, they will be a source of much discomfort. The great secret of having lamps in good working order is to keep them clean and to use good oil. Have a regular place and time for trimming the lamps. Put a folded newspaper on the table, so that any stray bits of burned wick and drops of oil may fall upon it. Wash and wipe the chimneys and shades. Now take off all loose parts of the burner, washing them in hot soap-suds and wiping them with a clean soft cloth. Trim the wicks and turn them quite low. With a soft, wet cloth, well soaped, wipe the burner thoroughly, working the cloth as much as possible inside the burner, to get off every particle of the charred wick. Now fill the lamps within about one inch of the top, and wipe with a damp towel and then a dry one. Adjust all the parts and return them to their proper places.

Whenever a new wick is required in a lamp, wash and scald the burner before putting in the wick. With a student lamp, the receptacle for waste oil, which is screwed on the bottom of the burner, should be taken off at least once a week and washed. Sometimes a wick will get very dark and dirty before it is half consumed. It is not economy to try to burn it; replace it with a fresh one. The trouble and expense are slight, and the increase in clearness and brilliancy will repay the extra care. When a lamp is lighted, it should not at once be turned up to the full height; wait until the chimney is heated. Beautiful shades are often cracked or broken by having the hot chimneys rest against them. Now, when lighting a lamp be careful that the chimney is set perfectly straight, and does not touch the shade at any point. The shade should be put in place as soon as the lamp is lighted, that it may heat gradually.

Take Good Care of the Plumbing.

The care of the plumbing is an important duty; yet, provided there be nothing wrong about the plumbing at the start, and the supply of water be constant and generous, this duty will not be found a hard one. The housekeeper should impress upon the younger members of her family the importance of thoroughly flushing the water-closets. She should at least once a day personally see to it that there is sufficient flushing. The best time for this is after the morning work is done.

The laundry tubs should be thoroughly rinsed after washing. Be free with the water, that no trace of suds shall be left in the pipes.

After the midday work is done, and again at night, the pipe in the kitchen sink should be thoroughly flushed with hot water, if possible. In case there be no hot water, be generous with the cold. Once a week put half a pint of washing soda in an old saucepan, and add six quarts of hot water. Place on the fire until the soda is all dissolved; then pour the water into the pipes, reserving two quarts of it for the kitchen sink.

Have an old funnel to use in the bath-tub and basins, that the hot soda shall not touch any of the metal save that in the pipes.

Particles of grease sometimes lodge in the sink-pipe and cause an unpleasant odor. The hot soda dissolves this grease and carries it away.

Copperas will remove odors from drain-pipes. Put one pound of the crystals in a quart bottle and fill up with cold water. Cork tightly and label, writing " Poison " on the label. Pour a little of this into the pipes whenever there is any odor.

If thorough flushing and an occasional use of the hot soda will not keep the pipes sweet, there is something wrong with the plumbing, and it should be attended to at once.

It seems as if one need not caution people in regard to throwing into either water-closet or basin anything that may clog the pipes, but it is because of ignorance or carelessness on the part of the people who use these conveniences that much of the trouble with the pipes arises. Here are some of the things that should never have a chance to get into the pipes: hair, lint, pieces of rags, no matter how small; matches, fruit peelings, etc.

If for any reason there should be a bad odor from the drain, two tablespoonfuls of carbolic acid, mixed with a cupful of cold water and poured into the pipes, will prove a good disinfectant. A small bottle of carbolic acid, plainly labelled, always should be kept in the house, out of the reach of the children.

About the Bath-room.

The bath-room should have special attention daily, and once a week a thorough cleaning. A woollen carpet is not desirable for this room. The floor may be of tiles, or of hard wood, stained or painted, or be covered with lignum or oil-cloth. Of course, there must be a rug or two. The Japanese cotton rug is cheap and pretty for this purpose; or, one can make rugs from pieces of carpet.

Not only should the wash-basin be washed clean and the bowl in the water-closet washed every day, but, if the bath-tub has been used, this too should be washed and carefully wiped dry. Dust the room, and hang the soiled towels where they will dry before being put in the hamper provided for such things.

Once a week give the room a thorough cleaning. Wash the toilet articles. Wash all the marble with soap and water, and if there be any spots that are not easily removed, put a little sand soap on the wash-cloth and rub the spot well. The bowl in the water-closet should have a good scrubbing with sand soap. Rub the bath-tub with whiting, wet with household ammonia, and then wash it with plenty of hot water and wipe dry.

Never use for the bath-tub sand soap, or any substance that would scratch, unless it be an enamel tub, in which case no harm will be done. Clean the faucets with whiting. Take a long-handled boot-buttoner and draw from the waste-pipes all the bits of lint that have gathered there. Dust the room and wash the floor, wiping very dry. Now lay down the rugs, which already should have been well beaten and aired.

Do not Neglect the Garbage Barrel.

The garbage barrel or tub should be thoroughly washed once a week. In summer, after the barrel has been cleaned, sprinkle into it one teaspoonful of carbolic acid mixed with half a cupful of cold water. This will keep the barrel free from offensive odors even in the hottest weather.

WASHING DISHES.

Sort the dishes and scrape them free from fragments. Have two pans, one for washing and the other for rinsing. Have also a large tray on which to drain the dishes. Wash the glassware first.

Proper Care of Glassware.

It must be remembered that even a scratch on the surface of a piece of glass often will cause it to break at that point under the slightest shock; therefore, it is essential that it shall not come in contact with a sharp, hard substance. A grain of sand on the bottom of the dishpan, or on the cloth with which the article is washed or wiped, may be the means of breaking a valuable dish. When possible, a wooden or paper tub should be used in washing glass. A soft silver-brush, soft cloths for washing, and soft linen towels for wiping, also are necessary. Have the water cool enough to bear the hand in comfortably. Make a strong suds with hard soap. The second dish of water should be of the same temperature. Wash each piece carefully, rubbing with the soft cloth; then put in the rinsing water. When four or five pieces have been washed, spread a coarse towel on an old tray, and place the glass on this to drain. Wipe the hands dry, and then wipe the pieces of glass with a perfectly clean, dry towel. Rub gently, to polish. Hold the glass up to the light, to see if it is perfectly clear, then place on a clean tray. Always keep the towel between the hands and the glass, and as soon as the towel becomes damp change it for a dry one. The glass should not drain long enough to become cold; for this reason it is best to wash only a few pieces at a time. If the glass be cut, or an imitation of cut, use the soft silver-brush to cleanse all the grooves. As it is almost impossible to get the deeply cut

SOME THINGS TO BE LEARNED EARLY. 39

glass perfectly dry, it should not be placed at once on a polished-wood surface. It is a good plan to have a soft cloth on which to place cut pieces for ten or fifteen minutes after they have been wiped. Glass that is ornamented with gold must be treated with great care, to prevent the ornamentation from wearing off. Use only castile soap, and do not have the suds strong. Wash one piece at a time, and wipe immediately.

It will be seen by the foregoing that the care of glass can be summed up in a few words : wash in clean warm suds and wipe perfectly dry, using clean dry linen towels ; be careful not to scratch nor hit a piece of glass, and do not expose the surface to sudden heat or cold.

Other Dishes and Utensils.

After the glass the silver should be washed and wiped. Next wash the china in hot suds, and then rinse in the second pan of hot water. Drain on the tray, and wipe while yet warm. The kitchen crockery should follow the china, then the tins, and finally the iron cooking dishes. Change the dish-water often, having the first water very soapy and the rinsing water hot. Be as careful to have clean water and clean dry towels for the pots and kettles as for the china, and wash in the same way as a piece of china, having the outside as clean as the inside. Some kind of sand soap or mineral soap is necessary to keep the tins, granite-ware, and iron saucepans perfectly clean and bright. After wiping such utensils with a dry towel, place them on the hearth, to become perfectly dry, as they rust easily and quickly.

Now rub the steel knives with either Bristol brick, wood ashes, or sand soap. Wash them, and wipe perfectly dry. Next wash the tray, the rinsing pan, the table, and the sink. Finally wash the dish-towels, and then the dishpans.

Some Special Cautions.

Pitchers, bowls, pans, and other utensils used for milk, should have cold water stand in them for half an hour or so, then be washed in plenty of clean soapy water. After this they should be scalded with boiling water, wiped dry, and placed in the sun and open air, if possible, for several hours.

Teapots, coffee-pots, chocolate-pots, and the like, should be washed in hot soapy water and be rinsed in boiling water. Use a wooden skewer to remove every particle of sediment that may lodge in the spouts or creases of the pots. Wipe perfectly dry, and expose to the sun and air, if possible, for an hour or more.

Pans in which fish or onions have been cooked, should be washed and scalded; then they should be filled with water, in which should be put a teaspoonful of soda for every two quarts of water. Place them on top of the stove for half an hour or more. This will insure the removal of the flavor of fish or onions.

Care of Silver.

Silver that is properly washed and wiped every day will require very little extra cleaning. Remove it from the table on a tray and then put it into a wide-mouthed kitchen pitcher containing warm water. When ready to wash it, have a pan of hot soap-suds and a clean soft dish-cloth. Put all the silver, except the knives, into the suds, and wash a few pieces at a time, rubbing well with the cloth. Wipe the silver, while it is still warm, with a fine soft silver-towel, rubbing it until perfectly dry and bright. Always keep the towel between the hands and the silver. As fast as a piece is finished lay it on the tray, and when all the work is done wipe the hands perfectly dry, and then put the silver away.

Should there be any tarnish on any of the pieces, rub with

a little wet whiting and a piece of chamois skin. Wash again in the hot suds, and wipe.

When the silver is to have a regular cleaning, put it in a pan of hot suds and wash well. Spread several thicknesses of paper on the table. Have at hand a saucer of French whiting, finely powdered and sifted. Wet a little of this with water, unless the silver is very much tarnished, in which case use half water and half alcohol; or, instead of the alcohol, half household ammonia. Rub the article with this and then with dry whiting and a chamois skin, finally using a soft silver-brush to clean out all the chasing and creases. When all the silver has been cleaned in this manner, wash it in clean hot suds, wipe on a towel kept for silver, and put away.

Do not put silver in woollen bags, as the sulphur in this cloth tarnishes the metal. Rubber should not be placed near silver.

Only substances which are well known have been suggested for the cleaning of the various articles of silver. There are preparations in the market which many housekeepers use because they consider them harmless, and great savers of labor. Each one will decide for herself in these matters.

Do not Slight the Knife Blades.

In nearly all cases the blade of the knife requires different treatment from the handle. If it be of unplated steel it must be thoroughly polished every time it is used. If it be of silver, or be silver-plated, a careful washing with soap and water, and a thorough drying, will be all the daily care that is required, — a thorough cleaning about once a week sufficing to keep the blade perfectly clean. There should be a knife-board for the steel knives. Boards covered with leather that come for this purpose may be purchased at any first-class kitchen furnishing store.

To clean the knives have at hand a pan of clean, soapy

water and a soft cloth. Hold the knives in the left hand and wash the blades with the cloth, only wiping the handles with the wet cloth, unless they be silver, in which case wash them thoroughly with the soap-suds and cloth. Sprinkle the board with some knife-polish. Hold the blade flat on the board and rub back and forth until it is polished. If the stain be hard to remove, dip a cork in the strong soap-suds, then in the polishing powder, and, laying the blade of the knife perfectly flat on the board, rub with the cork until the stain disappears. Now wipe the polish off with a soft cloth and rub the blade with a piece of chamois skin. The handles of the knives should be protected while the blades are being polished. Have a long, narrow bag of Canton flannel to slip over the handle while the blade is being rubbed.

Rust and Other Annoyances.

If it should happen that the steel of knives or forks becomes rusted, dip them in sweet oil and let them stand for twenty-four hours, then rub them with powdered quicklime, and the stain will be removed. If the handles of the knives be ivory, and they become stained, rub them with whiting and spirits of turpentine. This will remove all ordinary stains. Still, the appearance of the ivory will be greatly improved by a vigorous rubbing with the whiting and turpentine. Frequent wettings with hot water and soap will dull the mother-of-pearl handles, which should be wiped with a damp cloth and rubbed dry with a soft towel. Silver handles should be rubbed frequently with whiting. Celluloid, ivorine, bone, etc., require the same general treatment as ivory and pearl. The handles of knives, no matter what the material, should never be allowed to stand in water. The water, particularly if it be hot, loosens the handles from the tang, and also dulls them. A tin or granite-ware pail or pitcher should be kept exclusively for knives. When used, it should have some water in it, but not enough to come up to the handle of the knife. As soon as the table is cleared the knives should be put in this, to remain until the time for washing them.

If you have no regular case for the knives, they may be kept in one made of Canton flannel. To make this take a piece of flannel about three quarters of a yard wide and cut off twenty-one inches. Fold over eleven and a half inches of the selvage end, leaving a single thickness of about four inches at the other end. Baste the doubled part together; then stitch it into twelve compartments. Bind the bag with tape, and sew tapes on the single flap at the centre. Of course, the flannel is on the inside. When steel cutlery is to be put away for any length of time, melt pure mutton suet, and dip the steel part of the knives and forks in it. When cool, wrap in tissue paper, and then in thicker paper or Canton flannel.

CHAPTER V.

WORK ON WASHING DAY.

ON washing day arrange the white clothes in this manner: Half fill two tubs with warm suds. Put in one tub the pieces soiled the most; put the remainder of the articles in the second tub. Have a third tub half full of warm water and the wash boiler half full of cold water. Wash the cleaner clothes first, rubbing soap on the parts which are soiled the most. Wring from this water and drop into the tub of clean warm water. When all are done, rinse the clothes well in the warm water; then wring out and soap the parts that were badly soiled. Put these same pieces in the boiler of cold water and set on the fire. Let the water get almost boiling hot; then take up the clothes and put them in a tubful of cold water. Rinse them from this into another of warm water and from this into a third of bluing water. Wring them as dry as possible; then shake them out and hang on the lines. They should become perfectly dry before they are folded. All the white clothing should be washed in this manner. The second tubful can, of course, be rubbed out and rinsed while the first is being scalded. If clothes be not thoroughly rinsed and bluing be used, the soap will combine with the bluing to give a yellow tinge to the clothing. This is especially the case when liquid bluing is used. A thorough rinsing is really one of the most important steps in all the work.

Satines, Ginghams, and Prints.

These kinds of goods look better when no soap is used and they are not starched in the usual way. For two dresses make one gallon of starch by mixing one cupful of flour with one pint of cold water. Pour on this three quarts and a half of boiling water. Pour half of this mixture into a tub containing four gallons of warm water. Wash one of the dresses in this, rubbing the fabric the same as if soap were used. Now rinse in two clean waters and hang out to dry. The starch cleans the fabric, and enough is held in the cloth to make it about as stiff as when new. Wash the second dress in the same way. This method is not for light cambrics, but only for satines, ginghams, and dark prints.

If the colors run, put half a cupful of salt in the second rinsing water. If the color of the fabric be blue and faded, put two tablespoonfuls of acetic acid, or twice as much vinegar, into the last rinsing water. This will often restore the color, but not always, as it depends upon the chemicals used in the dyeing. The acid can be used in the last water in which faded blue flannels are rinsed. Colored goods should be dried thoroughly and dampened only a few hours before you are ready to iron them. They should be ironed on the wrong side.

How Flannels should be Washed.

Have a tub half full of strong soap suds, in which has been dissolved a tablespoonful of borax. Shake all the dust and lint from the flannels, and then put them into the suds. Wash them by rubbing with the hands and sopping them up and down in the water. Wring them out of this water and put them into a tub of clean hot water. Rinse thoroughly in this water, then in a second tubful. Wring dry, shake well, and hang on the lines. When nearly dry, take them in and fold, rolling them very tightly. Wrap a clean cloth around them, and, if possible, iron the same day. Do not have the irons very hot, but press the flannels well. Have clean suds for the colored flannels. To prevent shrinking, the temperature of the water should be the same in all the tubs.

Never use yellow soap for washing flannel, and never rub any other kind of soap upon the cloth.

To wash blankets, make strong suds with some white soap. To every three gallons of water add a tablespoonful of powdered borax. Have the suds as hot as the hands will bear comfortably. Shake the blankets, and, if the bindings be of colored silk, rip them off. Put the blankets in the hot suds and sop them up and down until the suds show that the dirt has been removed. If there be any stains on the blankets, rub the spots well between the hands, but remember the caution not to rub soap on such goods. Have a tub half full of clear water as hot as the suds. After squeezing the suds from the blankets, put them in the rinsing water. Sop them well in this, and then squeeze out the water; finally rinse in a tub of bluing water, having the temperature still as hot as the suds. Press all the water possible from the blankets and hang them on the lines to dry, shaking out all the wrinkles. When dry, fold smoothly and lay on a clean board. Put another board on top, and on this place some heavy weights. In a day or two the blankets will be pressed.

Wash only two blankets at a time, and select a clear day for this work, — a windy day, if possible.

The Right Way to Wash Silk Undergarments.

To three gallons of warm water add three tablespoonfuls of household ammonia. Let the silk garments soak in this for twenty minutes; then rub soap on the parts which are the most badly soiled, and wash the articles with the hands. Never rub them on a board. Rinse in two waters, wring dry, and hang on the line. When nearly dry, take in and fold, and, if possible, iron within a few hours. Never let an iron come in contact with the silk; lay a piece of cloth over the fabric, and iron on that.

The ammonia may be omitted, and the silk garments be

washed in strong suds made with white castile soap and warm water.

How to Launder Washable Curtains.

There are many inexpensive cotton or cotton and silk fabrics used for curtains which launder very well if treated properly. Shake out all the dust. Make weak suds with white castile soap. Wash the curtains in this, and rinse them in two waters; then wring dry. Next dip them in a preparation made as follows: Soak half an ounce of isinglass in one quart of cold water for an hour or more. Steep one ounce of saffron on the fire in two quarts of hot water for two hours. Stir the soaked isinglass and half an ounce of alum into this, and then strain into a bowl. Put one fourth of this mixture into another large bowl, and dip one curtain into it, sopping it well, that the color and stiffening may be equally distributed. Shake out and hang on the line to dry.

When the curtains are dry, sprinkle them, making them very damp. Draw out evenly; then fold, and roll up in a cloth; finally iron them, being careful to move the iron lengthwise of the curtain, and to get the fabric very dry.

The alum and saffron may be omitted, and the stiffening be used for washable dresses or thin muslin curtains.

Cleaning Lace Curtains.

Lace curtains will not bear rubbing. All the work must be done carefully and gently. For two pairs of curtains half fill a large tub with warm water, and add to it half a pound of soap, which has been shaved fine and dissolved in two quarts of boiling water; add also about a gill of household ammonia. Let the curtains soak in this over night. In the morning sop them well in the water, and squeeze it all out; but do not wring the curtains. Put them into another tub of water, prepared with soap and ammonia, as on the night before; sop them gently in this water, and then, after squeezing out the water, put them in a tub of clean warm water. Continue to rinse them in fresh tubs of water until there is no trace of soap; next, rinse them in water containing bluing. After pressing out all the water possible, spread the curtains over sheets on the grass; or, if you have no grass, put them on the clothes-line. When they are dry, dip them in hot thick starch, and fasten them in the frame that comes for this purpose. If you have no frame, fasten a sheet on a mattress, and spread the curtains on this, pinning them in such a manner that they shall be perfectly smooth and have all the pattern of the border brought out. Place in the sun to dry. If it be desired to have the curtains a light écru shade, rinse them in weak coffee; and if you want a dark shade, use strong coffee.

If the curtains be dried on a mattress they must be folded smoothly, the size of the mattress. Lace curtains can be spread two or three thicknesses in the frame.

Points on Starching and Ironing.

In making and using starch have all the utensils and the water perfectly clean. Mix the dry starch with cold water enough to make a thin paste. Pour on this the required amount of boiling water, stirring all the while. To each quart of starch add a teaspoonful each of salt and lard. Boil the starch until it looks clear, which will be in about ten minutes. Strain it through a piece of cheese-cloth (it will have to be squeezed through the cloth). White articles should be dipped into the hot starch, but have it cooled a little for colored articles. For collars, cuffs, shirts, etc., have the starch very thick; for white skirts it should be rather thin; for dresses, aprons, and children's clothing also, the starch must be thin, and for table linen only the thinnest kind imaginable should be used.

Always have starched clothes thoroughly dried; then

sprinkle evenly with enough cold water to make them very damp. Fold smoothly and roll up in a clean cloth for several hours. In ironing, begin with the plain pieces, like the sheets and pillow cases. This will get the irons in condition for the starched clothes, which should be done next; and after these finish the plain pieces. Have the ironing blanket and sheet spread smoothly on the table and tacked in place, and have some fine salt spread on a board. Tie a large piece of beeswax in a cloth, and after rubbing the hot iron on the salt, rub the beeswax over it. Finally wipe the iron on a clean cloth. This process will make the iron clean and smooth. Starched clothes must be made very damp; other articles should be dampened only slightly. Starched clothes must be ironed until perfectly dry. In ironing, do the rubbing lengthways when possible, — that is, with the selvage.

A Rule for Making Hard Soap.

18 pounds of clarified grease.	3 pounds of potash.
3 tablespoonfuls of powdered borax.	4 quarts of cold water.

Put the fat on the back part of the range, where it will melt slowly. The potash is put into a large earthen or stone bowl or jar. Upon this is poured three quarts of cold water, and three tablespoonfuls of powdered borax is added. This mixture is stirred with a wooden stick until the potash is dissolved; then it stands until cold.

When the fat is melted pour it into a butter tub. It must not be hot when the potash is added; should it be, it must stand until so cool that it will hardly run when poured. When the potash mixture is perfectly cold pour it in a thin stream into the fat, stirring all the while. When all has been added, continue stirring for about ten minutes, when the soap should begin to look thick and ropy. At this stage pour it into a box, having it about three or four inches deep.

Let it stand a few hours; then cut it into bars, and the bars into pieces of a convenient length for handling. It will still be soft, and should not be removed from the box for at least two days. It will be hard and white.

If you attempt to combine the fat and potash mixture while the latter is at all warm it will take a long time to make the soap, and the result will not be so satisfactory. It is well to put paper under the soap tub and the bowl in which the potash is prepared. Remember that potash is very strong, and do not spatter it on yourself or on the floor.

This is a hard soap, — a most desirable quality.

Borax Soap.

> 2 pounds of good white soap.
> 3 ounces of borax.
> 2 quarts of water.

Shave the soap and put it in a porcelain kettle with the water and borax. Place on the fire, and stir frequently until the soap and borax are dissolved and combined. Pour the hot mixture into a clean butter tub, and when cold, cover. This soap is excellent for washing flannels, blankets, etc.

Soft Soap.

It is best to make the soap a few weeks before you wish to use it, as it is rather hard on the hands when new. Here is a good rule for making the soap without heating the grease : —

Put fourteen pounds of crude — not concentrated — potash in a wooden pail and pour over it enough boiling water to cover it. Stir well, and let the mixture stand over night. In the morning pour this mixture into a large kettle and place on the fire. Now add another pail of boiling water, and stir frequently with a stick until all the potash is dissolved. Next put ten quarts of soap grease in a water-tight barrel and gradually pour in the hot potash. Stir until all the grease is united with the potash. Let this stand for three hours; then add a pailful of hot water and stir well. Add another pailful three hours later. After this add a pailful each day for the next six days, stirring well with a long stick each time. The soap should be stirred every day for the next three weeks, when it will be ready for use.

Be sure the potash is pure.

CHAPTER VI.

IN THE DINING-ROOM.

ONE'S dining-room should be large enough to enable a person to pass around the table comfortably when the family or guests are all seated. It should also be light and sunny, and easily heated and ventilated. The most essential pieces of furniture are a table of generous width, capable of being enlarged, comfortable chairs, and a sideboard. After that, if the room be large enough and the purse will admit of the purchase of a cabinet or two, with glass fronts and sides, so much the better. In these there can be kept dainty bits of china and glassware. These cabinets will brighten a dining-room more than anything else you can put into it, possibly excepting pictures. If there be no room for a cabinet, a corner cupboard and some hanging shelves will be a great addition. Pictures that suggest pleasant things are, of course, always desirable. A few thrifty ferns, flowering plants, or evergreens add a great deal to the brightness and beauty of any room, but particularly the dining-room. Have them there if you possibly can.

Setting the Table.

The table should stand in the middle of the room. Cover it with a thick felt or a double-faced Canton flannel cloth. Over this spread the white damask cloth, having the centre fold come exactly in the centre of the table. Pass the hand over the cloth to make it lie smooth. If there be a centrepiece, carving, or tray cloths, or table mats, have them lie perfectly straight and smooth on the cloth. At each seat place on the right the knives, spoons, and glasses; on the left, the forks and napkins. Have the edge of the knife toward the plate. Lay the forks with the tines up, and the spoons with the bowls up. Have the spacing between the seats regular, and the space between the knife and fork about seven inches. Set the glasses at the points of the knives. If individual salt-cellars and pepper bottles be used, they are to be placed at the head of the plates; otherwise, place the cellars and bottles at the corners of the table. The tablespoons may be placed at the corners of the table, or near the dishes where they will be required in serving. In the centre of the table there may be set a dish of flowers or fruit.

These general directions apply to the setting of the table for any meal. Nearly all housekeepers have their own ideas about the arrangement of the table, thus securing variety and individuality.

Refinement not Exclusively for the Rich.

The incomes and style of living in this country have such a wide range that it would be impossible to give here directions for the table service which would meet the wants of all classes. The woman of limited means who does her own work could not serve her meals the same as one who keeps one or more servants. As far as possible she will so arrange her meals that it shall not be necessary to rise from the table more than once or twice. Indeed, it is possible to have everything on the table for breakfast, tea, or luncheon, but at dinner time the meat, vegetables, and soiled plates should be removed before the dessert is put on. No woman, no matter how simply she lives, should get into a slipshod way of serving her meals. The table can be made, and should be, a means of refinement and pleasure. Do not have it ceremonious, yet strive for neatness, brightness, and order. No one has a right to mar the sociability of a meal by bringing a gloomy countenance or disagreeable subject to the table. When the housekeeper has done all she can to make the meal suitable and appetizing, each member of the family should do his or her share to bring life and sunshine into the conversation.

The directions which follow may, it is hoped, be helpful in some degree to the young housekeeper, no matter what her manner of living may be. It is easy to omit all but one or two courses, thus making the table arrangement and service simple; but the general principles may be observed just the same.

At the Breakfast Table.

Breakfast being the plainest meal of the day, the arrangement of the table should always be simple. The cloth should be spotless. At each person's seat place a knife, fork, teaspoon or dessert spoon, tumbler, and napkin, and if fresh fruit is to be served, a finger bowl, if there be no servant. If you have a waitress, she will place the finger bowls on as you finish with the fruit. If fresh fruit be served, there must also be placed at each seat a fruit knife and plate. Have the dish of fruit in the centre of the table. Have a tray cloth at each end of the table. Place a little butter plate near the top of each plate. Put four tablespoons on the table, either in two corners, or beside the dishes where they will be used in serving. Put the carving knife and fork at the head of the table, and the cups and saucers, sugar and cream, coffee-pot, hot-water bowl, and the mush dishes at the other end.

The mistress of the house serves the mush, and when the fruit and this course have been served, the dishes are removed and the hot plates and other food brought in; the head of the house serving the hot meats, etc., while the mistress pours the coffee. It sometimes happens that a man of business lacks time to serve breakfast, in which case the mistress of the house attends to that duty. If there be a waitress, she passes the plates when they are ready; also the bread, butter, and coffee. The hostess usually puts the sugar and cream in the coffee, first asking each one if he will have these additions. After all have been served, it is quite common to dismiss the waitress, ringing for her if her services be again required. When there is but one servant, the family help each other after the breakfast has been placed upon the table. Fresh water is good for most people, and each person should be served with a tumblerful on taking a seat at the table. If there be hot cakes or waffles, they should come after the meats, and there should be a fresh set of warm plates, as well as of knives and forks.

The Dinner Table.

The silver required depends upon the number of courses to be served, but a few suggestions may help one to decide what is proper for her own table. The silver for all the courses except the dessert may be put on the table when it is set, or it may be placed there by the waitress as needed for each course. Dinner plates are placed on the table or not, when it is set, as one pleases. The silver needed for an ordinary course dinner would be a small fork for raw oysters, tablespoon for soup, fork for fish, knife and fork for meat, and fork for salad; carving knife and fork at the head of the table, soup ladle at the head of the mistress's plate, and, if the dinner be served from the table, spoons for serving.

In the centre of the table set rather a low dish containing flowers or ferns. On each side of it place some small dishes of pretty design for olives, salted almonds, confectionery, and such things; or these small dishes may be set in the corners of the table. If the dinner is to be served on the table, the small dishes should be put in the corners; but if it is to be served from the sideboard, such dishes may be placed wherever they look best and are most convenient. Lay the tablespoons in pairs; in the corners, of course, if the dinner is to be served on the table. In the fold of each napkin lay a small square of bread or a small roll. The fruit and dishes for the dessert may be disposed on the sideboard. All the dishes for a handsome dinner service may be of one pattern, or for each course a different kind of china may be used. For the olives, almonds, etc., it is desirable to have bits of cut glass, or pretty little china dishes. Such wares are used much more than silver. The dishes on which fish, meats, and entrées are served may be round, oval, square, plain white, or richly colored Chinese or Japanese ware. The plates for the several courses are, of course, carefully to be kept hot or cold, as each course may require, until serving time. After-dinner coffee cups, when all are of different patterns, give a remarkably pretty effect. Indeed, there is so much that is beautiful in table-ware nowadays that one can have a handsome service with means either large or limited.

Luncheon and Tea.

Family luncheons and teas are rarely served in courses. Tea, cocoa, or chocolate is, as a rule, served at these meals, so that the table is set in practically the same manner as for breakfast; but the plates are placed for each person, and unless there be meat to carve, the carving knife and fork are not put on. The bread, butter, cake, preserves, etc., are placed on the table when it is set. If hot meats, vegetables, soup, or cakes be served, the cold plates must be changed for hot ones. When meats, vegetables, or salads have been served at these meals, the plates should be changed before the cake and preserves are passed.

For luncheon, such dishes as these are suitable: eggs in any form, soups, salads, cold meats, with baked or warmed up potatoes, any kind of broiled meat or fish, any simple made dish, fresh fruit, stewed fruit, preserves, cake, gingerbread, etc.

Any dish (except soup and fresh fruit) that you serve for luncheons will be suitable for tea.

Duties of the Waitress.

Although every housekeeper may have some methods peculiarly her own in the matter of waiting upon the table, still there are some customs that are almost universal in refined households.

If the water has not already been poured, the waitress pours it as soon as the guests sit down at the table. If there be raw oysters, they should be served first. Usually they are arranged on the plates, and placed at each person's seat before the guests come in.

When the oyster plates have been removed, the soup tureen and hot soup plates are placed before the hostess. The waitress lifts the cover off the tureen, inverting it at once, that no drops of steam shall fall from it, and carries it from the room. The hostess puts a ladleful of soup into each plate and hands it to the waitress, who places it before the guests, going in every case to the right hand side. Some hostesses always serve the ladies first, while others serve the guests in rotation.

The meat is set before the host, the vegetables being placed before the hostess or on the sideboard, as one chooses. The waitress passes each plate as the host hands it to her. She then passes vegetables, bread, sauce, etc.

The salad is to be served by the hostess. After that the table is brushed and the dessert is brought in and placed before the hostess. The coffee follows. If fruit be served, it is passed before the coffee.

Finger bowls are brought in after the made dessert has been served. A dainty doily is spread on a dessert plate and the finger bowl placed on this. The bowl should be about one quarter full of water. Each guest lifts the bowl and doily from the plate and places them at the left hand side. The doily is never to be used to wipe the fingers.

A good waitress will not pile one dish upon another when removing them from the table. She should be provided with a tray for all the smaller dishes, and should remove the plates one or two at a time.

All dishes from which people help themselves, such as vegetables, bread, butter, etc., should be passed at the left; those that are set before people, such as soup plates, clean plates, water glasses, finger bowls, etc., should be passed at the right.

Serving Meals without a Servant.

A housekeeper who keeps no servant is often puzzled as to how to serve dessert, how to serve the other dishes at dinner, whether the plates should be distributed on the table or placed beside the carver, and so forth.

The conditions are so different in different families that no arbitrary rules can be given for these things, but here are a few suggestions which may be helpful. Have everything ready in the kitchen to put on the table without delay, and place the dishes where they will keep hot until wanted. Eggs in any form must, of course, be served as soon as cooked; therefore they must be timed very carefully. The mush should be put on the table at the housekeeper's own place, and served in saucers or little dishes that come for that purpose. Any one who does not eat mush or fruit may decline it, and wait for the next course. After the mush has been served, remove the dishes, and place the rest of the breakfast on the table. The plates should be hot, and be piled before or at one side of the carver. While he is serving, pour the coffee. When there is another member of the family who can put the second course on the table, the housekeeper should be relieved of this part of the work. It is hard on a woman not only to have to prepare the breakfast, but also to rise from the table, bring in the second course and serve this, as she often must, since, as a rule, men are in a hurry in the morning and cannot assist their wives in serving the breakfast.

CHAPTER VII.

BUYING FOOD AND CARING FOR IT.

Going to Market.

WHEN a housekeeper understands just what to do, and can spend the time to go to the market herself, she will find that she can have a better table, with greater variety and at less expense, than when she orders from the provision man who comes to the house each day. It is true that there are a great many housekeepers who have neither time nor strength for daily or even weekly visits to the markets, but the average housekeeper has the time, and she will find that in the end it will add to her mental and physical health, as well as to the attractiveness of her table.

In ordering at the house it is a difficult matter to keep in mind all the things that the provision man briskly calls off. Even if he should not miss many little things that one might choose for the sake of economy and variety, it would be almost impossible to remember them all when giving him the order. In the market, however, the articles are spread out before you, and one thing suggests another. Here the prices can be kept in mind when selecting the food; and should the thing that you have decided upon be too expensive, something else that you will find to be nearly or equally good may be substituted. For example, you may have planned to have halibut for dinner, and found that, instead of being eighteen cents, it has gone up to twenty-five or thirty cents. You will naturally hesitate before adding fifty per cent to the expense of the dish. A cod, haddock, whitefish, red-snapper, or something else of moderate price, will make a satisfactory substitute. Although the prices of beef, mutton, pork, etc. are not subject to great changes, the prices of fresh fish, vegetables, fruit, and game fluctuate constantly. Then again, many little savory dishes are suggested by the sight of the various little odds and ends found in the stalls. The sight and odor of a piece of smoked bacon may give you visions of the many savory dishes to which it will give relish, — liver and bacon, chicken livers en brochette, and rashers of bacon with chops or beefsteak.

FIRST FIVE RIBS.

In the market, too, perhaps you will see sheep's hearts, which when boiled make a cheap and savory breakfast, luncheon, or supper dish. Calves and lambs' tongues are both cheap and good. They may be kept in brine for a week or two and then boiled, the same as beef tongue; or they may be boiled while fresh. They make an attractive dish when served in jelly, or they may be braised, and served with vegetables à la jardinière, making an elegant as well as an economical dish. Sheep and lambs' kidneys are delicious when broiled, stewed, or sautéd. They are always cheap.

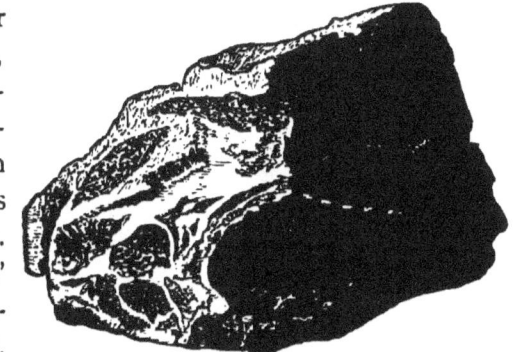
CHUCK RIBS.

Perhaps you may see a piece of honeycomb tripe which would make a pleasing dish

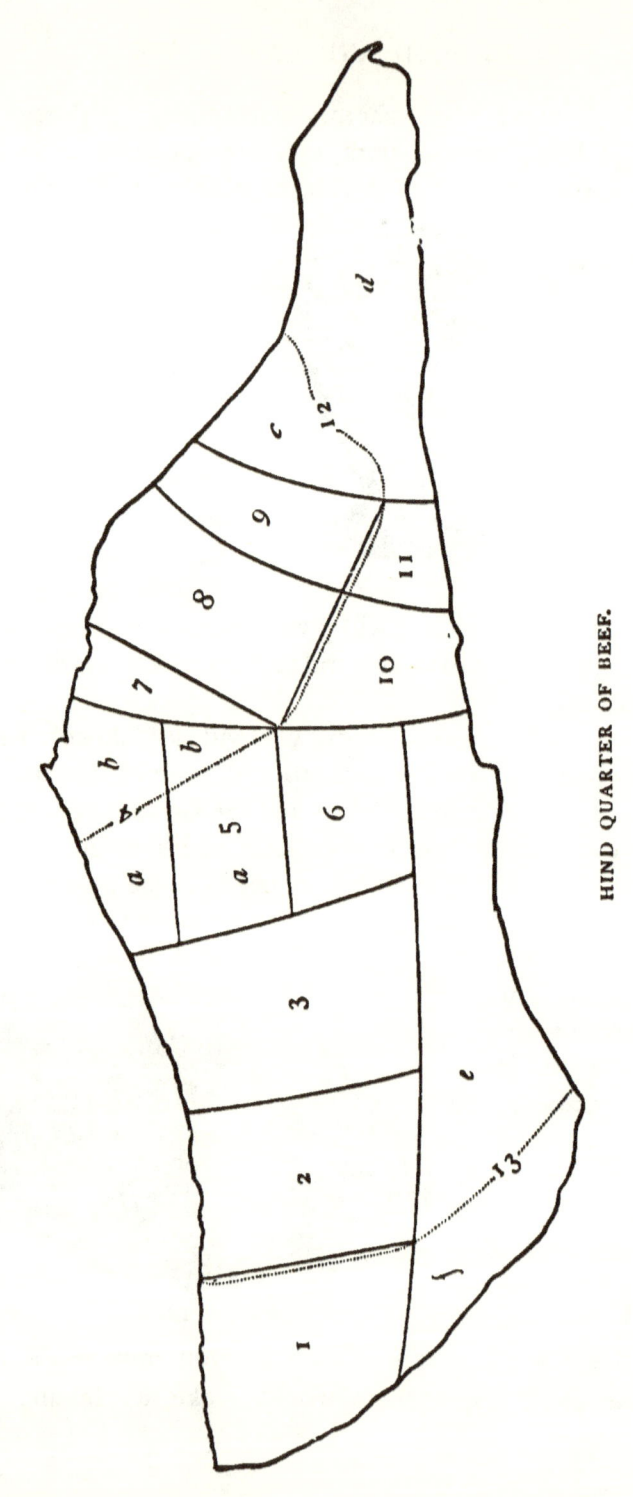

HIND QUARTER OF BEEF.

BUYING FOOD AND CARING FOR IT. 63

EXPLANATION OF DIAGRAM.

	BOSTON.	NEW YORK.	PHILADELPHIA.
1.	Tip end of sirloin.	First cut of ribs.	First cut of ribs.
2.	Second cut of sirloin.	Porter-house steak or sirloin roast.	Sirloin roast or steak.
3.	First cut of sirloin.	Flat-boned sirloin steak or roast.	Sirloin roast or steak.
4.	Back of rump.	(*a*) Large sirloin steaks or roasts.	Hip roast; also rump steak
5.	Middle of rump.	(*a*)	Middle of rump.
6.	Face of rump.		Face of rump.
7.	Aitchbone.	Aitchbone.	Tail end of rump.
8.	Best round steak.	(and 4*b* and 5*b*) Rump steak or roasts.	Best round steak.
9.	Poorer round steak.	(and 12*c*) Round steak.	Poorer round steak.
10.	Best part of vein.	Best part of vein.	Best part of vein.
11.	Poorer part of vein.	Poorer part of vein.	Poorer part of vein.
12.	Shank of round.	(*d*) Leg of beef.	Leg.
13.	Flank.	(*e*) Flank.	(*e*) Flank.

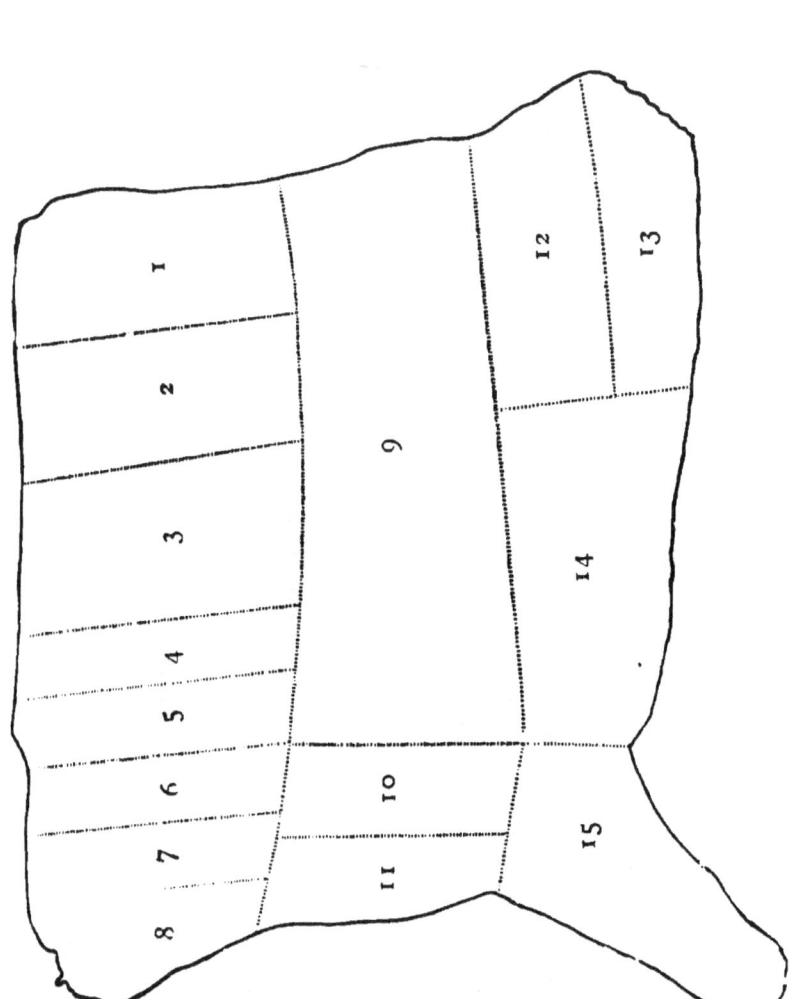

FORE QUARTER OF BEEF

EXPLANATION OF DIAGRAM.

	BOSTON.	NEW YORK.	PHILADELPHIA.
1.	First cut of ribs.	First cut of ribs, with tip of sirloin.	First cut of ribs, with tip of sirloin.
2.	Second cut of ribs.	Second cut of ribs.	Second cut of ribs.
3.	Third cut of ribs.	Third cut of ribs.	Third cut of ribs.
4 and 5.	Best chuck ribs.	Best chuck ribs.	Best chuck ribs.
6 and 7.	Poorer chuck ribs.	Poorer chuck ribs.	Poorer chuck ribs.
8.	Neck piece.	Neck piece.	Neck chuck.
9.	Rattle-ran.	Plate piece.	Plate piece.
10.	Shoulder of mutton.	Shoulder of mutton.	Shoulder of mutton or boler piece.
11.	Sticking piece.		Sticking piece.
12.	Middle cut or rib plate.	Navel end of brisket.	Navel end of brisket.
13.	Navel end of brisket.		
14.	Brisket piece.	Brisket piece.	Brisket piece.
15.	Shin, thick end of brisket, part of sticking piece.	Shin and thick end of brisket.	Shin and thick end of brisket.

for breakfast. The liver of nearly all animals is used, but beef, calves, and pigs' livers are the most common. Sheep and lamb's livers are delicious.

Perhaps you want just about two pounds of the neck of mutton for a broth. You see it cut off and are sure to get nearly what you want. It may be you want a pound or two of the round of beef chopped for a Hamburg steak or for beef tea. If you see it cut, you will not get three or four pounds instead of two. This is true of all the cuts of meat and fish. It is a rare thing that the provision man, who takes your order at the house, does not bring you more than you want. In the fish, vegetable, and fruit market there is constant change, and we cannot be well supplied with the best and cheapest except by a personal visit to the sales place.

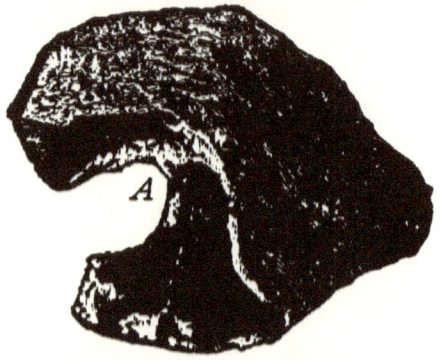

SIRLOIN ROAST, — SECOND CUT.

If one have a large and cold room to keep stores in, and the family be large, it will pay to buy in quantity, provided the housekeeper knows what to do with the supplies when she gets them.

In cold weather I often buy a hind quarter of mutton. To give the housekeeper an idea of what can be done with such a piece of meat, let me explain how I use it. This is for a family of three, with an average of one guest for one meal each day. It must be kept in mind that the part of the hind quarter which will spoil first is the flank; next come the ribs and loin; the leg will keep many weeks if hung in a cold dry place. When the piece of mutton is sent home, I cut off the flank and the thin end of the ribs, leaving the rib and loin chops quite short. Should I want to cook any of the chops that day or the next I cut

BUYING FOOD AND CARING FOR IT. 67

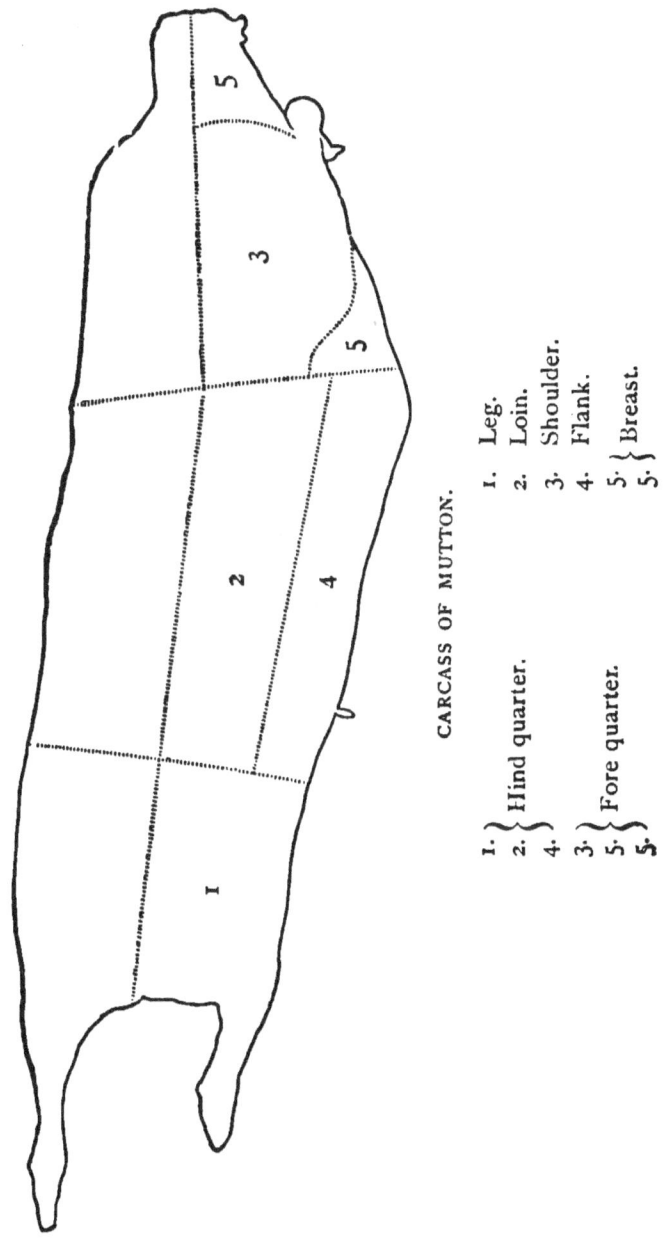

CARCASS OF MUTTON.

1. } Hind quarter.
2. }
4. }

3. } Fore quarter.
5. }
5. }

1. Leg.
2. Loin.
3. Shoulder.
4. Flank.
5. } Breast.
5. }

off the required number, but if I do not care to use them for several days, they are not cut off until that time. The piece of meat is now hung in my cold room, and cut from as required. The flank and thin ribs are freed from every bit of fat ; the lean meat is cut into cubes and placed in a stewpan with four tablespoonfuls of chopped onion, a generous half-cupful of pearl barley, two level tablespoonfuls of salt, one level teaspoonful of pepper, and three quarts of cold water. These materials for a soup are placed on the fire and skimmed carefully when they begin to boil ; then the stewpan is set back where the contents will just bubble for

SIRLOIN ROAST.
A, Tenderloin. B, Back of Sirloin. C, Flank. D. Suet.

three hours. The bones are placed in another stewpan with one quart of cold water. They cook for two hours and then the water is strained into the soup in the other stewpan. When the soup has been cooking for three hours, two tablespoonfuls of butter are put into a small frying-pan and set on the fire. When this becomes hot, two tablespoonfuls of flour are stirred into it, and when the mixture becomes smooth and frothy it is added to the soup; after which a tablespoonful of chopped parsley is added. The result is a gallon of the most delicious Scotch broth. This soup is just as good when warmed over as when first made, and it is so substantial that it answers for luncheon, no meat, fish, or vegetables being required. From the remainder of the hind quarter I get fourteen chops, cutting the last four from the leg, and a good roast. All the fat is rendered for soap grease; and as I make my own soap, this is quite an item.

The weight of the hind quarter described is about twenty pounds, and I save about one third what it would cost me to buy the soup meat, chops, and roast separately. One must have a good sharp knife, a meat-saw, and a cleaver to cut up meats in this manner.

Before going to market one should look through her supplies, and then make a list of things for use with them. A list of the meals that are to be arranged, and such purchases as must be made for these meals, is next in order. One may find it best to make radical changes in her plans

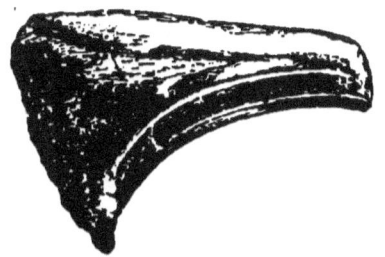 

RIB CHOP BEFORE TRIMMING.   RIB CHOP AFTER TRIMMING.

when she gets to the market; still, the list will be a great aid as a guide. With it, one is not likely to buy too much or too little.

In some places it is a great pleasure to go through the markets, especially on the regular market days. This is particularly true where there is a large German or French population. The women of these nationalities have stalls where they sell eggs, butter, cheese, poultry, fruit, vegetables, and flowers, — the product of their own and neighbors' farms. Nothing can be brighter or more picturesque than are such markets in the spring, summer, and fall, when flowers and vegetables are in abundance. Even the poor laborer's wife takes home her little growing plant, or a bunch of fresh flowers. Going to market has not been all prose to that poor woman, although she had to calculate very closely in her purchases for her table; for has she not had the sight and odor of the plants and green vegetables, and did not their beauty and freshness fill her mind with visions of a beautiful and fragrant country? What a pity there are not such markets in all our cities!

If you have never made a practice of going to market, try the plan now. It will pay you.

Buying Food for a Small Family.

A woman who has to provide for a large family can plan and buy with greater economy than if her family consisted of only two or three. This is especially the case with meats and some kinds of fish. In buying meats, if the family be small, it is wiser to get only the parts actually wanted than to buy large pieces, simply because they are cheaper by the pound. When planning to cook a large piece of meat or fish, its adaptability to being made over into various little dishes should be considered. Pork is the least desirable of the fresh meats for such purposes. For warming over in various ways the following-named meats are the most valuable: poultry, veal, lamb, mutton, and beef. The white meats are better than the red for this purpose. This is also true of fish; the white, dry varieties are much better for made-over dishes than the dark, oily kinds.

LOIN.

The smallest prime roast of beef is one of the short ribs, weighing from three to four pounds. There are two of these short ribs. In Boston they are called the tip of the sirloin; outside New England, the short ribs or first cut of the ribs. The two ribs are included in the cut, but it is possible to get the cut divided.

A small loin of lamb, mutton, or veal, weighing about three or four pounds, makes a roast that will not last forever. Great care must be used in treating these small roasts. The heat must be moderate after the roast is browned and there must be a generous and frequent basting, else the meat will be dry.

RUMP.

A turkey weighing between six and seven pounds is about the smallest one can find in the market, but it can be served in so many ways that one need not grow to hate the sight of turkey before it is all gone.

In the season of lamb it is possible to get a small leg from which there can be cut one or two cutlets. The remainder of the leg can be roasted the following day. If there be a cold room where meats can be hung, a leg of mutton can be used for several meals. Cut off about one third for a roast. In about two or three days cut off a thick slice, to be breaded and fried, and served with tomato sauce. In four or five days the remainder of the leg can be roasted. The leg of mutton that one can get small enough for this purpose will probably be what butchers call yearling lamb. It is not possible to get the best kind of beef or mutton in so light a weight that it can be used to advantage in a small family.

One grouse or partridge, a chicken, duck, or rabbit, a pair of pigeons or of quail, all can be used as a roast in a family of two.

Here are some of the things that can be bought in small quantities: half a pound of sausages, a thin slice of ham that will not weigh more than half a pound, a quarter of a pound of dried beef, a quarter of a pound of smoked bacon, a quarter of a pound of smoked salmon or halibut, one pound of salt codfish, which will answer for three or four dishes, — fish-balls, fish in cream, fish hash, etc.; one thin slice of round steak, weighing about a pound, can be used for beef olives or roll; a slice of veal from the leg can be used in the same way; a piece of beef, cut from the shoulder, and weighing about two or three pounds, can

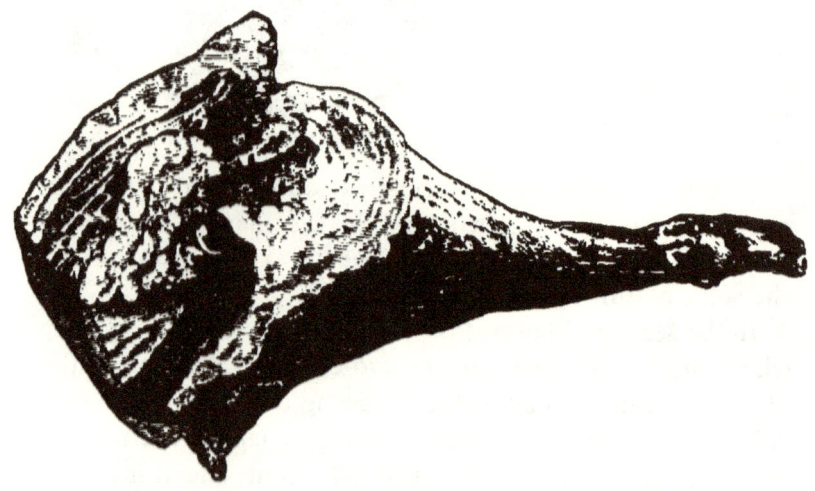

LEG OF MUTTON.

be braised; about a pound and a quarter of fresh beef, cut from any of the tough parts of the animal, can be prepared in a stew; mutton and veal can be used in the same way.

A short porter-house steak may be made to answer for two meals. Cut out the tenderloin, broil it, and serve with brown or mushroom sauce. The remainder of the steak should be put in a cold place and used a day or two later.

In summer vegetables should be bought from day to day, as they are required. In the fall and winter tuberous vegetables may be bought in larger quantities, if there be a cool place in which to store them. The common white potatoes may be purchased by the barrel, but as the sweet potato decays rapidly, it is best to buy it by the pound. Carrots, turnips, beets, onions, squash, etc., are vegetables that can be stored, and if one live in a country town it will be well to store them; but for the housekeeper in the city it will be economy to purchase these vegetables only as she requires them.

Squash spoils quickly after it has been cut. Since one can purchase as small a quantity as two or three pounds, it would, therefore, be unwise to buy a whole squash simply because it costs a little less per pound than when bought in a small quantity.

If one have a cold cellar, it would be well to put in one or two barrels of apples late in the fall; but as all fruits as well as vegetables require a low, dry temperature, it would be unwise to make large purchases unless one have a proper place to keep them in.

Butter, Eggs, and Milk.

Butter is an expensive article, and should be selected with care. If one have the proper place for storing it, and can get it direct from some trustworthy dairy, it would be economical to purchase the winter's supply in October. About fifty pounds will be enough for a family of two for six months. This should be put up in two or three small tubs. It must be kept in a cool, sweet place.

Eggs, of course, are best fresh. It is wise economy for the young housekeeper to pay the extra price, and always be sure of the quality of her supply.

Pure milk is a most important adjunct to the table. As far as it is in her power to do so, the housekeeper should see that the supply comes from a wholesome source, and then do her part to keep the milk good by having the vessels perfectly clean and the surroundings such that the milk shall not be contaminated.

About Groceries.

Flour, if stored in a cool, sweet, dry place, will be better for bread-making if kept several months after being made. All the meals are better when fresh, and only a small quantity should be purchased at a time. Sugar is about the same price, whether you buy it in small or large quantities. It saves much bother to buy the granulated and cut sugar in sufficient quantities to last a month or more. Powdered sugar "cakes," and only a small amount should be kept in store. English breakfast tea improves with age, while the lighter teas do not. The green coffee berry grows better as it grows older; but after coffee is roasted it quickly loses strength and flavor, so that only a small quantity of the roasted berry should be bought at one time.

Buy flavors, spices, etc. in small quantities, and get only the purest. The store closet should always contain macaroni, rice, fine breakfast hominy, tapioca, barley, corn-starch, arrowroot, farina, chocolate, breakfast cocoa, tea, coffee, some of the cereal preparations for mush, white and red pepper, mustard, a small supply of whole spices, such as cinnamon, clove, nutmeg, mace, allspice, and pepper; also ground cinnamon, mace, and allspice. The less ground clove one uses the better. It is well to have on hand a bunch each of dried thyme, savory, and sage, and half an ounce of bay leaves, which can be purchased at the grocer's or druggist's, a few packages of gelatine, and a small package of sea-moss farina, which insures a foundation for a cold dessert at short notice.

For emergencies, the store closet should always contain some canned peas, tomatoes, corn, fruit, chicken, salmon, a box of fancy crackers, some plain soda crackers, a bottle of olives, and a can of condensed milk. One need never be at a loss to prepare a good meal at short notice with this supply in reserve.

CARE OF FOOD.

One may buy food with good judgment, and yet fail to be an economical provider because she does not take proper care of it. Perfect cleanliness is essential for the best preservation of food. The cellar, pantries, storerooms, refrigerators, and all the receptacles in which food is kept, should be frequently inspected and thoroughly cleaned. Heat and moisture tend to cause decay; therefore it is important that all foods should be surrounded with pure, cool, dry air. When it is possible, expose every closet and food receptacle to the sun and air several times a week.

All kinds of cooked food, particularly the animal foods, spoil quickly when covered closely while still warm. All soups, meat, fish, bread, etc., that are to be kept for many days or hours, should be cooled thoroughly and quickly in a current of cold air. In hot weather it is a good plan, when cooling soups, milk, or any liquid mass, to place the vessel containing the food in another of cold water, — with ice, if convenient, — and set it in a cool draught.

All meat, when not hung up, should be placed on a dish and set in a cool place. If poultry be drawn, and a few pieces of charcoal be placed in the body, it will keep longer than if hung undrawn. It must not be washed until it is to be cooked. The dryer the meat is kept the better.

A dish of charcoal placed in the refrigerator or pantry helps to keep the atmosphere dry and sweet.

Milk and butter should be kept in a cool place, and away from all strong odors.

Bread and cake must be thoroughly cooled before being put in boxes or jars; if not, the steam will cause them to mould quickly. The bread box should be washed, scalded, and thoroughly aired in the sun, twice a week. The crusts and stale pieces of white raised bread, for which there is no other use, should be put in a pan, be dried slowly in a warm oven, and then be pounded, sifted, and put in glass jars for future use.

All the trimmings of fat should be rendered while they are sweet; then strained into jars or pails kept for that purpose. Put beef, pork, and chicken fat together; this will answer for deep frying. Ham, bacon, and sausage fat answers for frying potatoes, hominy, mush, etc. All the strong-flavored fats, such as mutton, duck, turkey, and the skimmings from boiled ham, are to be kept by themselves for making soap.

It should be remembered that pure fat will keep sweet many months, but if water or any foreign substance be left in it, it will spoil quickly. When rendering or clarifying fat, cook it slowly until there are no bubbles. As long as bubbles form, you may be sure that there is water in the fat. If put away in that condition it will become rancid.

Clarifying Fat.

To clarify fat that has been used for frying, put it into a frying kettle, being careful not to let the sediment go in, and place the kettle on the fire. When the fat becomes hot, add three raw potatoes cut into slices, and stir well. The impurities gather on the potatoes. Three potatoes will be enough for four pounds of fat. Whenever there are any trimmings of fat from any kind of meat cut them in bits and place in a frying-pan on the back part of the stove, where they will cook slowly until all the liquid fat has been extracted. Strain this into a pot kept for this purpose.

As soon as the fat is skimmed from soups, gravies, and the water in which meat has been boiled, it should be clarified, as the water and other objectionable particles contained in it will cause it to become rancid if it stands a long time. Put it on the stove, in a frying-pan, and heat it slowly. When it becomes melted, set it where it will simply bubble, and keep it there (being careful not to let it burn) until there is no motion, and all the sediment has fallen to the bottom of the pan. When this stage is reached the fat is clarified.

Sometimes fat that has been used several times for frying, and has not been strained, will become dark and unfit for use. This may be put into a kettle with about six times as much hot water, boiled for twenty minutes, turned into a large pan, and set in a cold place. When the contents of the pan become cold, the fat will be found in the form of a solid cake on the surface of the water. It must be removed, and clarified in the manner already described.

To clarify butter, put it in a stewpan, and set it on the back part of the range, where it will heat slowly. When a clear, oily substance is found on top, and a cloudy sediment at the bottom of the pan, lift the pan gently and pour off the clear substance, which will be the clarified butter.

When the fat is ready to strain, draw it back where it will partially cool; then strain it through a piece of cheese-cloth.

Tin or stoneware vessels are the best in which to keep fat. The pails in which lard comes are very good for soap grease, because, knowing their exact capacity, one knows just how much grease there is on hand. Have the pails covered, and keep them in a cool place.

Save for stock all the bones and trimmings from fresh meat, the bones from roasts or broils, and such pieces of cooked meat as are too tough or hard to serve cold or in made dishes. Put these in a stewpan, with water enough to cover them, and simmer for five or six hours. Strain into a bowl, and cool quickly. No matter how little bone or meat there may be, cook it in this way while it is fresh and sweet. A gill of stock has great value in warming over meats, fish, and vegetables.

Odds and Ends.

It is true that the care of remnants and their preparation for the table is not a slight matter; but in the household where attention is given to this matter there is no waste, and a pleasant change of fare can be made daily. If a housekeeper looks into her larder each morning, and avails herself of the opportunities she finds to make little dishes of the bits of food which she sees before her, the work of caring for the odds and ends may become a pleasure rather than a burden; the preparation of this food giving a bright woman an opportunity to exercise much taste and skill in producing dainty and healthful dishes.

Pieces of cold meat or fish may be divided into small pieces, and warmed in a white or brown sauce; or the sauce and meat or fish may be put in a small baking dish, covered with grated bread crumbs, and then browned in the oven. If there be not enough fish or meat to serve to the entire family, use an extra quantity of sauce, and fill up the dish with either well seasoned mashed potatoes, hominy, rice, or macaroni. Cover lightly with grated bread crumbs, and dot with butter. Bake this for half an hour in a moderately hot oven.

Cold meat or fish may be hashed fine and mixed with potato, rice, or hominy, and a sauce, and made into croquettes.

Bits of cooked ham or sausages may be minced fine and mixed with hashed potatoes; the mixture being then well seasoned and put into a frying-pan, with a little butter or sweet drippings, and browned. If there be a little gravy of any kind, it may be added to any of the above-mentioned dishes.

Nearly all kinds of vegetables may be combined in a salad or a hash.

Tough pieces of meat and bones may be used in making little stews or a little soup stock. All kinds of meats may be combined in making a stew or soup.

A few spoonfuls of almost any kind of meat, fish, or vegetable may be heated in a sauce and spread over a plain omelet, just before rolling it up, thus giving a change in this dish of eggs.

A soft-boiled egg left from a meal may be boiled until hard, and then used in a salad or an egg sauce.

Pieces of bread may be used for puddings and griddle-cakes, and, in the form of dried crumbs, for breading.

Pieces of cake and gingerbread may be used in puddings.

Gravies, sauces, and soups, no matter how small the quantity, should be saved to use in warming over meat, fish, or vegetables.

A few tablespoonfuls of cold rice or hominy are often a pleasing addition to muffins or griddle-cakes. Indeed, it is rarely necessary to waste a particle of food if the proper attention be given to the little details of kitchen management.

CHAPTER VIII.

SOUPS.

A Good Plain Stock.

7 quarts of cold water.	1 teaspoonful of pepper-corns.
A shin of beef weighing ten pounds.	A tiny bit of mace.
	6 whole cloves.
4 tablespoonfuls of butter.	½ pint of minced onion.
1 generous tablespoonful of salt.	4 tablespoonfuls of minced carrot.
A piece of cinnamon two inches long.	4 tablespoonfuls of minced celery.
	A bouquet of sweet herbs.

Have the butcher cut the shin of beef into several parts. Wash it in cold water, and then cut off any particles that do not seem perfectly sweet. The lower end of the leg, near the hoofs, is apt to be a little tainted. Cut all the meat from the bones, and then cut it into small pieces. Put one tablespoonful of the butter in the soup pot, and place on the hottest part of the fire. Put the meat in the pot, and stir frequently until it is browned. It will take about half an hour for this. At first the juices are drawn out of the meat, making a great deal of liquid in the pot. The cooking must be continued until all this juice has evaporated, leaving a dry, brown substance on the bottom of the pan. Now add one pint of the water, and stir the meat well, scraping the brown substance from the bottom of the pot. Add the remainder of the water and the salt and bones. As soon as the soup comes to the boiling point, skim carefully several times. Lay a piece of cheese-cloth in a strainer and place in a bowl. Skim into this, and when the soup has ceased to throw up any more scum, pour back into the soup pot the clear liquid which will be found in the bowl. Draw the soup pot back where the contents will bubble gently for eight hours.

Put the minced vegetables and three tablespoonfuls of butter in a small frying-pan, and cook slowly for half an hour. At the end of that time draw forward to a hotter part of the range and stir until they begin to brown; then draw them to one side of the pan and press out the butter. Add them to the soup, and pour the butter into a cup, as it will be useful in making sauces.

Tie up the spice and the bouquet of sweet herbs in a piece of cheese-cloth and put into the soup pot. Cook the soup for an hour and a half longer; then strain through a coarse napkin into two or three bowls, and cook rapidly. Set away in a cold place and it will become a jelly. When about to use it, remove all the fat and turn into a saucepan, being careful to keep back any sediment there may be at the bottom of the bowl. It will then be ready to serve as a clear soup; or it can have any kind of a garnish added to it, such as cooked rice, macaroni, vegetables, etc. It may require a little more salt and pepper.

This soup may be kept for months if sealed in jars. Have the jars hot and the soup boiling hot. On filling the jars, seal at once, and keep in a cool, dark place.

Second Stock.

Put away in a cold place the meat and bones which were left from the strained stock. In the morning add six quarts of water to it, and cook gently for six hours; then strain and put away to cool. This stock lacks the fine flavor of the first stock, but it is useful for thick soups, sauces, and made-over dishes.

Macaroni Soup.

1½ pints of clear soup.
4 sticks of macaroni.
1 teaspoonful of salt.

Break the macaroni into small pieces and throw it into one quart of boiling water containing the teaspoonful of salt. Let it boil for twenty-five minutes with the cover off the stewpan. Drain off the water and add the macaroni to the hot stock. Cover, and cook for ten or fifteen minutes, being careful to have the soup only bubble at one side. It may require a little more salt and pepper.

Vermicelli and any of the smaller forms of Italian paste may be added to the clear stock and cooked gently for about twenty minutes.

Rice Soup.

Wash two tablespoonfuls of rice and cook it the same as the macaroni; then drain it, and add to the pint and a half of hot stock. Cook the mixture gently for ten minutes.

Beef Soup.

2 pounds of beef from the round.
2 quarts of water.
2 tablespoonfuls of minced onion.
1 tablespoonful of minced carrot.
1 tablespoonful of minced celery.
½ pint of potatoes, chopped fine.
½ gill of barley.
1 clove.
2 tablespoonfuls of butter.
1 tablespoonful of flour.
⅙ teaspoonful of pepper.
1 teaspoonful of salt.

Free the meat from fat and cut it into fine pieces. Put it in the soup pot with the cold water and heat slowly to the boiling point. Skim carefully, and set back where the soup will just bubble at one side of the pot. Wash the barley and put it on to cook in one pint of cold water. At the end of half an hour pour off the water and add the barley to the soup. When the soup has been cooking for three hours put the butter, minced onion, carrot, and celery into a frying-pan and cook slowly for fifteen minutes. Skim the vegetables from the butter and put them in the soup. Stir the flour into the butter remaining in the pan. Cook until brown, stirring all the while; then add to the soup. Now add the potatoes and salt and pepper, and cook for half an hour longer.

Oxtail Soup.

1 oxtail.
1 quart of water.
1 pint of stock.
1 heaping tablespoonful of corn-starch.
1 tablespoonful of minced celery.
2 tablespoonfuls of minced onion.
1 tablespoonful of minced carrot.
20 pepper-corns.
2 whole cloves.
A tiny bit of mace.
A small piece of cinnamon.
1 bay leaf.
1 small leaf of sage.
1 small sprig of parsley.
1 small sprig of thyme.

Free the oxtail from fat and cut into small joints. Wash these in several waters and then put them in a stewpan with the cold water. Place on the range and heat slowly to the boiling point; then skim, and move the stewpan back where the water will just bubble at one side of the stewpan. Cook for one hour. Tie the vegetables, herbs, and spice in a piece of netting, and put them in the stewpan. Add the salt, and cook for one hour longer. Strain the broth into a bowl and set away in a cold place. Rinse the oxtail in cold water and put in a cold place.

When the broth is cold, skim off all the fat. Put the soup stock and skimmed broth in a stewpan, and set on the fire. When this boils, add the corn-starch, mixed smoothly with a gill of cold water. Cook for fifteen minutes; then add the oxtail and cook for ten minutes longer. Taste, to see if seasoned enough, and serve very hot.

A few tablespoonfuls of sherry will improve this soup for many tastes. It should be added just before the soup is poured into the tureen.

Veal Broth.

2 pounds of the poorer parts of veal.	1 level tablespoonful of salt.
2 quarts of water.	¼ teaspoonful of pepper.
3 tablespoonfuls of minced onion.	¼ teaspoonful of celery seeds.
1 tablespoonful of minced carrot.	2 tablespoonfuls of butter.
1 whole clove.	2 tablespoonfuls of flour.
1 inch piece of cinnamon.	1 pint of raw potato cubes.

Cut the veal into cubes and put the bones and meat into a stewpan with the water, seasoning, and vegetables. Place on the fire, and when the soup comes to the boiling point, skim carefully, and then set back where it will just bubble. Heat the butter in a small saucepan, and add the flour to it. Stir until the mixture is smooth and frothy; then stir it into the broth. Simmer the broth for two hours and a half, and, after adding the pint of potato cubes, cook for half an hour longer.

The potatoes may be omitted and a quarter of a cupful of rice be added when the broth has been cooking for an hour and a half.

Scotch Broth.

1½ pounds of neck or shoulder of mutton.	1 tablespoonful of butter.
1 tablespoonful of pearl barley.	1 tablespoonful of flour.
1 tablespoonful of minced onion.	1 heaping teaspoonful of salt.
1 tablespoonful of minced carrot.	¼ teaspoonful of pepper.
1 tablespoonful of minced turnip.	1 teaspoonful of chopped parsley.
1 tablespoonful of minced celery.	3 pints of water.

Remove all the fat from the mutton and cut the lean meat into cubes, which should be put in a stewpan with the chopped vegetables, salt, pepper, and the barley, well washed. Tie the bones in a piece of coarse white netting and put them in the stewpan with the other ingredients. Add the three pints of cold water and cover the stewpan.

Place the soup on the stove where it will heat slowly to the boiling point. When it reaches that temperature, skim it and set back where it will only bubble slightly at one side of the pan. Cook in this manner for three hours, being careful not to let it more than bubble gently in all that time. At the end of the three hours take out the bones. Now put the butter in a little saucepan and set on the fire to heat. When hot, stir in the flour, and cook — stirring all the time — until the mixture is smooth and frothy. Stir this into the broth; then add the chopped parsley, and cook ten minutes longer.

Vegetable Soup.

1 pound of beef.	¼ pint of potato cubes.
2 quarts of water.	1 tablespoonful of rice.
1 gill of minced carrot.	1 tablespoonful of flour.
1 gill of minced turnip.	1 generous teaspoonful of salt.
½ gill of minced onion.	⅛ teaspoonful of pepper.
1 tablespoonful of minced celery.	

Cut the meat into cubes; then put it in a stewpan and set on the fire with the cold water. When this boils, skim carefully. Mix the flour to a smooth paste with one gill of cold water, and stir into the boiling ingredients. Next add the rice. Move the stewpan back where the contents will bubble at one side for one hour; then add the onion and carrot. Cook for one hour longer, and then put in the turnips, potatoes, salt, and pepper, and simmer for half an hour longer. Serve hot.

Two quarts of the water in which the bones and hard pieces of meat have been cooked may be substituted for the beef and water. If one choose, half a pint of finely shred cabbage may be added at the same time the onions and carrots are put in the soup.

Chicken Soup.

3 pints of the water in which a fowl was boiled.	2 tablespoonfuls of minced onion.
2 tablespoonfuls of rice.	2 tablespoonfuls of minced celery.
1 tablespooonful of butter.	1 teaspoonful of salt, — generous.
1 tablespoonful of minced carrot.	⅛ of a teaspoonful of pepper.
	½ teaspoonful of parsley.

Wash the rice and put it in a stewpan with the chicken stock. Place on the fire and cook for two hours. The soup must not boil in that time; keep it where it will be at the point of boiling, but do not let it bubble. At the end of two hours put the butter and vegetables in a small frying-pan and set on the fire, to cook slowly for twenty minutes. Now draw the pan to a hotter part of the range, and stir for one minute. After pressing the butter from the vegetables, put them with the soup. Put the flour with the butter remaining in the pan, and stir until smooth and frothy; then stir the mixture into the soup. Add the salt, pepper, and chopped parsley, and cook the soup for thirty minutes longer, allowing it to bubble at one side of the saucepan.

If you have a little cold chicken, cut it into small cubes and add it to the soup at the same time the vegetables are put in. If you cannot get celery, take half a teaspoonful of celery salt, and in that case use only half a teaspoonful of the common salt.

This soup can be made with the stock from boiled fowl, or that obtained by boiling the bones of roast chicken.

Cream of Rice Soup.

Make this in the same way as chicken soup, with the addition of one tablespoonful of rice, a slight grating of nutmeg, a tiny bit of mace, and a piece of stick cinnamon about an inch long, and the omission of the parsley.

When the time required for the cooking has expired, take out the spice and pour the soup into a fine sieve. Rub all

SOUPS. 87

the rice through, using a wooden vegetable masher. Put the strained mixture in a clean saucepan with a pint of milk, and let it boil up once.

If you have cream in plenty, use half cream and half milk. The soup will be much smoother if it is strained a second time, after the milk has been boiled with it.

Mock Bisque.

1 pint of stewed tomatoes.
1 pint of milk.
1 tablespoonful of flour.
1 tablespoonful of butter.

½ teaspoonful of soda.
¼ teaspoonful of pepper.
1 teaspoonful of salt.

Reserve half a gill of the milk and put the remainder on to cook in the double-boiler. Put the tomatoes on to cook in a stewpan. Mix the flour with the cold milk and stir into the boiling milk. Cook for ten minutes; then add the salt, pepper, and butter. Stir the soda into the hot tomatoes and stir for half a minute; then rub through a strainer. Add the strained tomatoes to the thickened milk, and serve at once.

If canned tomatoes be used, stir the contents of the can before measuring, that the proper proportion of the juice of the tomatoes shall be used. If it be inconvenient to serve the soup when the tomatoes and thickened milk are done, keep them hot in their separate stewpans, and do not mix until just before the time to serve.

Tomato Soup.

1 pint of canned tomatoes.
½ pint of stock or water.
1 teaspoonful of salt.
⅛ teaspoonful of pepper.
1 teaspoonful of sugar.
1 tablespoonful of minced carrot.

2 tablespoonfuls of minced onion.
2 tablespoonfuls of butter.
1 tablespoonful of flour.
1 heaped teaspoonful of cornstarch.
2 whole cloves.

Put the tomato and stock in a saucepan and set on the fire. Cook the vegetables slowly in the butter for twenty minutes; then press out the butter and put the vegetables in the soup. Into the butter remaining in the pan put the flour, and stir until smooth and frothy; then add to the soup. Mix the corn-starch with four tablespoonfuls of cold water, and stir into the soup. Add the other ingredients, and simmer for one hour. Strain, and serve with toasted or crisped bread.

Tomato Soup, No. 2.

1 pint of canned tomatoes.	½ teaspoonful of salt.
½ pint of water.	1 teaspoonful of sugar.
1 tablespoonful of butter.	⅛ teaspoonful of pepper.
1 tablespoonful of flour.	

Put the tomato, water, and seasonings in a stewpan and set on the fire. Beat the butter and flour together until creamy. When the soup begins to boil, stir this mixture into it, and cook for ten minutes. Strain, and serve with toasted or fried bread.

Tomato and Macaroni Soup.

1 pint of meat stock.	1 gill of cold water.
1 quart of stewed tomatoes.	2 tablespoonfuls of corn-starch.
1 teaspoonful of sugar.	½ pint of broken macaroni.
2 teaspoonfuls of salt.	1 tablespoonful of butter.
¼ teaspoonful of pepper.	

The stock can be made with any bits of dry hard meat, or the bones from roasted or broiled meat; or one can take the water in which a fowl was boiled.

Put the tomatoes and stock in a stewpan and set on the fire. Mix the corn-starch with the cold water, and stir into the boiling liquid. Add also the sugar, salt, and pepper.

SOUPS.   89

Put the macaroni in a stewpan with a quart of boiling water and boil for twenty minutes. Pour off the water, and put the macaroni in the soup. Add the butter at the same time, and cook for ten minutes longer.

If the soup be preferred smooth, it can be strained before the macaroni is added.

Corn Soup.

½ can of corn.
1½ pints of milk.
1½ tablespoonfuls of butter.
1 tablespoonful of flour.

1 level teaspoonful of salt.
⅙ teaspoonful of pepper.
1 tablespoonful of minced onion.

Mash the corn as fine as possible, and then put it in the double-boiler. Reserve one gill of the milk, and, putting the remainder with the corn, cook for fifteen minutes. Cook the butter and onions together for ten minutes, and add to the corn and milk. Mix the cold milk with the flour, and stir into the hot mixture. Add the salt and pepper, and cook for ten minutes longer. Strain, and serve hot.

Potato Soup.

4 potatoes of medium size.
1½ pints of milk.
2 tablespoonfuls of minced celery.
4 tablespoonfuls of minced onion.
1 tablespoonful of flour.

1 teaspoonful of salt.
¼ teaspoonful of pepper.
1 tablespoonful of butter.
½ teaspoonful of minced parsley.

Pare the potatoes, and, placing on the fire in enough boiling water to cover them, cook for thirty minutes. Reserve one gill of the milk, and put the remainder in the double-boiler with the onions and celery, and place on the fire. Mix the cold milk with the flour, and stir into the boiling milk. When the potatoes have been cooking for thirty minutes, pour off all the water and mash them fine and light. Gradually beat into them the milk. Now add the salt, pepper, and butter, and rub the soup through a sieve. Return to the fire, and add the minced parsley. Cook for five minutes, and serve immediately.

Hub Soup.

½ pint of baked beans.
½ pint of stewed tomatoes.
1 pint of water.

1 level teaspoonful of salt.
⅕ teaspoonful of pepper.
½ teaspoonful of mustard.

Put all the ingredients into a stewpan and simmer for half an hour, with the stewpan covered; then rub the mixture through a coarse sieve and return to the fire. Simmer for ten minutes, and serve with toasted crackers or bread.

Lima Bean Soup.

½ pint of beans.
½ pint of milk.
2 quarts of water.
3 tablespoonfuls of minced onion.
1 tablespoonful of minced carrot.
1 tablespoonful of minced celery.

1 bay leaf.
2 whole cloves.
3 tablespoonfuls of butter.
1 tablespoonful of flour.
1 teaspoonful of salt.
¼ teaspoonful of pepper.

Soak the beans over night in two quarts of cold water. Pour this water off and rinse the beans in fresh water. Now put them in a stewpan with two quarts of cold water. Cook slowly for two hours. Cook the vegetables in the butter for twenty minutes. On taking them out, add them to the soup. Put the flour into the butter remaining in the pan, and stir until smooth and frothy. Add this mixture to the soup. Now add the other seasonings, and cook for one hour longer. At the end of this time take out the spice and rub the soup through a fine sieve. Return to the fire and add half a pint of hot milk. Stir the soup until it boils; then serve.

Dried Pea Soup.

½ pint of peas.
2 quarts of water.
4 tablespoonfuls of minced onion.
1 tablespoonful of minced carrot.
1 tablespoonful of minced celery.
2 tablespoonfuls of drippings or butter.

1 ounce of ham, or a ham bone.
½ pound of cold roast or broiled meat.
1 tablespoonful of flour.
¼ teaspoonful of pepper.
1 teaspoonful of salt.
1 bay leaf.

Soak the peas over night in two quarts of cold water. In the morning pour off the water, and put the peas, the meat and bone, and two quarts of fresh water in the soup kettle, and place on the fire. Cook gently. At the end of three hours put the drippings and vegetables in a small saucepan, and cook slowly for half an hour. When the vegetables have been cooked for this time, draw the saucepan forward where they will cook a little faster for one minute. Stir all the time; then draw them to the side of the pan to press out the fat, and after that put them with the soup. Into the fat remaining in the pan put the tablespoonful of flour, and stir until the mixture becomes smooth and frothy. Stir this into the soup, and add the salt, pepper, and bay leaf. Cover, and cook for three hours longer. At the end of that time take out the meat and bay leaf, and rub the soup through a coarse sieve or colander. Return to the fire and make very hot. Serve with crisped bread.

The soup must be stirred from the bottom frequently all the time it is cooking, and it must never more than bubble gently. If it cooks too rapidly it will get too thick and be in danger of scorching.

Cream of Dried Pea Soup.

Make the same as the dried pea soup; and, after straining, add a pint of milk and a little more salt and pepper. Stir all the time until it boils; then strain again, and serve.

Bean Soup.

½ pint of white beans.	3 tablespoonfuls of drippings or butter.
¼ pound of lean salt pork.	1 tablespoonful of flour.
3 quarts of water.	¼ teaspoonful of pepper.
4 tablespoonfuls of minced onion.	Salt to taste.
1 tablespoonful of minced carrot.	
1 tablespoonful of minced celery.	

Make this the same as the dried pea soup.

Cream of Bean Soup.

Make the same as bean soup; then add a pint of hot milk, and boil up once. Strain, and serve.

Oyster Soup.

1 pint of oysters.	¼ teaspoonful of pepper.
1 pint of milk.	2 tablespoonfuls of butter.
½ pint of cold water.	Salt.
2 level tablespoonfuls of flour.	

Put a strainer over a bowl and turn the oysters into it. Pour the water over the oysters and stir with a spoon until all the liquid has passed through the strainer. Turn the oysters into a dish and set in a cold place.

Reserve a gill of the milk, and, pouring the remainder in the double-boiler, set it on the fire. Put the oyster liquor in a stewpan and heat slowly, being careful not to burn. Mix the cold milk with the flour, and, stirring into the boiling milk, cook for ten minutes. When the oyster liquor boils, skim it. When the flour and milk have cooked for ten minutes, add the oysters, butter, salt, pepper, and oyster liquor, and continue cooking until the oysters curl on the edge and are plump. Serve at once.

It is well to provide toasted or crisped crackers with this soup.

Clam Soup.

1 pint of clams.	1 heaping tablespoonful of flour.
1 pint of milk.	1 heaping tablespoonful of butter.
½ pint of water.	1 teaspoonful of salt.
2 tablespoonfuls cracker crumbs.	¼ teaspoonful of pepper.

Separate the heads from the clams, and put them on to simmer with the water for fifteen minutes. Beat the flour and butter together, and stir into the water in which the heads of the clams are cooking. Now add the seasoning and milk; and when the mixture boils, strain into another stewpan. Chop the soft parts of the clams and add them to the soup. Now add the cracker crumbs. Boil the soup for three minutes, and serve.

Clam Chowder.

1 pint of clams.	2 tablespoonfuls of minced onion.
1 pint of water.	1 tablespoonful of flour.
1 pint of milk.	2 teaspoonfuls of salt.
3 gills of potato cubes.	⅓ teaspoonful of pepper.
2 ounces of sliced salt pork.	3 Boston butter crackers.

Wash the clams in the water and turn both into a strainer which has been placed over a bowl. Cut the soft parts of the clams from the hard, and put away in a cold place. Chop the hard parts fine and put them in a stewpan. Strain on these, through a piece of cheese-cloth, the clam water; after which place it on the fire and cook gently for twenty minutes. Fry the sliced pork for ten minutes; then add the onion, and cook ten minutes longer. Take the pork and onions from the pan and add to the chopped clams. Put the flour into the fat remaining in the pan, and stir until smooth and frothy. Add this mixture to the clam broth and cook for ten minutes longer. Now put the potato cubes in a stewpan and strain the clam broth over them. Season with the salt and pepper, and cook for twenty minutes. Split the crackers and soak them in the milk for four minutes. Add the soft parts of the clams and the milk and crackers to the cooking mixture. When all boils up, serve.

The milk may be omitted and half a pint of strained tomato be added when the potatoes and broth have been cooking for ten minutes.

Fish Chowder.

2 pounds of fish.	½ pint of milk.
3 ounces of salt pork.	1 tablespoonful of flour.
3 tablespoonfuls of minced onion.	⅓ teaspoonful of pepper.
3 gills of potato cubes.	2 teaspoonfuls of salt.
1 pint of water.	3 Boston butter crackers.

First, skin the fish; and after cutting all the flesh from the bones and cutting it in small pieces, cook the bones with the water for ten minutes. Cut the pork into thin slices and fry until crisp and brown. On taking it from the pan, put the onions into the fat, and cook slowly for ten minutes. Put a layer of fish in a stewpan and sprinkle half the potatoes, fried onions, and salt and pepper on this. Put in the remainder of the fish, and finish with the rest of the potatoes, onions, salt, and pepper. Into the fat remaining in the frying-pan put the flour, and stir until smooth and frothy. Gradually pour on this the water in which the fish bones were boiled. Stir until it boils; then pour on the fish mixture.

Lay the slices of pork on top, and cook gently for twenty minutes. Split the crackers and soak them in the milk for four minutes. Remove the slices of pork and turn crackers and milk into the chowder. When this boils up, serve.

For a change, the milk may be omitted and half a pint of tomatoes be added. Any kind of light fish will answer, such as cod, haddock, catfish, whitefish, etc.

Salt Codfish Chowder.

1 pint of milk.	¼ teaspoonful of pepper.
½ pint of shredded codfish.	1 tablespoonful of flour.
3 gills of potato cubes	Salt.
3 ounces of salt pork.	3 Boston crackers.
2 tablespoonfuls of minced onion.	

Wash the fish and cut it into two-inch lengths. Tear these in pieces, and, covering with cold water, soak for three or four hours. Slice the pork, and cook in the frying-pan for ten minutes. Add the onion and cook for ten minutes. Now add the flour, and stir until smooth; after which, stir in one gill of water. Put the potatoes in a stew-pan and pour the mixture in the frying-pan over them. Season with the pepper and half a teaspoonful of salt. Place on the fire and cook for ten minutes; then take out the slices of pork and add the fish, milk, and the crackers split. Cook gently for half an hour, being careful to let the chowder only bubble at one side of the stewpan. At the end of the half-hour, taste before serving, to be sure to have it salt enough.

CHAPTER IX.

FISH.

FRESH fish should frequently be substituted for meat. For those who live in seaboard towns there is no trouble in obtaining a variety. Every inland place has its own peculiar species, which should have precedence over other kinds; for the first thing to be taken into account is freshness. Fish brought from a distance deteriorates with the handling it receives and the time it is out of the water.

The lighter the fish, the greater the variety of modes by which it may be cooked. It also may be served more frequently without one's becoming tired of it. For example, at the Isles of Shoals visitors are offered broiled scrod every day in the week, yet they do not weary of the dish in a stay of months. At Nantucket broiled bluefish is served daily, and it is so delicious that its appearance three times a day would at first be hailed with pleasure; but after a short time the appetite would become palled, because the fish is rich. It would be the same with the freshest and most toothsome salmon and mackerel. A rich fish satiates much sooner than a lighter and poorer kind, and for this reason it is advisable to avoid having the richer varieties frequently. Of course, the poorer kinds require more and richer sauces than salmon, mackerel, or bluefish. White-fish, like cod, haddock, cusk, halibut, and flounders, is improved by the addition of sauces made of milk, cream, or white stock.

Boiling is the least desirable mode of preparing fish, because it causes the greatest loss of flavor and nutriment. A fine sauce is needed to make the dish satisfactory. But boiling has one merit: the remains of the fish after the first meal are in better form for use in little dishes of many kinds than they are if any other way of cooking be employed. Small fish, like brook trout, smelts, etc., are best when fried.

How to Boil Fish.

Fresh fish should always be put on to cook in salted boiling water. A little lemon juice or vinegar in the water makes the flesh of the fish firmer and improves the flavor. For some tastes the flavor is improved still more by putting in the water, tied in a piece of cheese-cloth, a few spoonfuls of minced onion, carrot, and celery, two bay leaves, a sprig each of thyme, parsley, and summer savory, a small bit of cinnamon, and two whole cloves. There should be only water enough to cover the fish. If there be a fish-kettle with a tray, lay the fish in the tray and do not wrap it in a cloth. If, however, there be no regular fish-kettle, pin the fish in a piece of cloth, put a large plate in the bottom of a large flat saucepan, and lay the fish on this. A thick square of fish will take longer to cook than the same number of pounds cut from a long, slender fish. A small cod, haddock, bluefish, lake trout, salmon trout, whitefish, etc., weighing from three to five pounds, will require thirty minutes' cooking. The water should bubble only at the side of the saucepan. A large fish of the same kind, weighing six or eight pounds, would require only ten minutes' more time. A thick square or cube of halibut or salmon, weighing from three to five pounds, would require forty minutes' cooking; and if it weighed six or eight pounds, it would require an hour. If the fish be put into cold water the juices will be drawn out. The fish will be broken if the water be allowed to boil hard during the cooking. A good sauce should always be served with boiled fish.

Baked Fish.

½ pint of cracker crumbs.
½ pint cold water.
1 teaspoonful of salt.
¼ teaspoonful of pepper.
2 tablespoonfuls of butter.
½ teaspoonful of summer savory.

1 teaspoonful of minced parsley.
½ teaspoonful of onion juice.
3 ounces of fat salt pork.
A fish weighing about four or five pounds.

For the dressing, mix the cracker crumbs, herbs, salt, pepper, and butter together; then moisten with water, and add the onion juice. Have the fish split and drawn, but leave on the head and tail. Cut off the fins and scrape off any scales that may still cling to it. Wash and wipe dry; then rub one tablespoonful of salt into it, put the dressing in the opening, and pin together with a skewer. Cut slits on the top of the fish, about two inches long and half an inch deep. Cut the salt pork in strips and fit them into these slits.

Butter a flat tin sheet and place in the dripping-pan. Lay the fish in the pan, having uppermost the side containing the pork. Dredge with pepper, salt, and flour. Put enough hot water in the pan to cover the bottom, and place in the oven. Bake for forty-five minutes, basting every fifteen generously with the gravy in the pan and lightly with salt, pepper, and flour. When done, lift the tin from the dripping-pan and slide the fish upon a warm dish. Serve with brown, tomato, or Hollandaise sauce.

Fish that cannot be stuffed, such as halibut, may be cooked in the same way. Three pounds of halibut would be equivalent to a five-pound cod or haddock.

In giving the rule for so large a fish, allowance was made for the leaving of enough cold fish to make a dish of escaloped fish the next day.

Baked Salt Mackerel.

1 salt mackerel of medium size.	1 level tablespoonful of flour.
3 gills of milk.	⅛ teaspoonful of pepper.
1 tablespoonful of butter.	

Wash the mackerel and soak it in a pan of cold water, having the split side down. In the morning put the fish, split side up, in a shallow baking pan. Pour the milk over it, and place in a moderate oven. When the mackerel has been cooking for twenty minutes, mix the butter, flour, and pepper, and stir the mixture into the milk in the pan. Cook ten minutes longer; then slide the fish out on a hot dish and pour the sauce over it. Serve hot.

This dish is suitable for breakfast, luncheon, dinner, or supper. Serve with it potatoes in some form.

How Fish should be Broiled.

Simple as is the work of broiling a piece of fish, it is more often done badly than well. If not cooked enough the fish is extremely disagreeable to the taste, and if cooked too much it is hard and dry. It is always best to have an exact rule as to the time it shall be cooked; when the fish is put on the fire, look at the clock, and take it off as soon as it is done.

A split fish, such as shad, whitefish, mackerel, scrod, bluefish, etc., should be timed according to the thickness. If the fire be bright and hot, a fish an inch thick can be cooked twelve minutes. If two inches thick, it will take twenty minutes. Of course, when the fire is dull it will take longer.

Always season fish with salt and pepper before cooking. A fish with the skin on should be broiled with the skin side from the fire until the last five minutes of cooking, when that side can be turned to the fire; but it must be watched closely, that it shall not burn.

It is only dry halibut that requires the butter and flour before broiling. Many people prefer to dip the slice of fish in olive oil rather than butter. If the oil be used it must not be heated, and it is well to apply it to the fish an hour or more before the cooking.

Various sauces are often served with broiled fish, but there is nothing better than sweet butter, salt, pepper, a little lemon juice, and perhaps a little chopped parsley; or, the lemon juice may be omitted and a fresh lemon be cut into six parts as a garnish for the dish. Each person can then use as much of the acid as pleases him.

Broiled Halibut.

1½ pounds of halibut.
2 tablespoonfuls of butter.
1 teaspoonful of lemon juice.

1½ teaspoonfuls of salt.
¼ teaspoonful of pepper.

Have the halibut cut in a slice about an inch thick. Put half the butter, salt, and pepper in a hot soup plate, and stir until the butter is melted. Wash and wipe the fish, then lay it in the plate of seasoned butter. When one side is coated with the butter, turn it down and season the other. Dredge lightly with flour, place in the double-broiler, and cook over a hot, bright fire for fourteen minutes. Put on a hot dish and season with the remaining salt, pepper, butter, and the lemon juice, all mixed. Serve very hot.

Fried Fish.

2 pounds of fish.
3 ounces of fat salt pork.
¼ teaspoonful of pepper.

1 teaspoonful of salt.
Flour.

Have the fish cut in slices about an inch thick. Season these with the salt and pepper, and roll in flour. Cut the pork in thin slices and fry until crisp and brown. Take the pork from the pan, and put the fish in the hot fat.

When it has become browned on one side, turn it and brown the other side. It will take about twelve minutes to fry the fish. Arrange on a hot dish and lay the slices of pork on top. Serve hot.

All small fish, such as trout, perch, and smelts, may be cooked in this manner. Draw and wash them, but leave on the heads and tails of the smelts and trout. Some kinds of small fish need to be skinned, but this is done at the market.

Breaded Fish.

½ pint of dried bread crumbs.
1½ teaspoonfuls of salt.
⅙ teaspoonful of pepper.

1 egg.
2 pounds of any kind of fish.
Fat for frying.

Have the fish free from skin and bones, and cut it into handsome pieces. Season it with the salt and pepper. Beat the egg in a soup plate and dip the fish in it, one piece at a time, getting every part covered with the egg; then roll in the crumbs and lay on a plate. Have enough fat in the frying kettle to float the fish. When it becomes so hot that blue smoke rises from the centre, put in the fish and cook for five minutes. Drain on brown paper and serve very hot.

Tartar sauce is particularly good to serve with breaded fish. Smelts are especially palatable when cooked in this manner.

Escaloped Fish.

½ pint of cooked fish.
1 teaspoonful (scant) of salt.
⅛ teaspoonful of pepper.
1 tablespoonful of butter.

½ tablespoonful (scant) of flour.
1½ gills of milk.
4 tablespoonfuls of grated bread crumbs.

Use any kind of cold cooked fish; but the white kinds, such as halibut, cod, haddock, etc., are the best. Have it broken into flakes and freed of bones and skin. Season it with half the salt and pepper. Put a generous half of the butter in a small pan and set on the fire. When it is hot add the flour, and stir until the mixture is smooth and frothy; then gradually add the milk. Boil up once, and stir in the remainder of the salt and pepper. Put a layer of this sauce in a small baking dish, then a layer of the fish, and follow with a second layer of sauce. Now put in the rest of the fish and cover with the remainder of the sauce. Sprinkle with the bread crumbs and dot with the other half tablespoonful of butter. Bake in a moderately hot oven for twenty minutes, and serve at once.

The baking dish should hold nearly a pint.

Salt Codfish in Cream.

½ pint of fish, solidly packed.
1½ gills of milk.
1 teaspoonful of butter, generous.
1 teaspoonful of flour.
⅓ saltspoonful of pepper.

Cut the salt fish into pieces about an inch and a half long, and tear these pieces into thin strips. Wash them and, putting them in a bowl with one pint of cold water, let them soak over night, or at least four or five hours. In the morning put the fish and water in a saucepan and set on the fire. Heat to the boiling point, but do not let boil. Drain off the water, and, after adding the milk, heat again to the boiling point.

Beat the butter and flour together until light and smooth. Stir this mixture in with the fish, and boil up once. Add the pepper, and also some salt if any be required. Set back where the fish will continue to cook, but not boil, for twenty minutes.

If cream be plentiful use half cream and half milk. Serve baked or mashed potatoes with this dish.

Fish Balls.

1 cupful of raw salt codfish.	½ teaspoonful of salt.
6 potatoes of medium size.	¼ teaspoonful of pepper.
1 egg.	1 level tablespoonful of butter.

Tear the raw fish into fine shreds, and measure out a cupful. Pare the potatoes, and put them in a large stew-pan. Sprinkle the fish on top and cover with boiling water. Cover, and cook for just thirty minutes. Pour off every drop of the water, and mash the fish and potato together until light and fine; then beat into the mixture the salt, pepper, butter, and the egg, which should first be well beaten. Shape into small balls, and, putting them in the frying-basket, cook in deep fat until brown, — say for about four or five minutes.

Great care must be taken to follow the directions exactly, and to have the fat so hot when the fish balls are put in that blue smoke rises from the centre. If the fat be not hot enough, or the water be not all drained off, or if too much butter be used, the fish balls will absorb fat and be spoiled. If all the work be done carefully, the dish will be perfect.

Fish Cakes.

1 pint of minced salt codfish.	1 tablespoonful of butter.
1 pint of hot mashed potatoes (about six potatoes of medium size).	¼ teaspoonful of pepper.
	½ teaspoonful of salt.
½ gill of hot milk.	2 ounces of fat salt pork.

Wash the fish and soak it over night, in one piece. In the morning put it in a saucepan and on the fire, with enough cold water to cover it. When the water is heated to the boiling point set the saucepan back where the water will keep hot, but not boil. Cook the fish in this manner for one hour; then take from the water and cool. When cold, remove the skin and bones and chop the fish fine. Pare the potatoes, and put them in a stewpan with boiling water enough to cover them. Cook for just thirty minutes; then drain off the water, and mash and beat the potatoes with a fork. Beat the fish, butter, salt, pepper, and milk into the potato. Shape the mixture into round, flat cakes, and fry brown on both sides in pork fat.

The pork is cut into slices and fried rather slowly until crisp and brown. The pan is then placed on a hotter part of the fire, and the pork removed; and as soon as the fat is smoking hot, the cakes should be put in to brown. Serve the cakes on a hot dish, garnishing them with the slices of crisp pork.

This is a generous amount for three people, and in some families it may be found that half the amount will be enough.

When the fish cakes are for breakfast, cook, cool, and mince the fish the day before. Pare the potatoes, and let them stand in cold water over night. These preparations will insure having the fish cakes on time and in perfection for an early breakfast.

Fresh Fish Cakes.

½ pint of cooked fresh fish.
½ pint of hot mashed potato.
1 tablespoonful of butter.

1 level teaspoonful of salt.
⅛ teaspoonful of pepper.
2 tablespoonfuls of pork fat.

Free the cold fish from skin and bones, and shred it fine with a fork. Season it with the salt and pepper. Mash the potato fine and beat the butter and fish into it. Shape into flat cakes. Have the pork fat smoking hot in the frying-pan and put in the fish cakes. When brown on one side, turn and brown on the other. Serve immediately.

FISH. 105

Fried Scallops.

1 dozen scallops.	⅕ teaspoonful of pepper.
1 egg.	½ pint of dried bread crumbs.
1 teaspoonful of salt.	Fat for frying.

After seasoning the scallops with the salt and pepper, dip them in the beaten egg and roll them in the dried bread crumbs. Put the scallops in the frying-basket and immerse the basket into fat so hot that blue smoke rises from the centre. Cook for two minutes. Drain on brown paper and serve very hot.

Do not put more scallops in the basket than can be spread on the bottom.

Tartar sauce is especially good for this dish.

Oyster Stew.

1 gill of water.	1½ tablespoonfuls of butter.
1½ pints of oysters.	¼ teaspoonful of pepper.
1½ pints of milk.	Salt.

Put a strainer over a bowl and turn the oysters into it. Drain off all the liquor, and then pour one gill of water over the oysters. Pour this liquor into a stewpan, being careful not to turn in the sandy sediment. Place where it will heat slowly, being careful not to burn. When the liquor boils, skim it, and set back where it will keep hot. Meantime heat the milk to the boiling point in the double-boiler. Add the hot liquor, oysters, butter, salt, and pepper to the boiling milk. Boil up once, and serve immediately.

Oysters on Toast.

1½ pints of oysters.	1/10 teaspoonful of pepper.
2 tablespoonfuls of butter.	Salt.
½ teaspoonful of lemon juice.	3 slices of toast.

Put the oysters in a frying-pan and set on the fire. When they begin to boil, skim them; then add the seasonings. Have the toast arranged on a hot dish and pour the oysters over it. Serve at once.

Oysters au Gratin.

1 solid pint of oysters.	1 tablespoonful of flour.
1 gill of oyster liquor.	½ teaspoonful of salt.
½ gill of milk or cream.	¼ teaspoonful of pepper.
1½ tablespoonfuls of butter.	½ pint of grated bread crumbs.

Heat the oysters to the boiling point in their own liquor; then turn them into a strainer, which should be placed over a bowl. Put a gill of the oyster liquor in a saucepan, and heat slowly. Beat one tablespoonful of the butter and flour together until light and smooth. Stir this mixture into the hot liquor, and cook for three minutes; then add the milk, salt, and pepper. Heat to the boiling point and add the drained oysters. Now turn the oysters into rather a shallow escalop dish. Sprinkle the crumbs over them, and over the crumbs sprinkle the half tablespoonful of butter, broken in bits. Bake for twenty minutes in a moderately hot oven. If the flavor of nutmeg and Parmesan cheese be liked, add to the sauce one teaspoonful of the grated cheese and a slight grating of nutmeg.

Escaloped Oysters.

1½ solid pints of oysters.	1½ gills of cracker crumbs.
2 generous tablespoonfuls of butter.	1 teaspoonful of salt.
	¼ teaspoonful of pepper.

Put half the oysters in a dish that will hold about one quart. Sprinkle over them half the salt and pepper and half a tablespoonful of butter, broken in bits. Spread half the cracker crumbs over this. Now put in the remainder of the oysters, salt, pepper, and half a tablespoonful of the butter. Spread the remainder of the cracker crumbs over this, and then dot with the remaining tablespoonful of butter. Pour the liquor on the cracker crumbs, and bake in a hot oven for half an hour.

Fried Oysters.

2 dozen large oysters.
3 gills of dried bread crumbs.
1 egg.
1 tablespoonful of milk.
1 teaspoonful of salt.
⅛ teaspoonful of pepper.

Drain the oysters, and season them with the salt and pepper. Put a few tablespoonfuls of the crumbs on a plate and roll the oysters in them. Beat the egg in a soup plate and afterward stir the milk into it. Dip the oysters, one at a time, in this mixture, and roll in plenty of bread crumbs. Place them on a platter and set in a cool place. When it is time to cook them, put a layer in the frying basket and plunge into fat so hot that blue smoke rises from the centre. Cook for one minute and a half, and serve at once.

Never place one breaded oyster on top of another before they have been fried.

The milk may be omitted, and two tablespoonfuls of tomato ketchup be used instead.

Creamed Oysters.

1½ pints of oysters.
3 gills of milk or cream.
1 tablespoonful of flour.
1 teaspoonful of salt.
⅛ teaspoonful of pepper.
A tiny piece of mace.
½ teaspoonful of onion juice.

Put the milk and mace in the double-boiler, and set on the fire. Mix the flour with three tablespoonfuls of cold milk, reserved from the three gills, and stir into the boiling milk. Cook for ten minutes. Heat the oysters to the boiling point in their own liquor; then skim and drain them. Put the oysters, salt, pepper, and onion juice into the thickened cream, and serve.

If milk be used, add a tablespoonful of butter to the thickened milk.

Lobster.

Lobster should be perfectly fresh. If it be cooked, the odor should be fresh and the shells look bright, and when the tail is drawn back it should spring into position again. If the lobster be bought alive, see that it moves lively. To boil it, plunge it into boiling water and cook gently from ten to twenty minutes. A very small lobster will cook in ten minutes and a large one in twenty. Cooking a lobster too long or at too high a temperature makes it tough, dry, and stringy. When it is impossible to get the fresh lobster, the canned article may be used instead, though it is of the greatest importance to buy only the goods put up by first-class houses.

Curry of Lobster.

1½ gills of lobster meat.
½ pint of meat stock.
2 tablespoonfuls of butter.
1 generous tablespoonful of flour.
1 teaspoonful of salt.

⅙ teaspoonful of Cayenne.
⅙ teaspoonful of white pepper.
1 teaspoonful of curry powder.
1 tablespoonful of minced onion.
3 slices of toast.

Cut the lobster into small pieces and season with half the salt and pepper. Put the butter and onion on the fire, in a frying-pan, and cook until the onion turns a straw color; then add the flour and curry-powder and stir until brown. Gradually add the stock to this, stirring all the while. Season with the remainder of the salt and pepper, and cook for three minutes. Strain this into a saucepan, and add the lobster. Cook for five minutes. Cut the slices of toast in strips and lay in a warm dish. Pour the lobster over these and serve at once.

The toast may be omitted, and a dish of boiled rice be served with the curry.

Fricassee of Lobster.

A fricassee of lobster is prepared the same as a curry; omitting, however, the curry-powder and onion. Milk may be substituted for the meat stock.

Breaded Lobster.

1 large lobster.	⅙ teaspoonful of pepper.
1 egg.	Dried bread crumbs.
1 teaspoonful of salt.	Fat for frying.

Split the claws and tail and set aside. Take the meat from the large joints and the body, and chop fine. Mix with this one fourth of the teaspoonful of salt and two tablespoonfuls of the "tom-alley." Shape this into three small flat cakes. Season the pieces of lobster with the salt and pepper. Beat the egg in a soup plate. Dip the pieces of lobster and the little cakes, one at a time, into the egg; then roll in the bread crumbs, and, after arranging on a plate, put in a cool place until the hour to cook them. When that time comes, put the breaded lobster in the frying basket and cook in fat until crisp and brown (about two minutes). Serve with Tartar sauce.

Escaloped Lobster.

3 gills of lobster.	1 teaspoonful of salt.
½ pint of cream or stock.	⅛ teaspoonful of Cayenne.
1½ tablespoonfuls of butter.	1 tablespoonful of flour.
½ pint of grated bread crumbs.	

Mix in a saucepan one tablespoonful of the butter and all the flour. Have the stock or cream hot, and pour it gradually on the butter and the flour, stirring all the time. Add half the salt and pepper, and cook for one minute. Have the lobster cut fine, and seasoned with the other half of the salt and pepper. When the sauce has cooked for one minute, add the lobster. Now pour the mixture into a shallow escalop dish. Sprinkle the grated bread crumbs on this, and then dot with the half tablespoonful of butter. Bake in a hot oven for fifteen minutes.

If cream be used, measure the flour lightly; but if stock be taken, allow a generous tablespoonful.

Escaloped Crabs.

Prepare the same as escaloped lobster; using, however, only half a pint of crab meat.

Escaloped Shrimps.

Prepare this dish in the same manner as escaloped lobster; substituting, however, shelled shrimps for the lobster.

Stewed Clams.

1 pint of shelled clams.
1 gill of milk.
1 tablespoonful of butter.
⅙ teaspoonful of pepper.

1 level teaspoonful of salt.
1 heaping teaspoonful of flour.
3 Boston butter crackers.

Put the milk on the fire in the double-boiler. Put the clams in a strainer and pour a quart of cold water over them. Let them drain for about one minute, and then, turning them into a stewpan, place them on the stove. Beat the butter and flour to a cream, and stir this mixture into the pan containing the hot clams. Add the hot milk, salt, and pepper, and cook for two minutes longer. Have the crackers soaked for two minutes in cold water, and then toasted. Lay them in the bottom of a deep dish, and when the clams are stewed pour them over the toast.

Roast Clams.

Wash the clam shells thoroughly and drain them in the colander for a few minutes. Spread them in an old dripping-pan and put them into a hot oven. The shells will begin to open in five or eight minutes. Take them from the oven, and, holding the shell over a warm dish, let the clam and juice drop out. Season with butter, salt, and pepper, and serve very hot, with thin slices of buttered brown bread.

When possible, get the clams twenty-four hours before they are to be used, and after washing them thoroughly put them in a pan with just enough cold water to cover them; then, for a peck of clams, sprinkle in half a pint of corn meal. This will make the clams plump and tender.

Steamed Clams.

Prepare the clams as for roasting, but put them in a dish and place it in the steamer. When the shells open the clams are done.

CHAPTER X.

HOW TO COOK MEAT.

BOILING.

IN boiling meats the temperature of the liquid should be kept at about the boiling point or a few degrees lower; that is, the water should bubble gently at one side of the pot or stewpan. Great care must be taken that the water shall never boil rapidly, and that the temperature shall not be much lower than that indicated by a slight bubbling at the side of the stewpan. The meat and liquid will both be spoiled if kept for any length of time in a closed vessel with the temperature too low. A piece of meat cooked in water that boils rapidly all the time will be hard, dry, and stringy, no matter how long it is cooked or how tender and good it was originally; but even a tough, dry piece will be tender and juicy if cooked at the temperature indicated by the water's bubbling at one side of the pot. All meats will be juicier if they be allowed to cool, or even partially to cool, in the liquid in which they were boiled. The dish in which a food material is cooling must always be *uncovered* until the substance is perfectly cold.

Boiled Leg of Mutton.

Wipe carefully with a damp cloth a leg of mutton weighing between eight and ten pounds, and put it in a deep kettle with enough boiling water to cover it. Set the kettle where the water will boil rapidly for a quarter of an hour. Skim the water when it begins to boil. At the end of the fifteen minutes draw the kettle back where the water will only bubble. If the meat be desired very rare, cook it for an hour and a half; but if you want it rather well done, cook it for two hours, being careful that the water only bubbles except during the first fifteen minutes.

When the mutton is done place it on a warm dish. Pour a few tablespoonfuls of butter sauce over it, and, if convenient, garnish with parsley. Send to the table at once with the caper sauce and vegetables.

Of course, this is more meat than three persons would want, but if only half a leg be boiled the result will not be very satisfactory; therefore it would be better to roast or steam a part of the leg, unless the family be large.

Steamed Mutton.

When the family is so small that it is necessary to cut a leg of mutton, it is better to steam than to boil it. Place the piece of mutton on a kitchen plate, the cut side down. Set the plate in the steamer and over a kettle of boiling water. Cover closely, and keep the water boiling until the meat is done. A piece weighing about four or five pounds will be cooked rather rare in one hour. If liked well done, cook it longer. Serve the same as boiled leg of mutton.

Boiled Corned Beef.

A piece of corned beef will take about the same time to cook, whether it weigh four pounds or ten. Wash the meat and put it into a stewpan with enough boiling water to cover it generously. When the water begins to boil, skim thoroughly; then draw the stewpan back to a place where the water will just bubble for five hours. Never let the water boil hard, but it must not get much below the boiling point at any time. If the meat is to be pressed, take it from the boiling water and place it on a flat dish. Put a tin pan or sheet on top of the hot meat, and on this place two bricks or some other weight. Set away in a cool place. When the meat is cold, trim the edges, using a sharp knife. The trimmings may be used for a corned beef hash.

Spiced Corned Beef.

6 pounds of the plate piece of beef.
1 pint of coarse salt.

3 pints of water.
3 dozen whole allspice.
2 dozen whole cloves.

This is a cheap and savory dish for luncheon and tea. Put the water and salt in a stewpan and set on the fire. Stir frequently until the water boils, and then skim carefully. Take from the fire and set away to cool. Remove the bones from the meat by slipping a sharp knife between the flesh and bone and cutting the meat from the bone. Place the beef in a stone jar or earthen bowl, and when the brine is cold pour it over the meat. Cover the dish and set it away in a cool place for six or eight days. At the end of that time remove the meat and wipe it. Spread it on a board and sprinkle the spice over it. Roll up and tie firmly. Place this roll in a kettle and cover it with boiling water. When the water begins to boil, (it will at first be somewhat cooled by the meat,) skim it carefully; then set the kettle back where the water will just bubble for six hours. At the end of that time take the beef from the kettle and place it on a large dish. Put upon it a tin pan and weights, (two bricks will be sufficient,) and set away in a cool place. The meat should be cut in thin slices when served.

In New York many of the marketmen salt and spice beef for their customers. If one can get a plate piece of corned beef that has not been too long in brine, it will answer just as well as a fresh piece, and save the housekeeper the trouble of corning it. Almost any marketman will willingly remove the bones for a customer.

Boiled Ham.

Wash the ham and then soak it in cold water for ten or twelve hours. Put it on to cook in cold water. When the water begins to boil, skim it, and draw the kettle back to a part of the range where the water will only bubble gently. Cook the ham for five hours; then take it up and draw off the skin. Place the skinned ham in a dripping-pan and sprinkle over it one cupful of fine dried crumbs mixed with two tablespoonfuls of sugar. Cook it slowly in the oven for one hour.

If only a part of a ham is to be boiled, it would be better to steam it than to put it in the water. Wash and soak it; then steam it the same as mutton, cooking it for six hours. Brown it in the oven if you like.

Fresh Tongue.

Wash the tongue and put it in a stewpan with boiling water enough to cover it generously. Add four tablespoonfuls of salt. When the water begins to boil, skim carefully and draw the stewpan back to a place where the water will bubble gently for five hours. Take the tongue from the boiling water and plunge it into cold water. Draw off the rough skin, beginning at the roots of the tongue. Place the tongue on a dish, cover it lightly with a coarse towel, and put it in a cold place.

Smoked Tongues.

Cook a smoked tongue exactly the same as a ham, except that it is not to be browned in the oven. It will require five hours' time to boil it.

Pickled Tongue.

Treat a pickled tongue the same as a piece of corned beef. It will require five hours' cooking.

SCIENCE IN ROASTING MEAT.

A roast of meat, be it rare or well done, should be juicy and tender. One should not roast a tough piece of meat; stewing, braising, or boiling is better, because the cooking can be continued for a long time at a low temperature, and this method will make the toughest piece of meat tender. The meat always should be exposed to a high temperature at first, that the surface may become hardened and the juices protected. If the high temperature be continued all the time of cooking, the meat will become hard, dry, and stringy, as far as the heat has penetrated. It will be seen, therefore, that the high temperature should be kept up only long enough to form a thin, hard crust on the meat. From twenty to thirty minutes will suffice for this. The temperature should then be lowered by closing the draughts of the range.

Basting is another important item in roasting. If one use no water in the dripping-pan, and baste only with the fat that drops from the meat into the bottom of the pan, the roast will have a beautiful glossy brown surface when it is done; but it must be remembered that fat can be heated to a much higher point than water, and that basting with this boiling hot fat will help to harden the piece of meat.

If a small quantity of water be kept in the bottom of the dripping-pan, the drippings from the meat, mingling with it, will be kept at a low temperature, so that, if the meat be freely basted with this mixture every fifteen minutes, the surface of the piece of meat will be kept moist, and at a lower temperature than when basted with the hot fat, or not basted at all. By basting with this mixture of drippings and water, the heat is driven from the surface to the centre of the piece of meat, insuring a roast that will be rare from a point about half an inch from the surface to the centre. Bear these facts in mind when roasting meats.

How to Roast Meat in the Oven.

Have a dripping-pan of Russian iron and a meat-rack three or four inches shorter than the pan.

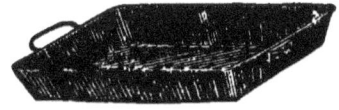   

DRIPPING-PAN.   MEAT-RACK.

Examine the piece of meat, and if there be any places that have become tainted trim them off with a sharp knife. Wipe the meat with a wet towel. Now season with salt and pepper, and dredge lightly with flour.

All the seasoning must be done with the meat resting on the rack, that the stray particles may fall to the bottom of the pan. Dredge flour over the bottom of the pan until the surface is white.

Have the oven very hot (about 400 or 450 degrees), and place the meat in it. Watch closely, and as soon as the flour in the pan turns dark brown pour in enough boiling water to cover the bottom of the pan. The flour may brown in five minutes, yet it may take ten or more for this process, the time depending upon the bottom of the oven. When the meat is brown on one side, baste well, and turn it over to brown the other side. When the meat has been in the oven for about thirty minutes, close the draughts to reduce the heat of the oven.

Baste the meat every fifteen minutes in this manner. With a long spoon, dip up the liquid from the bottom of the pan and pour it over the meat. Continue this until nearly all has been absorbed by the meat; then dredge lightly with salt, pepper, and flour. Now pour into the pan enough hot water to cover the bottom. The last time the meat is basted omit putting the water in the pan, and at the end of fifteen minutes all the liquid will be evaporated. Now take up the meat and place it on a hot platter. Take out the rack, and then pour all the fat from the pan into a cup. Put half a pint of hot water in the pan and set on top of the range. Scrape all the sediment from the sides and bottom, and thicken this gravy with a teaspoonful of flour smoothly mixed with a gill of cold water. Season with salt and pepper, and simmer for two minutes; then strain into a hot dish and serve with the roast meat.

The time of cooking a roast depends upon the shape in which it is cut and whether it is to be rare or well done. The rule of so many minutes for each pound is not a good one; for a long, thin, rib roast might weigh just the same as a short, thick piece cut from the round, rump, or shoulder, and, of course, the thin piece would cook much more quickly than the short thick piece.

A leg of mutton weighing eight or nine pounds should be cooked for an hour and three quarters, if to be served rare; if to be medium rare, two hours, but if well done (a pity it should ever be!) two hours and a quarter. Half a leg of mutton, weighing about four pounds, should be cooked for an hour and a quarter. The meat will be rare.

Roast Rib of Beef.

For three persons one rib will be enough. Wipe the meat with a damp towel. Place a meat-rack in a dripping-pan and lay the beef on it. Dredge with salt, pepper, and flour, turning the meat over in order that every part shall receive a portion of the coating. Dredge the bottom of the pan lightly with the flour and salt. Set the pan in a very hot oven, and watch carefully to prevent the flour on the bottom of the pan from burning. When the flour turns dark brown, pour in enough water to cover the bottom of the pan; this will be in from two to five minutes after the pan is placed in the oven. After the water has been added let the meat cook awhile, and then baste it. To baste, draw the pan out of the oven and tip it a little, that all the gravy shall flow to one end of the pan. With a long-handled spoon, dip up this gravy and pour it over the meat. Continue this until the entire piece is well moistened. Now dredge the meat lightly with salt, pepper, and flour. Pour into the pan enough boiling water to cover the bottom, and return to the oven. At the end of a quarter of an hour draw the pan out again, turn the meat over, and baste as before. Add some water and then set the pan in the oven. Now reduce the heat by shutting the draughts, and baste every fifteen minutes in the manner described. Do not use any water the last time. The meat should cook in all one hour if wanted rather rare. When the beef is done, take it up and place it on a warm dish. Pour all the fat from the dripping-pan, and, after setting the pan on the range, pour into it half a pint of boiling water. Scrape all the brown sediment from the sides and bottom of the pan. Mix one teaspoonful of flour with three tablespoonfuls of cold water, and gradually pour this mixture into the dripping-pan, stirring all the while. It may not take all the mixture of flour and water to thicken the gravy. Stop when the gravy is about as thick as cream. Season with salt and pepper, and strain into a hot bowl.

If all this work be properly done, the beef will be rare and juicy, and the gravy rich, brown, and smooth.

Roast Lamb.

Lamb, being immature meat, should be rather well done. The spring lambs are so small that a leg will not make a burdensome roast in a small family. The loin and breast make good small roasts. Roast the lamb according to the rule given for roast rib of beef. Serve with the made gravy and mint sauce. Asparagus, peas, young beets, summer squash, and any delicate summer vegetable, may be served with lamb.

Roast Mutton.

Mutton is roasted like beef. For a small roast the loin or breast is good. A leg of mutton may be cut into two parts, using one for a roast and the other for steaming. Mutton should always be cooked rare and served hot. Currant jelly should be provided with a roast. The most appropriate vegetables are potatoes, onions, mashed turnips, rice, squash, tomatoes in any form, sweet potatoes, Lima beans, canned corn, etc.

Stuffed Mutton.

Make the dressing given for roast veal, substituting a generous tablespoonful of butter for the chopped pork, and adding also one teaspoonful of onion juice. Have the bone removed from half of a leg of mutton. Cut deep incisions in the inside of the leg, and press the dressing into these. Sew up the leg, and roast the same as directed for roast beef, cooking the meat an hour and a half. The same vegetables as suggested for plain roast mutton are suitable for the stuffed leg.

Roast Veal.

5 pounds of loin or breast of veal.	1 teaspoonful of sweet marjoram.
1 pint of stale bread.	½ teaspoonful of sage.
3 ounces of salt pork.	Salt, pepper, flour.
1 gill of cracker crumbs.	

To make the dressing. Soak the bread in cold water for two or three hours. Press out nearly all the water; then add one ounce of salt pork chopped fine, one teaspoonful of salt, one third of a teaspoonful of pepper, the herbs, and crackers. Let this stand while the meat is being washed and seasoned.

The parts of the veal that are good for roasting are the loin, breast, and fillet. Veal requires a great deal of seasoning, and is almost always stuffed. It must be remembered that in the loin and breast there is a great deal of bone. On the other hand, the fillet has not a particle of waste except a small bit of round bone. Veal is delicious cold, and the cold roast meat can be prepared in many savory ways. For these reasons, if the family do not object to the meat in all forms, it would be well to get a roast of good size. This is a kind of meat that must be thoroughly done; not even a pinkish tinge should be seen after it is cooked.

For a family of three get a loin or breast weighing about four or five pounds. Wash it in cold water and wipe it with a clean towel. Rub into it one tablespoonful of salt, and sprinkle lightly with pepper. Stuff it, roll it up, and skewer it. Place on a rack in the dripping-pan, and lay upon it two ounces of salt pork cut in thin slices. Cook for two hours and a half, following the directions given for roasting.

Any of the following named vegetables may be served with roast veal: potatoes, rice, macaroni, spinach, asparagus, beets, turnips, parsnips, salsify, string beans, shell beans, grated horseradish, etc.

Roast Pork.

The piece termed the sparerib is the best for roasting. Wipe the meat with a damp towel. Season it with salt, pepper, and sage, using a teaspoonful of powdered sage to four pounds of pork. Follow the directions for roast rib of beef, cooking a four or five pound roast for two hours. Any of the following named vegetables may be served with roast pork: white potatoes, sweet potatoes, rice, hominy, squash, turnips, onions, etc.; and apple sauce always is desirable.

Roast Ham.

Prepare the ham the same as for boiled ham; boiling it for only three hours, however, and baking it slowly for three hours more.

BROILING.

There are several modes of broiling: over clear coals, before the coals, or under a bed of coals; also under a sheet of flame, as in a gas stove. No matter what the fuel may be or the mode of broiling, the principles are the same. A steak or chop, properly broiled, should have a thin, well browned crust. Beyond this crust the meat should be red and juicy; hardly a shade rarer at the centre than near the surface. A common mode of cooking a steak is to keep it over the coals until one side is rather well done; then turn it, and treat the other side in the same manner. The result of following this method is, that as far as the heat has penetrated the meat is hard and dry, and if the steak be thick it will be almost raw in the centre.

If the broiling is to be done on a range have the fire very bright and clear. Open every draught, that smoke and flame may be drawn up the chimney. Place the piece of meat in the double-broiler, and hold it as near the coals as possible until the surface is brown, turning frequently. It will take three or four minutes for this. Now raise the broiler several inches above the bed of coals, and continue the cooking until the meat is done. The broiler must be turned often. A good

DOUBLE-BROILER.

rule is to count ten slowly, then turn the broiler. A steak or chop, cut a little more than an inch thick, will cook rare in ten minutes; if liked medium well done, it should be cooked for twelve minutes. A chicken weighing about three pounds will require slow broiling for half an hour; or the chicken may be broiled over the fire until a rich brown, — say about fifteen minutes, — then put it in a shallow pan in a moderate oven for about twenty minutes.

Veal and pork must be broiled slowly until cooked thoroughly. Chops or cutlets cut about half an inch thick will cook in twelve minutes.

Steaks and chops which, before cooking, are dredged lightly with salt, pepper, and flour, will be much richer than those cooked without any seasoning. Both steaks and chops should be served the minute they come from the fire. Season them with salt and butter. Never put them in the oven for the purpose of melting the butter. It spoils the dish. If a steak or chop must wait a little time before it is served, keep it warm, but do not add the butter until serving time.

To Broil in a Frying-pan.

It sometimes happens that one has no means of broiling over coals or under heat. The next best thing is broiling in a pan. For example, have a steak cut about an inch thick. After making a frying-pan very hot, sprinkle in some fine salt, and lay the steak in the pan. Cook for two minutes; then lift the steak up and sprinkle the pan with salt. Turn the steak and cook for two minutes. Cook the piece of meat ten minutes in all, turning every two minutes. Put the meat on a hot dish, and season with salt and butter.

Broiled Chops with Bacon.

Bacon that is to be broiled should be boneless and fat, and the slices should be about as thin as the blade of a knife. The bars of the broiler should be very close, what is called an oyster broiler being best.

Place the slices of bacon in the broiler and over a clean fire, having all the draughts open. Cook the meat for about four minutes, turning constantly. The fat will blaze up continually, but will not hurt the bacon if that be turned all the while. Put the cooked bacon on a hot plate, and keep warm until the chops are cooked.

If the chops be cut an inch thick, cook them for nine minutes, turning almost continually. Season with salt and pepper, and place on a hot dish. Lay a slice of bacon on each chop, and arrange the remainder around the dish. Serve hot and on hot plates.

Beefsteak and Onions.

Steak for broiling.
1 pint of sliced onions.
1 level teaspoonful of salt.

3 tablespoonfuls of butter or drippings.

Pare and slice the onions. Put them in a stewpan with two quarts of boiling water and cook for fifteen minutes. Drain off all the water. Put the butter or drippings in a frying-pan and add the drained onions. Cover the frying-pan and place on the range. Cook for half an hour, being careful not to burn. Stir the onions frequently. Broil the steak rare and lay it on the bed of onions for five minutes, having the pan covered; then place the steak on a hot dish, and arrange the onions around it.

The onions need not be boiled, if a strong flavor be liked.

FRYING.

The word "frying" may mean either of two modes of cooking food: using a common frying-pan, with only a small amount of fat, or immersing the article to be cooked in a deep kettle of hot fat.

The first method is unhealthful, extravagant, and troublesome; the second saves time and is more economical and healthful. When a housekeeper once masters this method of frying, she will not return to the more unsatisfactory and indigestible mode.

There should be enough fat to float the article to be cooked. The fat must be so hot as to harden the surface

HOW TO COOK MEAT. 125

of the article of food the moment it is immersed, making it impervious to the fat or the juices contained in the food itself. Different articles of food brown at different temperatures, so that the frying temperature varies from 345° to 400° Fahrenheit. Most mixtures composed in part of flour, sugar, milk, or eggs — like fritter batters, doughnuts, etc. — may be cooked at 350°; whereas such articles as oysters, white-bait, croquettes, etc., require a heat of at least 400°. French fried and thin fried potatoes need ten minutes' cooking. The fat must have a temperature of about 370° when they are put into it, because the potatoes should stand in ice-water for some time before they are cooked. Moisture will cling to them; and this, with their chilliness, reduces the fat at least 20° as soon as the frying begins, making it then 350°. At this heat the potatoes may be cooked brown and crisp in ten minutes. As already stated, oysters require a heat of 400°. Drop a piece of stale bread into the fat; and if the temperature be right, the bread will become brown in half a minute. Oysters and white-bait should be cooked brown and crisp in one minute; longer cooking will make them rather tough and dry. A little lower temperature — say 380° — will do for croquettes, which should be fried for about two minutes. If the temperature be too low, croquettes will burst open during the cooking; particularly rice and potato croquettes.

Put the fat into a deep kettle (that called a Scotch bowl being best) and heat it slowly. When the time for frying the food is near at hand, set the kettle on the hottest part of the range, and watch to see the blue smoke rise from the centre of the surface of the liquid. The smoke indicates the temperature to be about 350°. Drop a piece of stale bread into the fat; and if one minute be required to brown it, the fat may be used at once for frying muffins, doughnuts, fritters, breaded chops, and indeed nearly all articles that require three or four minutes' cooking.

How to keep Fat.

When the frying has been finished, take the fat from the fire and let it cook slightly. Next place a piece of cheese-cloth in a colander or strainer, and, after setting this over a jar or pail, strain the fat through the cloth. This straining never should be omitted; for, with good care, the same fat may be used many times.

The Kind of Fat to use.

Olive oil would be the best liquid to use if the matter of expense were not to be considered. Any pure, clear fat that is free of strong odor will answer. Many folk use mutton and ham fat, and say that they do not find the flavor of the meat in the articles fried; but others would discover the taste at once, and consider it disagreeable.

But the housekeeper will select the material she will use according to her taste and means; and attention may as well be turned now to the conditions which will insure satisfactory and comparatively wholesome fried food. In the first place, the fat must be perfectly clarified. Even the purest and sweetest butter must go through this process before being used for frying. Oil and lard, when pure, already are clarified. When the fat to be clarified is that which has been skimmed from gravies, soups, or the water in which corned beef has been boiled, it will contain water and other impurities. While there is water in fat the latter cannot be heated to a temperature suitable for frying purposes; and if there be other foreign substances present, such as particles of meat, gravy, flour, or starch, they will burn at as high a temperature as 345°, blackening the fat and making it unfit for frying articles of food.

The Frying Basket.

While it is possible to fry food in deep fat without the use of the frying basket, that invention will be found a most valuable aid in this branch of cookery. The basket is made of fine wire, and has a bail across the top. Do not get one of coarse wire and open meshes.

THE WAY TO LOWER THE FRYING BASKET.

After the articles to be fried have been put into it, it should be lowered into the fat; gently, because the particles of moisture which cling to the food are instantly converted into steam, and this would expand beneath the surface and force some of the fat from the kettle if the basket were lowered quickly. The operation may be performed safely by hanging the basket on a long spoon or fork, and then letting it settle gently in the fat. Do not crowd into the basket the articles that are to be fried. When the food has been cooked as long as seems necessary, lift the basket with the spoon or fork, and, after allowing the fat to drip from it, place it on a plate. Remove the cooked articles, and lay them on brown paper that has been spread on a warm pan. If properly cooked, they will hardly stain the paper.

Breaded Chops.

Mutton or lamb chops may be breaded and served with tomato or brown sauce. Have the chops cut an inch thick.

Trim them, and season with salt and pepper. Dip them in beaten egg and roll in dry bread crumbs. Lay them in deep fat for six minutes if they are to be rare done, and for ten minutes if to be well done. Slices from the leg may be prepared in the same manner.

Breaded Veal Cutlets.

1 pound of veal, cut from the leg.	⅛ teaspoonful of pepper.
1 egg.	Dried bread crumbs.
1 teaspoonful of salt.	Fat for frying.

Have the cutlets about one fourth of an inch thick, and cut into pieces about four inches long and three wide. Season them with half the salt and pepper. Beat the egg in a soup plate, and season with the remainder of the salt and pepper. Dip the cutlets in the egg and roll them in the bread crumbs. Fry them in deep fat for ten minutes. Serve with tomato or brown sauce.

If you prefer, the cutlets may be fried in pork fat. In that case fry two ounces of fat salt pork. Take up the pork and put the cutlets into the fat remaining in the pan. When brown on one side, turn and brown on the other. They should be cooked for fifteen minutes.

Mutton Cutlets Sauté.

1 slice of mutton from the leg, or five chops.	¼ teaspoonful of pepper.
1 tablespoonful of butter.	1 tablespoonful of flour.
1½ teaspoonfuls of salt.	1 gill of stewed and strained tomato.

Trim most of the fat from the chops, and season them with half the salt and pepper. Put them in a hot frying-pan and cook them for four minutes, turning often. Sprinkle the flour over them and cook for two minutes longer, turning them twice in that time. Now add the tomato, butter,

HOW TO COOK MEAT.   129

and the remainder of the salt and pepper. Cook for three minutes longer, and serve very hot.

Breaded Sausages.

6 small sausages.
½ pint of dried bread crumbs.
The yolk of one egg.

1 tablespoonful of milk.
Fat for frying.

Beat the yolk of the egg in a soup plate, then beat into it the milk. Prick the sausages with a fork and roll them, one by one, in the egg, and then in the bread crumbs. Arrange them in the frying basket and cook for ten minutes in smoking hot fat. Drain and serve.

MISCELLANEOUS MODES.

Stewed Shin of Beef.

4 pounds of shin of beef.
1 small onion.
1 bay leaf.
1 whole clove.
1 sprig of parsley.
1 small slice of carrot.

½ tablespoonful of salt.
½ teaspoonful of pepper.
1½ tablespoonfuls of butter.
1½ tablespoonfuls of flour.
2 quarts of boiling water.

Have the butcher cut the bone into six parts. Wash the shank carefully, being sure to remove any particles of meat or gristle that are not perfectly sweet. They will be found at the small end, if at all. Put the shin in a stewpan with the onion, carrot, bay leaf, parsley, clove, salt, pepper, and water.

Place the stewpan on the fire, and when its contents begin to boil, skim the liquid carefully, and set the pan back where the meat will only simmer for six hours. At the end of five hours and a half, dip out one pint of the liquid; and after allowing this partially to cool, skim off the fat.

Put the butter in a saucepan and place it on the stove. When the butter begins to bubble, add the flour, and stir the mixture until it is smooth and brown; then gradually add three gills of the cold liquid. Cook for three minutes, stirring all the time. Season with salt and pepper, and set back where it will keep hot.

Take up the meat, removing it from the bones; also remove the marrow from the bones. Put the meat and marrow into the stewpan with the sauce. Draw the pan forward and let its contents boil up once. Serve on a hot dish with a garnish of potato cubes.

The remainder of the liquor in which the shin was boiled may be used for a soup the next day.

To prepare the potatoes, pare raw ones, and cut them into inch cubes. Put these in a stewpan, and cover with boiling water. Cook them for fifteen minutes, counting from the time the cover is placed on the stewpan. At the end of that time pour off all the water and sprinkle salt over the potatoes, — half a teaspoonful to a pint of the cubes. Place the stewpan on the fire for about one minute; then shake well. For three persons cook a pint and a half of cubes.

Pot Roast.

3 pounds of a tough piece of beef.	2 level tablespoonfuls of flour.
1½ teaspoonfuls of salt.	1 whole clove.
¼ teaspoonful of pepper.	1 pint of boiling water.
	1 gill of cold water.

Wipe the meat and season it with the salt and pepper. Put it in an iron or granite-ware stewpan, and set it on a part of the range where it will brown slowly. Turn it frequently. Cook the meat in this manner for thirty minutes. Now add a gill of boiling water, and draw the stewpan to a part of the range where the contents will cook slowly for four hours. Add a gill of boiling water whenever the liquid in the stewpan becomes low. When the meat has been cooking for three hours, mix the flour smoothly with a gill of cold water, and turn into the gravy in the stewpan. Add enough boiling water now to make the full pint; the whole clove also may be added. Cook the meat an hour longer; then serve on a warm platter, with a part of the gravy poured over it. Serve the remainder of the gravy in a bowl.

Braised Beef.

3 pounds of beef.	1½ pints of water.
2 ounces of fat salt pork.	2 tablespoonfuls of minced onion.
2 tablespoonfuls of flour.	2 tablespoonfuls of minced carrot.
3 teaspoonfuls of salt.	2 whole cloves.
½ teaspoonful of pepper.	1 sprig of parsley.

Cut the pork into thin slices and fry until brown and crisp. Take out the pork, and, putting the vegetables into the fat remaining in the pan, cook slowly for fifteen minutes.

Rub half the pepper and two teaspoonfuls of the salt into the piece of meat, and place it in a deep granite-ware pan. When the vegetables are cooked, put them with the meat, first pressing from them as much fat as possible. Into the fat remaining in the pan put the flour, and stir until it becomes a dark brown. Add the water gradually, stirring all the while. Season this gravy with the remainder of the salt and pepper, and boil for five minutes; then pour over the meat in the pan. Add the cloves and parsley. Cover the pan and set in a very moderate oven. Cook for five hours, basting every half-hour with the gravy in the pan. The oven must never be so hot that the gravy will bubble.

This long, slow cooking will make the toughest piece of meat tender; but if it be cooked too fast, the meat will become hard, dry, and stringy. Any of the tough pieces can be used for this dish.

Veal, mutton, chicken, and turkey all can be cooked in this manner. With the light meats use a little celery, if convenient.

Beefsteak Roll.

½ pint of strained tomato.
1 egg.
1½ pounds of round steak.
4 tablespoonfuls of pork fat or beef drippings.
1 tablespoonful of butter.
½ cupful of cracker crumbs.

1¼ pints of water.
2 tablespoonfuls of flour.
½ teaspoonful of thyme.
1½ teaspoonfuls of salt.
⅓ teaspoonful of pepper.
1 tablespoonful of minced onion.

Have the steak cut thin. Make a dressing by mixing together the cracker crumbs, thyme, half a teaspoonful of the salt, half the pepper, the butter, a little more than a gill of cold water, and the egg, well beaten. Season the slice of steak with half a teaspoonful of salt, and a little of the pepper. Spread the dressing on it, and roll up. Wind soft darning cotton around the roll, to keep it in place.

Put the pork fat in a frying-pan, and set on the fire. Dredge the roll with flour, and place it in the hot fat. Cook until brown on all sides, then place it in a stewpan. Put the onion and a tablespoonful of flour into the fat remaining in the pan. Stir until brown; then gradually add the scant pint of water, and stir until the sauce boils up. Add the remainder of the salt and pepper, and half a pint of strained tomato. Strain this on the beefsteak roll. Cover the stew-pan, and place where the sauce will bubble at one side for three hours. When done, take up, remove the strings, and place the roll on a warm dish. Pour the sauce over it, and serve.

This dish is suitable for luncheon or dinner. Any of the following named vegetables may be served with it: potatoes, rice, hominy, carrots, turnips, cabbage, or macaroni.

Beef Olives.

1½ pounds of round of beef.	3 tablespoonfuls of flour.
½ pint of cracker crumbs.	3 ounces of salt pork.
1½ teaspoonfuls of salt.	⅓ teaspoonful of thyme.
⅓ teaspoonful of pepper.	⅓ teaspoonful of summer savory.

Have the beef cut in a thin slice. Cut all the fat from this and chop it fine. Mix together the cracker crumbs, chopped fat, half a teaspoonful of salt, one sixth of a teaspoonful of pepper, the herbs, and a gill of cold water. Cut the slice of beef in pieces about four inches long and three wide. Season the meat with the remainder of the salt and pepper. Spread the cracker dressing on these strips of meat and then roll them up. Tie them with soft darning cotton and then roll them in the flour. Cut the pork in slices and fry until crisp and brown. Take out the pork and lay the olives in the fat remaining in the pan. Fry on all sides until brown; then put the olives in a small stewpan. Put into a frying-pan such flour as remained after the olives were rolled, and stir until brown. Gradually pour upon this one pint of cold water. Stir until it boils and then pour over the olives. Cover the stewpan and place where the contents will just bubble at one side for two hours. At serving time take up the olives, remove the strings, and arrange in the centre of a warm platter. Free the gravy from fat and pour over the olives. The dish may be served plain or with a border of either boiled rice, mashed potatoes, or strips of toast.

Hamburg Steaks.

1 pound of round, shoulder, or flank of beef.	¼ teaspoonful of pepper.
	1 teaspoonful of salt.

Have the butcher chop the meat very fine. Season it with the salt and pepper and make it into small cakes about half an inch thick. Rub the bars of the broiler with a bit of fat and lay the cakes in it. Broil over clear coals for six minutes, if the steaks be liked rare; or eight minutes, if to be well done. Place on a hot dish and season with butter and salt. Another method is to put into a frying-pan about a tablespoonful of butter or pork fat and cook the steaks for eight minutes. Place the steaks on a hot dish, and into the pan in which they were cooked put one tablespoonful of butter and half a tablespoonful of flour. Stir until smooth and brown; then add a gill of cold water, stirring all the time. Season this sauce with half a teaspoonful of salt and a little pepper. A gill of strained tomatoes will be an improvement. Pour the sauce over the steaks and serve at once.

Beef Stew from the Cold Roast.

The bones of the roast.	2 tablespoonfuls of minced celery.
About a pound and a quarter of meat.	1½ tablespoonfuls of flour.
	2 level teaspoonfuls of salt.
5 tablespoonfuls of liquid fat.	¼ teaspoonful of pepper.
1 large onion.	1 pint of boiling water.
2 tablespoonfuls of minced carrot.	1 pint of sliced potatoes.

Take the bones and the tough pieces left from a cold roast of beef. After cutting all the meat from the bones, remove all the fat from the meat and put it on the fire in a frying-pan. Cut the lean meat into small pieces. Place the bones in a stew-pan and lay the meat on top of them. Take from the frying-pan five tablespoonfuls of liquid fat and put it in another frying-pan. Add the minced vegetables, and cook slowly for half an hour. At the end of that time draw the pan forward to a hotter part of the range and cook rapidly for three minutes, stirring all the time. Now draw the vegetables to one side of the pan and press out the fat, then put the vegetables in the stewpan. Put the flour into the fat remaining in the pan, and stir until it becomes smooth and brown; then add the water, and stir until it boils. Add the salt and pepper and cook for three minutes. Pour this gravy into the stewpan, and, covering the pan, set it back where the contents will just bubble at one side for two hours and a half. The potatoes are then to be added and the stewpan brought forward to a hotter place. At the end of half an hour the stew will be done. Remove the bones and serve the stew on a warm dish. It may be garnished with a circle of small baking powder biscuit, or with dumplings.

Stew from Cold Lamb or Mutton.

With the bones and tough pieces of cold lamb or mutton a stew can be made the same as beef stew with cold roast beef. If you have the small white turnips use a gill of these cut in cubes and fried with the other vegetables.

Creamed Dried Beef.

3 ounces of smoked dried beef.	1 teaspoonful of flour.
1 heaping tablespoonful of butter.	1½ gills of milk.

Have the beef cut in slices as thin as shavings, and put it in a bowl. Pour upon it one pint of boiling water, and let it stand for two minutes; then turn off the water and drain the beef dry. Put the butter on the fire, in a frying-pan, and when it becomes hot add the beef. Cook for three minutes, stirring all the time. Now pour on one gill of cold milk. Mix the half-gill of milk with the flour, and stir it into the cooking mixture. Cook for two minutes, and serve.

Frizzled Smoked Beef.

2 ounces of dried smoked beef.	1 gill of milk.
3 eggs.	1 tablespoonful of butter.

Have the beef shaved thin and then cut it into small bits. Beat the eggs well, and add the milk to them. Put the butter on the fire, in a frying-pan, and when it becomes hot, add the beef. Stir the meat for three minutes; then draw the pan back to a cooler place and add the eggs and milk. Stir constantly until the egg begins to thicken; then turn into a warm dish and serve.

Veal Olives.

In making veal olives use a tablespoonful of butter in the cracker dressing, as there will be no fat to cut from the veal. Add half a dozen celery seeds when the gravy is put with the olives. With these exceptions proceed exactly as for beef olives.

Veal Cutlets Sauté.

1 slice of veal from the leg.	1 generous gill of cold water.
2 ounces of fat salt pork.	¼ teaspoonful of pepper.
1 tablespoonful of flour.	1½ teaspoonfuls of salt.
1 gill of strained tomatoes.	

Nick the edge of the cutlet with a sharp knife; this will keep the slice flat. Cut the pork in slices and cook slowly in the frying-pan for fifteen minutes. Draw the pan forward to a hotter part of the range and take up the pieces of pork. Season the cutlet with half the pepper and salt, and lay it in the hot fat. Cook slowly for fifteen minutes, turning frequently. Now take up the meat and put the flour into the gravy remaining in the pan. Stir until it turns dark brown; then add the cold water, tomatoes, salt, and pepper, stirring all the while. Cook the sauce for five minutes; then lay the fried cutlet in it and cover the pan. Set back where the sauce will hardly bubble at one side for half an hour. At end of that time place the cutlet on a hot dish and strain the sauce over it. Serve at once.

Fricassee of Veal.

1 pound of veal.	2 tablespoonfuls of flour.
2 ounces of fat salt pork.	3 gills of water.
⅛ teaspoonful of pepper.	1 gill of strained tomatoes.
½ teaspoonful of salt.	

Cut the pork in thin slices and fry brown. Have the veal cut in small, thin pieces. Season it with the salt and pepper, then roll it in the flour. Take the pork from the pan and lay the slices of veal in the hot fat. Let them fry until they have a good brown color, turning them when brown on one side. Take up the veal and stir the remainder of the flour into the fat. When the flour is brown, add the cold water, stirring all the time. When this gravy boils up put the browned veal into it and simmer for half an hour. Add the tomatoes and boil up once.

The flavor and appearance of this dish may be varied by changing the gravy. Measure the water generously, and omit the tomatoes, and you have a simple brown fricassee. Be scant in the measurement of water and tomatoes, adding the tomatoes to the gravy when the meat is put in; then, at the end of half an hour, add a gill of milk, and boil up once, and you have a bisque of veal. Or you may omit the tomatoes, and at the end of the half-hour add a generous gill of milk, and you have a white fricassee. In this case do not brown the flour when it is added to the fat.

Ragout of Mutton.

2 pounds of mutton from the shoulder or breast.	1 tablespoonful of flour.
1 pint of turnip cubes.	1 tablespoonful of corn-starch.
½ pint of carrot cubes.	1 level tablespoonful of salt.
2 tablespoonfuls of minced onion.	⅛ teaspoonful of pepper.
1 tablespoonful of butter.	1¼ pints of water.

Have the mutton free from bones. Cut off all the fat and put it in the frying-pan and on the fire. Cut the meat into pieces about two inches square. When there is about five tablespoonfuls of liquid fat in the pan, take out the solid pieces and move the pan to a part of the range where the fat will become smoking hot. Now put in the mutton, and stir until it becomes brown, — which will be in about six minutes. Take the meat from the fat and put it into a stewpan. Put the turnips, carrots, and onion in the fat remaining in the pan and cook for ten minutes, being careful not to brown them. Press all the fat from the vegetables and put them in the stewpan with the meat. Now, after pouring all the fat from the pan, put in the butter and flour, and stir until the mixture becomes smooth and dark brown; then draw back to a cooler place and gradually stir in one pint and a half of water. When this boils up add it to the contents of the stewpan.

Mix the salt, pepper, corn-starch, and a gill of cold water. Stir this mixture into the stewpan. When the ragout boils, skim it, and move the stewpan back where the contents will bubble gently at one side for three hours. Serve very hot.

If you choose, a pint of potato cubes can be added the last half-hour.

Blanquette of Cold Meat.

1 pint of cold white meat.
1 gill of milk or cream.
1½ gills of stock.
1 teaspoonful of salt.

1¼ teaspoonfuls of pepper.
1½ tablespoonfuls of butter.
1 tablespoonful of flour.

Veal, lamb, or any kind of poultry, will answer for this dish. Have the meat free from fat and bone, and cut into dainty pieces. Season it with half the salt and pepper. Put the butter in a frying-pan and set on the fire. When hot, add the flour, stirring until the mixture is smooth and frothy; then gradually add the stock. Cook for two minutes; then add the milk and cold meat, and simmer gently for fifteen minutes. Turn out on a warm dish and garnish with rice, toast, or pastry cakes. A teaspoonful of lemon juice, added just as the blanquette is being removed from the fire, is an addition that pleases most tastes. A teaspoonful of curry-powder may be stirred into the butter when the flour is added, thus changing the dish to a delicate curry.

Pork Chops.

1½ pounds of pork steak.
1½ teaspoonfuls of salt.
¼ teaspoonful of pepper.

½ pint of strained tomatoes.
1 tablespoonful of flour.

Season the chops with one teaspoonful of the salt and half the pepper. Put them in a hot frying-pan and cook them rather slowly for twenty minutes. Take up the chops and stir the flour into the fat remaining in the pan. When the mixture is smooth and frothy, add the strained tomatoes and simmer for five minutes. Season with the remainder of the salt and pepper. Arrange the chops on a warm dish and pour the sauce around them.

If a plain brown sauce be preferred, substitute cold water for the tomatoes.

Fried Salt Pork.

Have the slices cut about one fourth of an inch thick. Drop them into boiling water and cook for five minutes. After draining the pieces of pork, put them in the frying-pan and set them on the fire. Let them cook slowly at first; then draw the pan to hotter part of the range, and cook more rapidly until they are crisp and brown. Draw the pan back, and, taking up the pork, arrange it on a hot dish.

Pour all the pork fat, except about two tablespoonfuls, into a bowl. Put the pan back on the fire, and into the fat remaining put one tablespoonful of flour. Stir until the mixture is smooth and brown; then gradually add half a pint of cold water. Simmer for three minutes, and then taste to be sure it is salt enough. Serve this gravy in a sauce bowl.

A brown sauce made in this manner is much more healthful and appetizing than the clear pork fat.

Salt Pork in Batter.

6 slices of pork.	1 egg.
3 tablespoonfuls of flour.	¼ teaspoonful of salt.
5 tablespoonfuls of milk.	

Have the pork cut in thin slices. Drop it into boiling water and cook for two minutes. Take it up and drain; then put it in a frying-pan, and, setting it on the fire, cook until it turns a delicate brown, which should be in five minutes. Draw the pan back and take up the pork.

Make a batter with the flour, milk, salt, and egg. Dip the pork in the batter. Have the pork fat hot, and lay the masked pork in it. Cook until brown on one side; then turn and brown on the other. Serve at once.

Sausage Cakes.

1 pound of fresh pork.	½ tablespoonful of salt.
½ pint of stale bread.	½ teaspoonful of powdered sage.
¼ teaspoonful of pepper.	½ teaspoonful of powdered thyme.

Have the meat one fourth fat and three fourths lean, and chopped fine. Soak the bread in cold water until it is soft, then press out all the water. Mix the seasonings and the bread with the meat. When all the ingredients are thoroughly combined, shape into small flat cakes, and fry

HOW TO COOK MEAT.

until brown on both sides. It will take twenty minutes to cook the cakes thoroughly.

Stewed Kidneys.

1 beef kidney, or two pairs of sheep or lambs'.	¼ teaspoonful of pepper.
	1 tablespoonful of butter.
1 pint of water or stock.	1 level tablespoonful of flour.
1 teaspoonful of salt.	1 teaspoonful of lemon juice.

Draw the thin, white skin off the kidneys; then cut them into thin, round slices, removing the hard, white substance. Wash them, and soak them in salted water for half an hour. At the end of that time put them in a stewpan with the pint of water. Place on the fire; and when they begin to boil, skim carefully. Draw the stewpan to a part of the range where the water will only bubble gently for two hours. At the end of that time put the butter in a small pan, and set over the fire. Add the flour, and stir until the mixture is smooth and brown. Stir this into the pan containing the kidneys. Now add the seasonings, and simmer for half an hour longer. Serve toasted bread with the kidneys.

Kidneys Sauté.

2 pairs of sheep's kidneys.	1 teaspoonful of lemon juice.
1 tablespoonful of butter.	1 teaspoonful of salt.
½ tablespoonful of flour.	¼ teaspoonful of pepper.
1 gill of stock or water.	

Prepare the kidneys as for stewing. Drain and wipe them. Put the butter and flour in a frying-pan, and set on the fire. Season the kidneys with the salt and pepper. Put them into the pan with the butter and flour, and cook for two minutes, stirring all the time. Add the stock or water, *cold*. Stir until this boils up, then add the lemon juice. Turn the sauté into a warm dish, and garnish with points of crisp toast.

Broiled Kidneys.

2 pairs of sheep or lambs' kidneys.	1 teaspoonful of salt.
2 tablespoonfuls of butter.	¼ teaspoonful of pepper.
1 teaspoonful of lemon juice.	Flour.

Draw the thin skin off the kidneys; then cut each kidney almost in two. Cut out the hard, white substance from the centre. Wash the kidneys and soak them in salt and water for half an hour. At the end of that time wipe them dry. Melt one tablespoonful of the butter and add the lemon juice, salt and pepper to it. Dip the kidneys in this; then roll lightly in flour, and, placing them in the broiler, cook over clear coals for six minutes. Arrange on a hot dish and season with the remaining tablespoonful of butter; or, instead of the plain butter, use two tablespoonfuls of maître d'hôtel butter.

The kidneys may be rolled in fine bread crumbs instead of flour.

Stewed Sheep's Hearts.

2 sheep's hearts.	2 tablespoonfuls of flour.
2 ounces of fat salt pork.	¼ teaspoonful of pepper.
2 tablespoonfuls of minced onion.	1½ pints of water.
1 teaspoonful of salt.	

Split and wash the hearts. Season them with half the pepper and salt, and roll them in the flour. Fry the pork in the frying-pan. Put the onions with the fried pork and cook for ten minutes. At the end of that time take the pork and onions from the frying-pan and put them in the stewpan. Lay the hearts in the frying-pan, and cook until they are brown on one side; then turn them and brown the other side. After that, put them in the stewpan. Pour the hot water into the frying-pan and stir until all the sediment is mixed with it, then pour it over the hearts.

HOW TO COOK MEAT. 143

To the flour left after the hearts were rolled, add two tablespoonfuls of cold water, and stir until the mixture becomes perfectly smooth, when it should be stirred into the gravy in the stewpan. Add the remainder of the salt and pepper, and place the stewpan where the gravy will bubble gently at one side for three hours. The hearts will be tender and delicious if the cooking be slow, but if the gravy be allowed to boil hard, the meat will be tough and unsatisfactory.

At serving time arrange the hearts on a dish and strain the gravy over them. Serve boiled rice with this dish.

Fried Liver and Bacon.

2 ounces of breakfast bacon.
½ pound of liver.

1 teaspoonful of salt.
⅛ teaspoonful of pepper.

Have the bacon cut in as thin slices as possible and keep it cold until the time to cook it. Have the liver cut into slices about one third of an inch thick. If it be calf or sheep's liver, wash it in cold water and let it drain; but if it be beef liver, after washing it, cover with boiling water and let it stand for five minutes; then drain it.

Put the pieces of bacon into a hot frying-pan and turn them constantly until they are crisp; then take them up. Draw the pan back to a cooler part of the range, and, laying the slices of bacon in the hot fat, cook them for eight minutes, turning often. Season with the salt and pepper. Arrange the liver on a warm platter and garnish with the bacon.

Remember that slow cooking spoils bacon, and rapid cooking hardens and ruins liver.

Calf's Liver Sauté.

1 pound of calf's liver.
2 tablespoonfuls of butter.
2 tablespoonfuls of flour.
1½ teaspoonfuls of salt.

¼ teaspoonful of pepper.
1 tablespoonful of lemon juice.
½ pint of water.

Cut the liver in slices one third of an inch thick, and wash and wipe them. Season with one teaspoonful of the salt and half the pepper.

Put the butter into a frying-pan and set on the fire. When it becomes hot, stir in the flour, and then lay the slices of liver in the pan. Cook slowly for six minutes, turning often. At the end of that time add the water, stirring all the while. When this boils up, add the remainder of the salt and pepper and the lemon juice, and cook gently for two minutes.

The lemon juice may be omitted and milk be substituted for the water in making the sauce. Pig, sheep, and lamb's liver can be treated in the same manner.

Chicken Livers en Brochette.

4 chicken livers.
8 slices of breakfast bacon.

Cut the bacon as thin as possible. Cut the livers in two parts, and after washing them, season them with salt and pepper. Fold each piece of liver in a slice of bacon and fasten with a small bird skewer. Broil over clear coals for ten minutes. Remove the skewers and serve the liver and bacon on slices of toast.

Broiled Tripe.

1 pound of tripe.	¼ teaspoonful of pepper.
1 tablespoonful of butter.	A little flour.
½ teaspoonful of salt.	

Wash and drain the tripe. If it has been in pickle, put it in a saucepan with cold water enough to cover it, and place on the fire. Simmer gently for half an hour. If milk be plentiful use half milk and half water. If the tripe has not been pickled, fifteen minutes will be enough time for the simmering. Take it from the hot liquid and drain.

Melt the butter in a soup plate. Add the salt and pepper to it and then roll the piece of tripe in the mixture. Dredge the tripe with flour and broil over a hot fire for six minutes. Serve at once.

Tripe may be broiled without using the butter and flour, but it is apt to be dry. Get the thick, juicy part for broiling.

Fried Tripe.

1 pound of tripe.	1 level teaspoonful of salt.
2 tablespoonfuls of drippings.	¼ teaspoonful of pepper.
2 tablespoonfuls of flour.	1 gill of water or milk.

Wash the tripe and cut it into small pieces. Season it with salt and pepper and roll it in the flour. Put the drippings in the frying-pan and set on the fire. When hot, lay in the tripe, and cook for ten minutes, browning both sides. Take up the tripe, and into the fat remaining in the pan scrape such part of the flour as did not adhere to the tripe. Stir the mixture, and then add the cold water or milk. Cook for two minutes. Taste, to see if seasoned enough, because more salt and pepper may be needed. Strain this gravy over the tripe, and serve. If any one of the following named seasonings be liked it may be added to the gravy: half a teaspoonful of onion juice, one tablespoonful of tomato catsup, one teaspoonful of lemon juice, or one teaspoonful of vinegar.

Tripe Fried in Batter.

1 pound of tripe.	1 egg.
6 tablespoonfuls of drippings.	1 teaspoonful of salt.
3 tablespoonfuls of flour.	¼ teaspoonful of pepper.
5 tablespoonfuls of milk.	

Cut the tripe in small squares and season it with half the salt and pepper. Pour the milk on the flour, and beat to a smooth paste. Add the egg, well beaten, and the remainder of the salt and pepper, and beat for two minutes longer. Have the drippings smoking hot in the frying-pan. Dip the tripe in the batter and lay it in the hot fat. When brown on one side, turn and brown on the other. Serve at once.

The tripe may be fried in deep fat. In that case it will cook in three minutes.

Corned Beef Hash.

1 pint of hashed corned beef.	⅓ teaspoonful of pepper.
1 pint of hashed potatoes.	1 tablespoonful of butter.
1 teaspoonful of salt.	1 gill of milk.

Have the meat about one fourth fat and three fourths lean. Chop it rather coarse. Chop the cold boiled potatoes a little coarser than the meat and season them with the salt and pepper. Mix the potato and meat, stirring with a fork. Add the milk, and stir lightly. Put the butter in the frying-pan, and when it becomes hot put in the hash, spreading it lightly and evenly, but not stirring it. Cover the pan and set where the hash will cook slowly and evenly for half an hour or more. There should be a rich brown crust on the bottom. At serving time fold and turn out on a hot dish, and serve on hot plates.

Hash of Fresh Meat.

Any kind of meat can be used to make a meat-and-potato hash; but, of course, nothing is so good as corned beef. Cold roast, boiled, or broiled beef, mutton, lamb, veal, or tongue can be freed from skin, fat, and bones, seasoned highly with salt and pepper, and cooked like corned beef hash. Even two or three kinds of meat can be used. If it happens that you have a bit of steak, a part of a chop, and perhaps a slice of tongue, use them all.

Sausage Hash.

3 cold boiled potatoes.
2 cooked sausages.
½ teaspoonful of salt.

⅛ teaspoonful of pepper.
1 teaspoonful of butter.

Chop the potatoes rather coarse, and the sausage a little finer. Season the potatoes with the salt and pepper, and mix the sausage with them. Put the butter in a frying-pan, and when it becomes melted put in the hash. Spread lightly in the pan, but do not stir. Cover the pan and set on the back part of the range, where the hash will brown slowly. Cook for half an hour. Fold it, and, turning out on a hot dish, serve at once.

Baked Hash.

½ pint of hashed meat.
½ pint of cold mashed potatoes.
½ pint of milk or stock.
3 teaspoonfuls of butter.

1 teaspoonful of flour.
⅛ teaspoonful of pepper.
½ teaspoonful of salt.

Use any kind of cold cooked meat. Have it freed from fat and bones, and chopped rather fine. Season it with the salt and pepper. Put two teaspoonfuls of the butter in a small pan and set it on the fire. When the butter is hot, add the flour, and stir until the mixture is smooth and frothy. Gradually add the milk, and boil for three minutes. Add the meat to this, and boil up once; then put in a baking-dish. Spread the mashed potatoes over this and dot with the remaining teaspoonful of butter. Bake in a moderate oven for twenty minutes.

Cooked hominy or rice may be substituted for the potatoes.

Minced Meat on Toast.

½ pint of cold hashed meat.
¼ teaspoonful of pepper.
1 level teaspoonful of salt.
1 teaspoonful of flour.

1 tablespoonful of butter.
1 gill of stock or water.
3 slices of toast.

Have the meat free from fat and bones and hashed rather fine. Mix with it the salt, pepper, and flour. Put it into a small stewpan and stir in the stock or water. Cover the pan and set it on a part of the range where the hash will cook slowly for thirty minutes; then add the butter, and cook five minutes longer.

Have the toast crisp and brown. Dip the edges in boiling water. Cut each slice of toast into two triangular pieces. Spread the meat on these, and serve at once.

Tongue Toast.

1 gill of minced tongue.
1 gill of milk.
1 tablespoonful of butter.

½ teaspoonful of flour.
Salt, pepper.
3 slices of toast.

Use the dry end of a boiled tongue and mince very fine. Put the butter on the stove in a small frying-pan, and when it becomes hot, add the flour. Stir until smooth and frothy; then draw the pan back to a cooler part of the range, and gradually add the milk. Now move the pan to a hotter place and cook its contents for two minutes, stirring all the time. Add the tongue and seasoning, and simmer for five minutes. Toast the bread, and place it on a warm dish. Spread a little of the tongue and sauce on each slice, and serve at once.

Meat Cakes.

1 gill of finely minced cold cooked meat.
1 gill of mashed potato.
1 tablespoonful of butter.

½ teaspoonful of salt.
$\frac{1}{16}$ teaspoonful of pepper.
1 tablespoonful of sweet drippings.

Season the meat with the salt and pepper, and beat it and the butter into the hot mashed potatoes. Shape into round flat cakes and fry brown on both sides, using the drippings for frying.

Sanders.

½ pint of minced cold meat.	1¼ teaspoonfuls of salt.
½ pint mashed potatoes.	¼ teaspoonful of pepper.
½ pint of stock or milk.	½ teaspoonful of onion juice.
1½ tablespoonfuls of butter.	1 gill of grated bread crumbs.
1 heaping teaspoonful of flour.	

Almost any kind of cold cooked meat may be used; preferably veal, mutton, or lamb. Season it with half a teaspoonful of salt, half the pepper, and all the onion juice. Put one tablespoonful of butter in a small frying-pan and set on the fire. When hot, add the flour, and stir until brown; then draw the pan back and gradually add the stock or milk, stirring all the time. Season with half a teaspoonful of salt and the remaining pepper. Put the meat in this sauce. Divide the mixture into six parts and put each part into a little baking-dish or shell. Season the mashed potatoes with one fourth of a teaspoonful of salt and spread it over the little dishes. Sprinkle the crumbs over these and dot with the half tablespoonful of butter. Bake in a moderately hot oven for fifteen minutes, and serve at once.

Two potatoes of medium size will make the half-pint of mashed potatoes. If you have cold mashed potatoes on hand, use them. The crumbs may be omitted.

Cold boiled rice may be substituted for the potatoes.

Small Timbales.

3 gills of hashed cooked meat.	1 gill of stock.
1 level teaspoonful of salt.	1 egg.
¼ teaspoonful of pepper.	1 gill of fine bread crumbs.
¼ teaspoonful of onion juice.	A slight grating of nutmeg

Have the meat free from bone, fat, and gristle, and chopped very fine. Mix all the seasonings and the bread crumbs with it. Now add the stock, and let it stand in a cool place for one or two hours. At the end of that time beat the egg well and mix it with the other ingredients. Butter four small timbale moulds, — small cups will do, — and pack the mixture into them. Put them in a pan and surround them with tepid water. Lay a piece of thick brown paper over the top. Place the pan in a moderate oven and cook the timbales for twenty minutes. Turn them out on a warm platter, and pour a white, brown, or bisque sauce around them.

This mixture may be cooked in one mould. In that case allow ten minutes longer. At no time during the cooking should the oven be hot enough to have the water boil.

Mutton Croquettes.

½ pint of finely chopped cold mutton.	1 level teaspoonful of salt.
2 eggs.	⅙ teaspoonful of pepper.
1 gill of milk or cream.	½ tablespoonful of lemon juice.
1 tablespoonful of butter.	A few drops of onion juice.
½ tablespoonful of flour.	Bread crumbs.
	Fat for frying.

Add the seasoning to the meat. Put the milk in a small pan and set on the fire. Beat the butter and flour together, and stir into the boiling milk. Now add the meat, and cook for two minutes, stirring often. Add one of the eggs, well beaten, and take from the fire at once. Pour the mixture on a plate and set away to get chilled. When it is chilled, shape the croquettes, and bread and fry them.

The second egg and the crumbs are for use in breading.

Any kind of tender cooked meat may be used instead of the mutton.

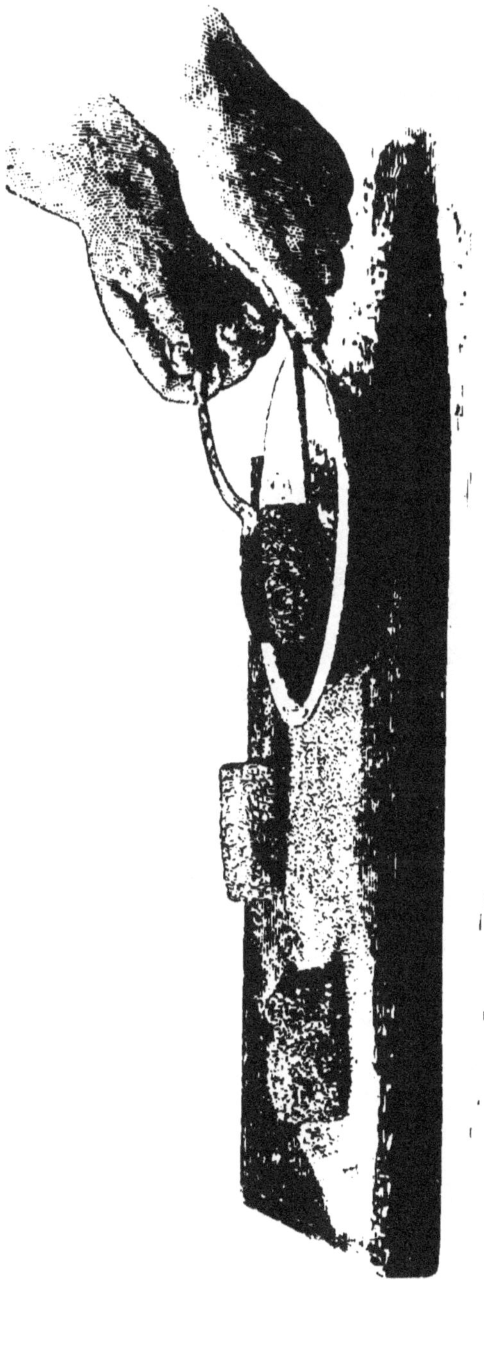

HOW TO COOK MEAT. 151

BREADING CROQUETTES.

Meat and Potato Croquettes.

1 cupful of cold meat, chopped fine.	½ cupful of milk.
1 cupful of cold mashed potatoes.	2 tablespoonfuls of butter.
1 teaspoonful of salt.	2 eggs.
¼ teaspoonful of pepper.	Dried bread crumbs.
	Fat for frying.

Mix the meat, potatoes, and seasoning. Put the milk and butter in a frying-pan, and when the liquid boils up put in the meat and potatoes, and cook for one minute. Beat one egg well and stir it into the hot mixture. Take from the fire immediately, and, after pouring out on a plate, set away

CROQUETTES READY FOR SERVING.

to cool. When cold, shape into cylinders about three inches long, and bread and fry.

The second egg and the crumbs are for the breading.

Hominy or rice may be substituted for the potatoes.

Meat Pie.

Filling.	*Crust.*
1½ pints of cold meat.	½ pint of flour.
1 pint of stock or water.	1 tablespoonful of butter.
1 tablespoonful of butter.	1 tablespoonful of lard.
1 teaspoonful of minced onion.	1 teaspoonful of sugar.
1 teaspoonful of minced carrot.	½ teaspoonful of salt.
1½ tablespoonfuls of flour.	1 teaspoonful of baking-powder.
1 teaspoonful of salt.	½ gill of cold water.
⅙ teaspoonful of pepper.	

Use any kind of cooked unsalted meat, and have it free from skin, bones, and fat. Put it in a stewpan. Put the vegetables and butter in a frying-pan, and cook for ten minutes. At the end of that time take the vegetables from the butter and put them with the meat. Into the butter remaining in the pan put half a tablespoonful of flour, and stir until smooth and frothy. Gradually add the stock or water, and stir until the sauce boils. Add this to the meat and vegetables, and place the saucepan on the fire. Mix the remaining tablespoonful of flour with four tablespoonfuls of cold water, and stir into the meat mixture. Add the seasonings, and cook for fifteen minutes. Turn this into a dish that will hold nearly two quarts, and set away to cool.

Now make the crust. Mix the salt, sugar, and baking-powder with the flour, and then rub through a sieve into a bowl. Add the butter and lard, and cut and mix through the flour, with a knife, until quite fine. Wet with the cold water, stirring all the time with the knife. Sprinkle the board lightly with flour, and turn out the paste upon it. Roll very thin; then fold and roll again into a thin sheet. Fold up, put in a tin pan, and set on the ice for an hour or more; or it may be used at once. Roll the paste into the shape of the top of the dish in which the pie is to be baked, only about an inch larger on all sides. Cut a small slit in the centre of the paste that the steam may escape. Cover the prepared meat with this paste, turning in the edges. Bake the pie in a moderate oven for one hour.

The bones and bits of gristle may be boiled in water to make a stock.

How to Clean and Truss Poultry.

Cut off the head, and then the legs, being careful in the latter case to cut in or below the joints. Now cut the skin on the back of the neck; then turn the skin over on the breast and cut off the neck. Take out the crop, being particular to remove all the lining membrane. Put the forefinger into the throat and break the ligaments that hold the internal organs to the breastbone. Next cut the bird open at the vent, beginning under the left leg, and cutting in a slanting direction toward the vent. Stop there. Insert the hand in this opening, and work around the organs until they are loosened from the bones. Gently draw all the organs out at once. Put the hand in to learn if either the windpipe or lights are left in the body. Cut the oil bag from the tail. This is a hard, yellow substance. Now singe the bird by holding it over a lighted newspaper. The paper should be drawn into a long, fluffy piece, then twisted lightly. Hold the burning paper over an open fire or a coal hod during the operation of singeing.

Wash the poultry quickly in cold water; then season it with salt, and fill the crop and breast with dressing. Draw the skin at the neck on to the back, and fasten it with a skewer to the backbone. Turn the tips of the wings under the back, and fasten them in that position with a long skewer. Pass a short skewer through the lower part of the legs, and then through the tail. Tie with long piece of twine. Turn the bird on its breast and bring the string up around the skewers that hold the neck and wings. Tie firmly, and the bird will be ready for cooking.

Boiled Fowl.

A boiled fowl is one of the most satisfactory and economical dishes of poultry. The meat can be used in making a great variety of dishes, and the water in which the fowl was boiled may be used in soups, or for the foundation of meat, fish, and vegetable sauces.

Select a short, plump, fat fowl. Singe and draw it, and wash it quickly in cold water. Put it in a stewpan, breast down, with boiling water enough to cover it. When the water begins to boil, skim thoroughly; then draw the stewpan back, where the water will bubble at one side of the pan, until the fowl is tender. This you can tell by pressing the wing back with a fork. If it breaks away from the breast readily, the fowl is cooked enough. Take the stewpan from the fire, and set it, with the cover off, in a cool, airy place. When cool, take up the fowl and put it away. Pour the water into a large bowl and set in a cool place for future use.

If the fowl is to be served hot, take it up when tender, place it on a platter and pour over it a little butter, bechamel, or parsley sauce. Serve the remainder of the sauce in a gravy bowl.

If the fowl is to be served hot for dinner, boil four ounces of mixed salt pork with it.

The time of boiling a fowl cannot be given, because it depends upon the age. A fowl about a year old will cook in two hours; one two or three years old may take three or four hours.

Cold boiled fowl may be used for a fricassee, blanquette, salad, pie, creamed chicken, croquettes, etc.

Roast Chicken.

1 chicken, weighing four or five pounds.	¼ teaspoonful of pepper.
2 tablespoonfuls of soft butter.	1 teaspoonful of minced parsley.
Salt, pepper, flour.	¼ teaspoonful of powdered thyme.
	¼ do. do. sage.
	¼ do. do. savory.
Dressing.	¼ do. do. marjoram.
1 pint of grated bread crumbs.	2 generous tablespoonfuls of butter.
1 level teaspoonful of salt.	

Have all the materials for the dressing mixed together in a bowl, cutting the butter into small bits. Remember that there is no liquid used in this dressing. Clean the chicken and stuff the crop and body with the dressing. Truss the chicken and dredge it with salt. Rub soft butter over the breast and legs, and dredge thickly with flour. Place a rack in the dripping-pan, and, after laying the chicken on it, put in half a pint of hot water. Set the pan in a hot oven and baste the chicken every fifteen minutes, pouring over it the gravy in the dripping-pan until every part is well moistened, and then dredging lightly with salt, pepper, and flour. At the last basting omit the gravy, and moisten instead with a tablespoonful of butter dissolved in a tablespoonful of hot water; then dredge lightly with flour. After the first half-hour the heat of the oven should be reduced. It will take an hour and a half to cook a chicken weighing four or five pounds. If the tin kitchen be used, the chicken should be prepared and basted in the same manner, but it will take fifteen minutes longer to cook it. Serve on a hot platter with a garnish of parsley.

Roast Turkey.

A turkey weighing eight or nine pounds.
4 tablespoonfuls of butter.

Salt, pepper, flour.
Double the amount of dressing given for roast chicken.

Prepare and cook the turkey the same as directed for roast chicken; cooking it, however, two hours and a half. It makes a pleasant change to stuff the crop with a mixture prepared as for sausage cakes. Fill the rest of the body with the usual dressing.

Chicken Gravy.

1½ pints of cold water.
1 tablespoonful of butter.
1 tablespoonful of flour.
1 teaspoonful of salt.

¼ teaspoonful of pepper.
The neck, liver, heart, and gizzard of the chicken.

Wash the giblets — that is, the neck, liver, etc. — and put them in a stewpan with the water. When the water boils, skim it. Simmer for two hours or more. There should be about half a pint of liquid at this time. Take up the giblets. Mash the liver until perfectly fine, and return to the liquid. Put the butter in a small frying-pan and place on the fire. When hot, add the flour, and stir until brown. Pour on this, gradually, the liquid in the saucepan, stirring all the time. Season with the salt and pepper. Pour this sauce back into the saucepan; cover, and set back where it will keep hot.

When the chicken is cooked, pour the gravy from the dripping-pan into this sauce. Serve in a hot dish.

Turkey gravy is made in the same manner.

Turkey or Chicken Dressing.

1½ pints of stale bread.	⅓ teaspoonful of sage.
1 gill of cracker crumbs.	½ teaspoonful of savory.
1 egg.	½ teaspoonful of marjoram.
1 teaspoonful of salt.	¼ teaspoonful of thyme.
⅓ teaspoonful of pepper.	⅓ cupful of butter.

Soak the bread in cold water until soft; then press out all the water. Add all the other ingredients to the bread, and mix well. Fill the breast of the turkey or chicken with this, and put the remainder in the body of the bird.

Breaded Chicken.

A young roasting chicken.	⅓ teaspoonful of pepper.
2 tablespoonfuls of butter.	1 gill of dried bread crumbs.
1 level tablespoonful of salt.	

Use a chicken weighing about three or four pounds, and have it split down the back. Singe and wipe it. Let the tips remain on the wings. Turn the wings back and skewer them into place. Fasten the neck under the body. Press the chicken out flat, and press the legs back on the body, skewering them in this position. Season with the salt and pepper, and place in a dripping-pan. Rub the soft butter over the breast and legs, and then sprinkle the crumbs over the chicken. Place the pan in a hot oven and cook for forty-five minutes. Reduce the heat after the first fifteen minutes.

Remember that the chicken is put in the bottom of the pan split side down, and that there is no water or basting of any kind used.

This dish is especially good served with a Tartar sauce, but it is very good without any sauce whatever.

Fried Chicken.

1 tender chicken.	1 generous teaspoonful of salt.
2 ounces of salt pork.	¼ teaspoonful of pepper.
3 tablespoonfuls of flour.	1 tablespoonful of butter.
½ pint of milk.	

Singe the chicken and wipe it with a damp towel. Cut it into handsome joints. Season it with the salt and pepper, and roll it in the flour. Cut the pork into thin slices, and fry it slowly until all the fat has been extracted, then take out the pork. Draw the frying-pan to a hotter part of the range, and when the fat begins to smoke lay in the slices of chicken. Fry the chicken brown on all sides. It will take about half an hour to cook it. When it is done, arrange it on a warm platter. Put the butter with the fat remaining in the pan, and add all the flour that did not cling to the chicken, stirring until smooth and frothy. Gradually add the milk, stirring all the time. When the sauce boils up, taste it, to learn if it requires more salt and pepper. Pour the sauce over the chicken and serve. If parsley be liked, add to the sauce half a teaspoonful, finely minced.

Creamed Chicken.

1 pint of cold boiled fowl or chicken.	1½ gills of milk or cream.
	⅕ teaspoonful of pepper.
1 heaped tablespoonful of butter.	1½ teaspoonfuls of salt.
2 level tablespoonfuls of flour.	A few drops of onion juice.
1 gill of chicken stock.	

Have the chicken free from skin, fat, and bones, and cut into long strips. Season it with half of the salt and pepper. Put the butter in a frying-pan and set on the fire. When hot, add the flour, and stir until the mixture is smooth and frothy. Now add the stock, stirring all the time, and when this boils gradually add the milk. Season the sauce with the remainder of the salt and pepper, and the onion juice. Put the chicken in this and simmer for ten minutes.

This dish is suitable for breakfast, luncheon, supper, or dinner.

Creamed Turkey.

Prepare and serve cold roast or boiled turkey the same as chicken.

Stewed Chicken.

1 chicken or fowl, weighing about three or four pounds.	3 tablespoonfuls of flour.
	3 pints of boiling water.
1 tablespoonful of butter.	1 tablespoonful of salt.
1 tablespoonful of minced onion.	½ teaspoonful of pepper.

Singe the chicken and cut it into handsome joints. Wash it, and, putting it in a stewpan with the water, place it on the fire. When the water begins to boil, skim carefully, and draw the stewpan back to a place where the liquid will just bubble at the side. Put the onion and butter in a small pan and cook gently for twenty minutes. Take the onions from the butter and add them to the chicken. Add half a tablespoonful of flour to the butter remaining in the pan, and cook until smooth and frothy. Add this to the stew. Mix the remainder of the flour smoothly with a gill of cold water, and stir into the stew. Add the salt and pepper. Cook gently for three hours. At the end of this time draw the stewpan to a hotter part of the range, and, after adding some dumplings, cook just ten minutes after the cover is put on the stewpan.

Chicken Pie.

1½ pints of cooked chicken.	¼ teaspoonful of pepper.
1 pint of stock.	1 teaspoonful of salt.
2 level tablespoonfuls of flour.	Half the materials named in the
2 tablespoonfuls of butter.	rule for delicate paste.

Have the chicken free from fat, skin, and bones, and cut it in delicate pieces. Season it with half the salt and pepper. Put the butter in a frying-pan and place on the fire. Add the flour to the melted butter, and stir until smooth and frothy. Gradually add the stock, stirring all the time. Season with the remainder of the salt and pepper. Stir the chicken into the sauce, and turn into the dish in which the pie is to be baked. Set away to cool. When it is time to finish the pie, roll the paste into the same shape as the top of the dish, but a little larger. Make a hole in the centre to allow the steam to escape. Cover the meat with this and bake in a moderately hot oven for one hour.

White Fricassee of Chicken.

Make this the same as the filling for chicken pie.

Roast Duck.

Singe and wash the duck, and then wipe it. Season it with salt and pepper, and put half an onion in the body. Truss it, and dredge lightly with flour. Roast it in a hot oven for half an hour, and serve it with a hot currant sauce. This time will cook the duck rare, which is the proper way to cook all kinds of ducks. If, however, you prefer to have it well done, stuff it, and treat it exactly like roast chicken.

Roast Grouse.

1 grouse.
1 small onion.
2 tablespoonfuls of soft butter.
1 ounce of fat salt pork.
Salt, pepper, flour.

Cut off the neck and wings close to the body. Cut off the feet in the joints, or just below; see that all the feathers are removed; then draw the bird and wash quickly in cold water. Peel the onion and cut it into four parts. Put these into the body of the bird and then truss it. Season with salt and pepper. Rub the butter over the breast and legs of the grouse, then dredge thickly with flour. Have the pork cut in thin slices and lay it over the breast, fastening it with small skewers or wooden toothpicks. Rest the grouse on its back on a tin plate and place it in a hot oven. Cook for half an hour, having the oven quite hot the first fifteen minutes, and then reducing the heat. When the bird is done, remove the skewers. Pour half a pint of bread sauce on a hot dish, and place the bird on this, breast up. Sprinkle fried crumbs over the bird and sauce, and garnish with a few sprays of parsley.

Roast Partridge.

Prepare and serve the same as grouse; but as it is white meat it must be well done. Cook it for forty-five minutes, and baste it every ten minutes with a gill of hot stock or water, in which have been melted two tablespoonfuls of butter.

Roast Ptarmigan.

Cook and serve this exactly the same as grouse, except that it should be cooked but twenty minutes, being smaller than grouse.

Broiled Small Birds.

All birds that are to be broiled must be split in the back; the necks must be cut off, the birds wiped, and the legs drawn up over the breast. This will give a compact form to the bird. Now season with salt. Spread soft butter over the breast and legs, and then dredge thickly with flour. Put in the double-broiler and cook over clear coals, having the buttered and floured side toward the fire at first, that the two materials may unite and form a paste on the bird. Cook quail or squab for ten minutes, and smaller birds six or eight. Partridge and grouse may be cooked in the same way, but the grouse should be cooked for twenty minutes and the partridge thirty. Serve the small birds on slices of crisp toast.

Fricassee of Rabbit.

1 rabbit.	1½ teaspoonfuls of salt.
4 tablespoonfuls of pork fat.	¼ teaspoonful of pepper.
1 pint of water.	6 tablespoonfuls of flour.

Have the rabbit skinned and drawn. Wash it, and then cut into joints. Next season it with the salt and pepper, and roll it in the flour, covering every part. Put the fat in a frying-pan and set on the fire. When hot, lay in the rabbit and cook it until brown on all sides. When the meat is well browned take it up. Into the fat remaining in the pan put such part of the flour as did not cling to the rabbit, and stir until brown. Gradually add the cold water, stirring all the time. When this boils up, taste it to see if it is seasoned enough; then lay the browned meat in the gravy and simmer gently for half an hour. Serve boiled rice or boiled hominy with this dish.

If one like the flavor of onions or herbs, a little may be added to the gravy.

Curried Rabbit.

Prepare the rabbit as for fricassee. Add to the gravy one teaspoonful of onion juice, one heaping teaspoonful of curry-powder, mixed with a little cold milk or water. Always serve boiled rice with this dish.

Broiled Venison.

Have a venison steak cut an inch thick, and cook it the same as beefsteak. Season with butter, salt, and pepper. Serve currant jelly with the steak.

Venison Steak Sauté.

1 pound of venison steak.	1 level teaspoonful of salt.
3 tablespoonfuls of butter.	$\frac{1}{16}$ teaspoonful of cayenne.
1 tablespoonful of currant jelly.	

Have the steak cut an inch thick. Put the butter in the frying-pan and set it on the fire. When hot, put in the steak. Cook for ten minutes, turning often. When it has been cooking for five minutes add the jelly and seasoning Serve hot.

CHAPTER XI.

SAUCES FOR MEAT AND FISH.

Brown Sauce.

½ pint of brown stock.	1 teaspoonful of salt.
2 tablespoonfuls of butter.	¼ teaspoonful of pepper.
1 tablespoonful of flour, generous.	

Put the butter in a frying-pan and set on a hot fire. When the butter becomes hot, add the flour, and stir the mixture until it becomes smooth and turns dark brown. Draw the pan back to a cool part of the range, and stir the mixture until it cools slightly. Now gradually add the stock, stirring all the time. Move the pan back to a hot part of the range, and stir the sauce until it boils. Add the seasoning, and simmer for three minutes. It will then be ready to serve.

Brown Sauce, No. 2.

2 tablespoonfuls of butter.	1 small slice of onion.
1½ tablespoonfuls of flour.	1 whole clove.
1½ gills of stock or water.	½ teaspoonful of salt.
1 bay leaf.	⅙ teaspoonful of pepper.

Put the butter in a frying-pan and set on the fire. When it becomes smoking hot, add the flour, and stir until it turns dark brown. Draw the pan back, and gradually add the cold stock or water, stirring all the time. Add the other ingredients, and simmer for ten minutes; then strain and use. If there be no stock, and water be used, add a teaspoonful of beef extract.

This sauce may be used with roasted or broiled meats, or when warming up meats; or it may be served with baked fish.

Mushroom Sauce.

Make a brown sauce and add to it half a small can of mushrooms, or four ounces of fresh ones. If canned mushrooms be used, simmer them for five minutes, but if fresh ones be used, simmer twice as long. Any large mushrooms should be cut up.

White Sauce.

½ pint of hot milk.
1 large tablespoonful of butter.
1 level tablespoonful of flour.
1 level teaspoonful of salt.

¼ teaspoonful of pepper.
½ teaspoonful of onion juice.
1 spray of parsley.

Beat the butter to a cream, and then beat the flour with it until light and creamy. Add the salt, pepper, and onion juice, and beat a little longer. Pour the hot milk on this. Add the parsley, and place the saucepan on the range. Stir until the sauce boils. Cook for two minutes; then remove the parsley, and serve. A slight grating of nutmeg may be added to this sauce, if the flavor be liked.

This sauce is good to serve with boiled fish and various kinds of meat and vegetables.

Bechamel Sauce.

½ pint of hot white stock.
1 gill of cream.
1 heaped tablespoonful of butter.
1 tablespoonful of flour.
Piece of onion the size of half a dollar.

Piece of carrot the size of a quarter of a dollar.
1 spray of parsley.
1 bay leaf.
A tiny bit of mace.
½ teaspoonful of salt.
⅙ teaspoonful of pepper.

Beat the flour and butter together. Pour the hot stock on the mixture. Add the seasonings, and place on the fire. Stir the sauce until it begins to boil; then move the saucepan back to a place where the contents will just bubble at the side for fifteen minutes. Add the cream; and when the sauce boils up, strain and serve.

Mustard Sauce.

1 gill of hot milk.	1 level teaspoonful of mustard.
1 large tablespoonful of butter.	¼ teaspoonful of salt.
1 teaspoonful of flour.	A grain of cayenne.

Beat the butter, flour, and mustard together until smooth and creamy. Pour the hot milk on this mixture, and place the saucepan on the range. Stir until the sauce boils. Add the salt and pepper, and serve.

This sauce is nice to serve with broiled lobster, roasted or steamed clams, and other fish.

Cream Sauce.

½ pint of milk.	½ teaspoonful of salt.
1 tablespoonful of butter.	⅛ teaspoonful of pepper.
½ tablespoonful of flour.	

Put the butter in a pan and set it on the fire. When it becomes hot, add the flour, and stir until smooth and frothy. Draw the pan back and gradually add the milk, stirring all the time. Set the pan back in a hotter place. Add the salt and pepper, and stir the sauce until it boils; then serve. It will not do to let this sauce simmer or stand for any length of time.

Parsley Sauce.

Put one teaspoonful of minced parsley with the cream sauce. If the sauce be liked richer, a teaspoonful of butter may be added with the parsley.

Egg Sauce.

1 hard-boiled egg.	1 teaspoonful of salt.
2 heaped tablespoonfuls of butter.	⅛ teaspoonful of pepper.
1 tablespoonful of flour.	1 scant half-pint of boiling water.

Boil the egg for ten minutes; then drop into cold water, keeping it there for five minutes. Remove the shell, and with a plated knife chop the egg rather fine. Put the butter in a small saucepan and beat to a cream. Beat the flour, salt, and pepper into this, and then pour on the boiling water. Cook for two minutes, and finally add the chopped egg and serve. This sauce is suitable for boiled fish.

Butter Sauce.

Make this sauce in the same way as directed for egg sauce, omitting the egg.

Caper Sauce.

3 tablespoonfuls of butter.	½ teaspoonful of salt.
2 tablespoonfuls of flour.	⅛ teaspoonful of pepper.
½ pint of water.	1½ tablespoonfuls of capers.

Set on the fire a small stewpan containing two tablespoonfuls of butter. When the butter gets hot, add the flour, and stir until the mixture becomes smooth and frothy, being careful not to brown it. Draw the pan back and gradually add the water. Stir the sauce until it boils; then add the salt, pepper, and the remaining tablespoonful of butter. Boil for one minute; then add the capers, first taking out a few spoonfuls of the sauce to pour over the mutton.

Curry Sauce.

1 heaped tablespoonful of butter.	⅛ teaspoonful of pepper.
1 tablespoonful of flour.	1 teaspoonful of salt.
1 tablespoonful of curry-powder.	½ pint of milk.
1 teaspoonful of minced onion.	½ pint of cooked meat.

Put the butter and onion in a frying-pan and set on the fire. Cook slowly until the onion begins to turn a light strawcolor. Now add the flour and curry-powder, and stir until frothy. Gradually pour in the milk, stirring all the while. When the sauce boils up, season with the salt and pepper, and add the half-pint of tender cooked meat, cut very fine. Chicken or turkey is particularly nice for this dish. Less meat can be used. Cook three minutes longer and serve with a dish of rice.

The mode of serving at table is to put a spoonful of rice on the plate and pour a spoonful of sauce over it.

Bisque Sauce.

3 tablespoonfuls of butter.
1½ tablespoonfuls of flour.
1 teaspoonful of salt.
½ pint of hot stock,—white if possible.
10 pepper-corns.
1 gill of strained **tomato**.
1 gill of milk.
1 small slice of onion.
1 sprig of parsley.

Beat the butter and flour in a saucepan until smooth and light. Pour upon this mixture the hot stock, stirring all the time. Now add the salt, pepper-corns, onion, and parsley, and stir until the sauce boils; then cover, set back, and cook gently for ten minutes. Add the tomato, and cook for three minutes longer. Finally add the milk, and stir until it boils. Strain and serve at once.

Hollandaise Sauce.

1 tablespoonful of lemon juice.
3 tablespoonfuls of butter.
1 gill of boiling water.
Yolks of two eggs.
½ teaspoonful of salt.
$\frac{1}{10}$ teaspoonful of cayenne.

Beat the butter to a cream; then beat in the unbeaten yolks of the eggs. Add the lemon juice, salt, and pepper.

SAUCES FOR MEAT AND FISH. 169

Place the bowl in a pan of boiling water, and beat the sauce for two minutes. Add the boiling water, and continue beating until the sauce is thick and light. It will take about five minutes for this. Serve either in a warm bowl, or poured around or over the fish, meat, or vegetable.

Tomato Sauce.

3 gills of canned tomatoes.	⅙ teaspoonful of pepper.
1 tablespoonful of butter.	2 whole cloves.
1 tablespoonful of flour.	A tiny bit of onion.
½ teaspoonful of salt.	

Put the tomatoes, onion, cloves, salt, and pepper in a stewpan and set on the range. Cook for ten minutes after the mixture begins to simmer. Put the butter in a small pan and set on the fire. When hot add the flour, and stir until smooth and frothy. Stir this into the tomatoes, and simmer for four minutes longer. Rub the sauce through a strainer fine enough to keep back the seeds. Serve hot.

Tartar Sauce.

½ gill of olive oil.	¼ teaspoonful of onion juice.
4 teaspoonfuls of vinegar.	½ tablespoonful of minced capers.
1 level teaspoonful of mustard.	½ tablespoonful of minced cucumber pickles.
½ teaspoonful of salt.	
⅛ teaspoonful of pepper.	1 egg yolk.

Beat the egg, salt, pepper, and mustard together until thick and light; then add the oil, a few drops at a time, beating after each addition of oil, until all is used. As the sauce thickens, add a few drops of vinegar to thin it. When the sauce is smooth and thick, stir in the minced pickle and capers.

Tartar sauce may be served with many kinds of breaded, fried, and broiled fish or meat.

Mint Sauce.

2 tablespoonfuls of mint.
1 gill of vinegar.
1 tablespoonful of sugar.

Wash the mint and chop it fine. Put it in a dish with the vinegar and sugar, and let it stand for twenty minutes or longer. If the vinegar be very strong, half vinegar and half water may be used.

Currant Jelly Sauce.

1 tablespoonful of butter.
1 teaspoonful of flour.
½ teaspoonful of salt.
⅛ teaspoonful of pepper.
1 teaspoonful of vinegar.

1 tablespoonful of currant jelly.
1 small bay leaf.
1 clove.
1 teaspoonful of minced onion.
1 gill of stock.

Cook the butter and onion together for five minutes. Add the flour, and stir until smooth and frothy. Gradually add the stock, stirring all the time. When the sauce boils up, add the other ingredients, and simmer for five minutes. Strain, and serve hot.

This sauce is for roast venison or mutton.

Maître d'Hôtel Butter.

2 tablespoonfuls of butter.
1 tablespoonful of lemon juice.
½ teaspoonful of salt.

¼ teaspoonful of pepper.
1 teaspoonful of minced parsley.

Beat the butter to a cream; beat the lemon juice into this; then add the seasoning and parsley.

This butter is not to be cooked. It should be spread on broiled meats or fish like plain butter. The heat of the food will melt it sufficiently.

Bread Sauce.

½ pint of milk.	⅙ teaspoonful of pepper.
1 generous gill of dried bread.	1 tablespoonful of butter.
½ teaspoonful of salt.	⅛ of a small onion.

The bread used should be stale, and it should be dried in a warm — not hot — oven. When it is so dry that it will readily crumble, place it on a bread board, and with a rolling-pin crush it lightly; for about two thirds of the bread, when done, should be in the form of coarse crumbs. Measure out half a cupful of these crumbs, and, putting them in the flour sieve, rub all the fine crumbs through. Put these fine crumbs in the double-boiler with the milk and onion. Place on the fire and cook for half an hour. At the end of that time take out the onion, and add the salt, white pepper, and half a tablespoonful of butter. Put the remaining butter in a frying-pan, and set the pan on the stove. When the butter becomes hot, add the coarse crumbs, and stir them until they are brown and crisp. Now spread the sauce on a warm dish, and place the bird or fowl on the same dish. Sprinkle the crumbs over all, and garnish with a few sprigs of parsley. Serve very hot.

CHAPTER XII.

SALADS.

A SALAD should be light, fresh, and crisp; no matter what it is made of, it should never be "mussy." Much decoration or handling will produce a heavy-looking dish.

Celery, lettuce, tomatoes, etc. should be thoroughly chilled before being combined in a salad. All meats and fish that are to be served in a salad must be seasoned with salt, pepper, vinegar, and oil before being combined with the green vegetable and the dressing. It is well to have this seasoning added several hours before the salad is to be served.

Mayonnaise Dressing.

½ pint of olive oil.	1 tablespoonful of lemon juice.
1 teaspoonful of mustard.	2 tablespoonfuls of vinegar.
½ teaspoonful of salt.	Yolks of two uncooked eggs.
½ teaspoonful of sugar.	A grain of cayenne.

Put the yolks of the eggs into a bowl, being careful not to let any of the white go in. Add the dry ingredients to the yolks, and place the bowl in a flat pan. Put a little cold water and ice in the pan. Beat these ingredients until light and thick; then begin to add the oil, a few drops at a time. Beat well between each addition of oil. When the mixture gets thick and ropy, a larger quantity of oil may be added each time. When the dressing is so thick that the beater turns hard, add a few drops of vinegar to thin it. When all the other ingredients have been used add the lemon juice, and beat for a few minutes longer. This sauce will keep for three or four weeks, if covered and kept in a cool place.

The secret of success in making a Mayonnaise dressing is to have everything cold, to beat the yolks of eggs and dry ingredients until thick, and at first to add the oil only in drops. It is also essential that the beating should be regular, and always in one direction.

If a milder flavor of the oil be liked, a gill of whipped cream may be stirred into the dressing when it is about to be used.

Cooked Salad Dressing.

1 gill of vinegar.
2 eggs.
1 tablespoonful of sugar.

½ teaspoonful of mustard.
½ teaspoonful of salt.
1 gill of rich cream.

Beat the eggs well, and stir into them the sugar, salt, and mustard, which should first be mixed together. Now add the vinegar, and place the bowl on the range in a saucepan of boiling water. Beat constantly with an egg-beater until the dressing becomes thick and light. Take from the fire at once, and turn into a cold bowl to prevent curdling; or the bowl in which it was cooked may be placed in a pan of ice water, and the mixture be stirred until cool.

Beat the cream to a thick froth, and stir it into the cold dressing. If you have no cream stir a tablespoonful of butter into the hot mixture. When cold, if too thick, add a few tablespoonfuls of milk.

French Dressing.

3 tablespoonfuls of oil.
1 tablespoonful of vinegar.

¼ teaspoonful of salt.
$\frac{1}{16}$ teaspoonful of pepper.

Mix these ingredients together and the dressing is made. French dressing is particularly good for lettuce and cooked vegetables.

Chicken Salad.

½ pint of chicken.	½ tablespoonful of oil.
1 gill of celery, white and tender.	½ teaspoonful of salt.
1 gill of Mayonnaise dressing.	⅛ teaspoonful of pepper.
1 tablespoonful of vinegar.	

Have tender cooked chicken, free from fat, skin, and bone, and cut into cubes. Season it with the vinegar, salt, pepper, and oil, and let it stand in the refrigerator for an hour or more. Clean the celery and cut it into thin slices. Put this in a napkin and surround it with ice. It should stand for ten or twenty minutes in the ice bath, and will then be crisp.

Mix the celery, seasoned chicken, and half the dressing. Heap in a dish and mask it with the remainder of the dressing. Garnish the dish with some of the tiny, bleached celery leaves.

In summer the salad may be made with lettuce. Put two or three tender bleached leaves together, and place a spoonful of chicken in the centre of the leaves. Drop a teaspoonful of dressing on the chicken. Arrange these lettuce nests on a flat dish, and serve at once.

Lobster Salad.

Make the same as chicken salad, substituting lobster for chicken and lettuce for celery.

Fish Salads.

Any kind of cold fish may be combined with lettuce and the Mayonnaise dressing or cooked dressing.

Oysters to be used for a salad should be heated to the boiling point in their own liquor; then skimmed, drained, seasoned, and thoroughly chilled before being combined with the celery or lettuce.

SALADS. 175

Vegetable Salads.

Any kinds of vegetables may be used in salads. They may be seasoned with the French or cooked dressing. A single vegetable may be used, or several kinds be combined.

Lettuce Salad.

Have the lettuce washed clean, and then let it remain for a little time in ice water to become crisp. Drain well, and dress it with the French, Mayonnaise, or cooked dressing. Serve at once.

If you prefer, the lettuce may be served plain, each one dressing it to please himself.

Tomato and Lettuce Salad.

1½ pints of canned tomatoes.
½ box of gelatine.
1 gill of cold water.
1 teaspoonful of sugar.

½ teaspoonful of salt.
1 head of lettuce.
½ pint of Mayonnaise dressing

Soak the gelatine in the cold water for two hours. Heat the tomatoes to the boiling point, and stir the gelatine, sugar, and salt into the vegetable. Turn this mixture into a mould, and set away to harden. Have the lettuce washed and chilled. Arrange it in a flat dish, and turn the mould of tomatoes out upon it. Heap the dressing at the base of the mould. This salad may be made in winter when it is impossible to get the fresh tomatoes.

Beet Salad.

Cold boiled beets may be cut into thin slices, and the slices into small pieces ; or the beets may be cut into small cubes. Season with Mayonnaise sauce or the cooked salad dressing, and serve.

Potato Salad.

1 pint of potato cubes.	1 tablespoonful of oil.
½ pint of celery.	1 tablespoonful minced chives, or
½ teaspoonful of salt.	1 teaspoonful of onion juice.
$\frac{1}{16}$ teaspoonful of pepper.	1 gill of cooked dressing.
1 tablespoonful of vinegar.	

Have the potatoes cut into cubes. Mix the oil, vinegar, salt, pepper, and onion juice together, and sprinkle over the potatoes. Stir lightly with a fork and set away in a cold place for several hours. At serving time add the celery and dressing, stirring lightly with a fork. Turn into a deep dish, and garnish with celery leaves or parsley.

Potato Salad, No. 2.

1 pint of potato cubes.	1 gill of cooked dressing, or the
½ teaspoonful of salt.	quantity of French dressing
⅛ teaspoonful of pepper.	made by the rule given.
1 teaspoonful of minced onion.	

Mix the seasonings and dressing with the potato cubes. Turn into a dish, and garnish with parsley. Let the salad stand for an hour or more before serving, that the seasonings may strike through the potatoes.

CHAPTER XIII.

VEGETABLES.

ALL vegetables should be put in boiling water when set on the stove to cook. Peas, asparagus, potatoes, and all delicately flavored vegetables should be only covered with water, but those with a strong flavor, like carrots, turnips, cabbage, onions, and dandelions, should be cooked in a generous quantity of boiling water. All green vegetables should be cooked with the cover partially off the stewpan. It gives them a better color and a more delicate flavor.

The average housekeeper is careless as to the time of cooking vegetables, yet a vegetable is as much injured by too much or too little cooking as is a loaf of bread or cake. When vegetables are underdone they are hard and indigestible, and when overdone they become dark, strong-flavored, and indigestible.

Now, although a potato will be hard if not cooked enough, even two minutes' cooking after the proper time will injure it. If potatoes be covered with boiling water and placed on the fire they will cook in thirty minutes. If they be very small, they may get done in twenty-eight minutes, and if they be large it may take thirty-two to cook them sufficiently. They should be kept boiling all the time after they once begin, but not at a furious rate, as a too rapid boiling breaks the surface of the potato before the centre is cooked. The time of cooking is to be counted from the moment the boiling water is poured over the potatoes. When the potatoes are done, the water should be poured off and the steam allowed to escape. Should it be necessary to keep them warm after that, cover them with a coarse towel, never with the pot cover; for if the steam does not have a chance to escape it will be absorbed by the potatoes, which will become sodden, dark, and strong-flavored. Baked potatoes take about forty-five minutes for cooking. A great deal depends upon the oven. If it be necessary to keep a baked potato warm, break it open, wrap it in a towel and put it in a warm place.

Now, as to turnips. The small white ones should be boiled, if cut in thin slices, for thirty minutes, but if they be cooked whole, forty minutes' time will be needed. Yellow turnips, when sliced, need forty-five minutes' cooking.

Carrots should be cooked for forty-five or fifty minutes; cauliflower, only thirty minutes; with peas and asparagus much depends upon the state of freshness and tenderness when picked, and the time varies from twenty to thirty-five minutes; indeed, peas sometimes require fifty minutes' cooking.

It is a pity that it is the fashion to serve such vegetables as peas and asparagus in a sauce. They have so delicate a flavor that only a little salt and good butter should be added to them. This is true, also, of turnips. Cauliflower, onions, and carrots, however, need a sauce.

Boiled Potatoes.

Pare five or six potatoes and let them stand in cold water for an hour or more. Forty minutes before dinner time put them in a kettle and pour boiling water over them, — enough to cover. Put the cover on the kettle and cook the vegetables for half an hour, counting from the moment the water is poured over them. When they have been cooking for fifteen minutes, add one teaspoonful of salt. At the end of the half-hour pour off all the water and set the pan on the back part of the range. Cover the potatoes with a clean, coarse towel. At serving time put the potatoes in a hot dish, and cover with a napkin. Never put the china cover on the dish. Cooked in the way described, the potatoes will be mealy and have a fine flavor.

Stewed Potatoes.

1 quart of sliced raw potatoes.	1 level teaspoonful of salt.
2 ounces of fat bacon.	1 tablespoonful of flour.
½ teaspoonful of onion juice.	1 gill of water.
¼ teaspoonful of pepper.	

Have the potatoes and bacon sliced thin. Spread half the meat on the bottom of a round baking dish. Put half of the potatoes into the dish and sprinkle half of the seasoning over them; then spread in the other half, and use the remainder of the seasonings. Mix the water with the flour, and pour this into the dish. Now spread the remainder of the bacon on top of the potatoes. Cover the dish closely, and, putting into a moderately hot oven, cook for forty-five minutes. At the end of that time take off the cover and bake twenty minutes longer. The bacon should become crisp and brown at the end of that time. Serve in the dish in which it is cooked.

Stewed Potatoes, No. 2.

1 quart of raw potatoes, cut in cubes.	1 teaspoonful of salt.
2 ounces of fat salt pork.	¼ teaspoonful of pepper.
1 tablespoonful of flour.	1 pint of water.

Pare and cut into cubes enough potatoes to make a quart, and let them stand in cold water for one hour. Cut the pork into thin slices, and fry slowly until crisp and brown; then take from the pan. Add the flour to the hot fat, and stir until smooth and brown; then gradually add the water, and boil for three minutes. Season with the salt and pepper. Drain the potato cubes free from water, and, after putting them in a stewpan, pour the sauce over them and lay the slices of pork on top. Cover the stewpan and place where the contents will just bubble for forty-five minutes; then turn into a warm dish and serve.

Potatoes au Gratin.

½ pint of cooked potato cubes.
1 gill of white stock.
½ gill of milk.
1 teaspoonful of flour.
1½ teaspoonfuls of butter.

¾ teaspoonful of salt.
⅛ teaspoonful of pepper.
3 tablespoonfuls of grated bread crumbs.

Have cold boiled potatoes cut into small regular cubes. Season them with half the pepper and salt. Put one teaspoonful of the butter in a small frying-pan and set on the fire. When hot, add the flour, and stir until smooth and frothy; then gradually add the stock. When this boils, add the milk and the remainder of the salt and pepper, and boil up once. Put a layer of this sauce in a small escalop dish; then put the potatoes in the dish and pour the remainder of the sauce over them. Sprinkle the grated bread crumbs over this, and dot with the half-teaspoonful of butter. Bake in a moderate oven for twenty minutes. A few drops of onion juice and one fourth of a teaspoonful of chopped parsley may be added to the sauce, if these flavors be liked.

Hashed Potatoes.

1 pint of sliced cold boiled potatoes.
1 teaspoonful of salt.

⅙ teaspoonful of pepper.
1 tablespoonful of butter.

Season the potatoes with the salt and pepper. Put the butter in the frying-pan and set on the fire. When hot, add the potatoes. Stir and cut the potatoes with a case knife until they are hashed fine and have become hot and slightly browned. Serve in a hot dish.

Ham, sausage, or pork fat may be substituted for the butter.

Nichewaug Potatoes.

1 pint of potato cubes.
1 tablespoonful of minced ham.
1 teaspoonful of salt.
¼ teaspoonful of pepper.
1 tablespoonful of fat.

Season the potato cubes with the salt and pepper. Put a tablespoonful of ham, bacon, pork, or sausage fat in the frying-pan, and set on the fire. When hot, put in the potatoes and stir frequently with a fork until they become brown. When the potatoes are done, turn them into a hot dish and sprinkle a tablespoonful of finely chopped cooked ham over them. Serve very hot.

Lyonnaise Potatoes.

1 pint of cold boiled potato cubes.
1 level teaspoonful of salt.
⅛ of a teaspoonful of pepper.
1 level tablespoonful of butter.
1 teaspoonful of finely-minced onion.
½ teaspoonful of minced parsley.

Season the potatoes with the salt and pepper. Put the butter and onion in the frying-pan, and cook slowly until the onion begins to turn a delicate straw-color. Now add the potatoes, and cook over a hot fire for five minutes, stirring with a fork. Add the parsley, and cook for one minute longer. Serve very hot.

Potato Cakes.

Shape cold mashed potatoes into round, flat cakes. For six cakes put one tablespoonful of butter in a frying-pan, and place on the fire. When the butter is hot, put in the potato cakes and cook until brown on both sides. A tablespoonful of either pork, ham, or sausage fat may be used instead of the butter.

Potato Croquettes.

3 potatoes of good size.	⅛ teaspoonful of pepper.
4 tablespoonfuls of hot milk.	1 egg.
1 tablespoonful of butter.	Bread crumbs.
½ teaspoonful of salt.	

Boil the potatoes for thirty minutes; then drain them and mash fine and light. Beat in the seasoning, milk, and butter. Let the mixture cool slightly; then roll into cylinders or balls. Beat the egg in a soup plate. Coat the croquettes, one at a time, with the egg, then roll in dried bread crumbs. When all are done, fry in hot fat until they are brown, — about a minute and a half. Drain on brown paper and serve at once.

Boiled Sweet Potatoes.

Potatoes of medium size should be cooked for one hour; very large ones should be boiled for an hour and a half, or be cut into several parts.

Baked Sweet Potatoes.

Wash the potatoes and bake from an hour to an hour and a quarter in a moderately hot oven. The longer they bake, the sweeter and moister they will be.

Browned Sweet Potatoes.

Boil for half an hour three potatoes of medium size. On taking them from the water pare them. Now cut them in two, lengthwise, and lay them in the pan under a piece of roasting meat. Season them with salt, and let them cook for half an hour. Serve in a hot dish.

Or, the potatoes may be boiled for three quarters of an hour, paired and split, then laid in a baking pan, seasoned with salt, and finally spread with soft butter. It will take one tablespoonful of butter for three potatoes. Bake in a hot oven for twenty minutes or half an hour.

Warming over Sweet Potatoes.

Cold boiled sweet potatoes may be warmed in several ways. Cut them in halves, season with salt, and put in the frying-basket. Fry in deep fat for five minutes; then season with salt and serve.

Another way is to cut them in thick slices lengthwise, dip them in melted butter, season with salt and pepper, dredge lightly with flour, and broil over clear coals. Serve on a hot dish.

Still another mode is to cut them in round slices, season with salt and pepper, and fry in pork or bacon fat.

Boiled Onions.

Put the onions in a saucepan with plenty of boiling water and cook for one hour. If milk be plentiful, pour off the water when the onions have been cooking for half an hour, and add just enough hot milk to cover them. Simmer for half an hour longer; then season with salt, pepper, and butter, and serve.

For half a dozen small onions use one tablespoonful of butter, one teaspoonful of salt, and one fourth of a teaspoonful of pepper.

Creamed Onions.

Boil three or four onions for one hour in two quarts of boiling water into which one teaspoonful of salt has been sprinkled. Pour off the water and cut up the onions. Put them in a hot dish and pour half a pint of cream sauce over them. Serve hot.

Onions au Gratin.

Prepare the creamed onions and put them in an escalop dish. Cover them with a gill of grated bread crumbs and dot with a teaspoonful of butter. Bake for twenty minutes in a quick oven.

Sliced Tomatoes.

Select smooth, ripe tomatoes. Drop them into boiling water for one minute, then into cold water. This will make the skin come off easily. Put them on a plate and in a cool place,— on the ice if possible. At serving time cut them in slices and place on a cold dish.

Stewed Tomatoes.

1 pint of canned tomatoes.	⅛ teaspoonful of pepper.
½ gill of fine cracker crumbs.	½ tablesponful of sugar.
½ teaspoonful of salt.	½ tablespoonful of butter.

Put all the ingredients, except the butter, in a stewpan, and cook for twenty minutes. Add the butter, and cook for ten minutes longer.

One pint of fresh tomatoes may be cooked in the same manner. The crackers may be omitted. Long cooking makes the tomatoes thicker and dark, but for most tastes this is not desirable.

Tomatoes au Gratin.

1 pint of stewed tomatoes.	1 teaspoonful of sugar.
1 gill of dried bread crumbs.	½ teaspoonful of salt.
3 tablespoonfuls of grated bread crumbs.	⅙ teaspoonful of pepper.
	1½ teaspoonfuls of butter.

Reserve the grated bread crumbs and half a teaspoonful of the butter. Mix all the other ingredients together and turn into a small baking dish. Sprinkle the grated bread crumbs over this. Cut the butter into small bits, and sprinkle over the crumbs. Bake in a moderately hot oven for half an hour, and serve hot.

Beets.

Beets, when young and fresh, will cook in forty minutes, but as they grow larger they require longer cooking. The time has to be increased as the season advances, and in winter beets require from two to three hours' boiling. Wash them in cold water, being careful not to break the skin or little tendrils. Put them in boiling water and cook until done, — the time depending upon the season. Lay them in cold water and rub off the skin; then slice them into a hot dish, and season with salt and butter. Serve hot.

Boiled Turnips.

1 quart of white turnip cubes.	1 level tablespoonful of sugar.
1 tablespoonful of butter.	1 heaped teaspoonful of salt.

Pare and cut up enough of the small flat white turnips to make one quart. Let them stand in cold water for an hour or more. Pour off all the water and turn the turnips into a stewpan containing two quarts of boiling water. Cook for just thirty minutes and then pour off all the water. Put into the saucepan with the turnips, butter, sugar, salt, and one gill of boiling water. Place the saucepan on the hottest part of the fire and cook the turnips rapidly until all the liquid has been absorbed, shaking the pan frequently to prevent the turnips from burning. Turn into a hot dish and serve.

Mashed Turnips.

Pare one yellow turnip or six white ones and cut in slices. Put in a large stewpan with a generous supply of boiling water. If white turnips be used, cook them for half an hour; but if the yellow kind be taken, cook for fifty or sixty minutes. Too little water and too much cooking will make any turnips strong-flavored, and give them a dark color. When the turnips are done, drain off all the water and mash them well. Season with salt, pepper, and butter.

Boiled Carrots.

Scrape and cut into cubes enough raw carrots to make a quart. Cook them for one hour in three quarts of boiling water, and then proceed as directed in the rule for boiled turnips. White stock may be substituted for the gill of boiling water.

Turnips, carrots, and green peas, cooked in this manner, and then mixed together, make a handsome and savory dish.

Success in cooking these vegetables depends upon their being boiled in plenty of water, and for only the time mentioned; also in cooking very rapidly after the seasonings are added.

Parsnips.

Scrape and slice the parsnips, and let them stand in cold water for an hour or more. Drain them and put them in a stewpan with plenty of boiling water. Cook them, if fresh, for forty-five minutes; but if they have been out of the ground any length of time they will require an hour's cooking.

When they have been boiling for half an hour, add a teaspoonful of salt for about a pint of the parsnips. Drain, and season them with salt and butter; or, pour a butter or Bechémal sauce over them.

Salsify.

Cook this vegetable the same as parsnips.

Boiled Cauliflower.

1 cauliflower of medium size.	½ pint of cream or Bechémal sauce.
2 tablespoonfuls of salt.	

Remove the leaves from the cauliflower, and place it head downward in a pan of cold water, to which add one tablespoonful of salt. Let it stand in a cold place an hour or more. Have about three quarts of boiling water in a stewpan and put the cauliflower into it head down. Cover, and cook gently for thirty minutes. At the end of this time drain the cauliflower and put it in a deep dish. Dredge lightly with salt, and pour the sauce over it.

Cauliflower au Gratin.

3 gills of cold boiled cauliflower.	⅛ teaspoonful of pepper.
½ pint of cream sauce.	1 teaspoonful of butter.
½ teaspoonful of salt.	1 gill of grated bread crumbs.

With a fork, break the cauliflower into small pieces; then sprinkle the salt and pepper over it. Put a layer of sauce in a small escalop dish, next a layer of cauliflower, then a second layer of sauce, then cauliflower, and finish with sauce. Cover this with the bread crumbs and dot with the butter. Bake in a moderately hot oven for twenty minutes.

Green Corn.

The fresher the corn is, the less time it will take to cook. It should be freed from husks and the silk threads. Have a large saucepan nearly full of boiling water. Drop the corn into this, and cook for ten minutes. Serve in a napkin.

Canned Corn.

1 can of corn.	1 tablespoonful of butter.
1 gill of milk.	1 teaspoonful of salt.

Put all the ingredients in the double-boiler, and heat to the boiling point; it will take about ten minutes. Serve at once. Too much cooking spoils this dish.

Corn Oysters.

½ pint of grated green corn.	½ teaspoonful of salt.
2 tablespoonfuls of milk.	⅛ teaspoonful of pepper.
1 gill of flour.	2 tablespoonfuls of butter.
1 egg.	

Mix the flour, seasoning, and corn together. Add the butter, melted, and beat well. Beat the egg till light, and add to the mixture. Fry on a griddle, in cakes a little larger than a silver dollar. Serve with the meat course at breakfast.

String Beans.

String the beans and then break them into pieces about an inch long. Wash them, and let them stand in cold water for an hour or more. Cook them in plenty of boiling water for two hours. When they have been cooking for one hour add one teaspoonful of salt for each quart of beans. When done, pour off all the water and add to the beans one tablespoonful of butter and four tablespoonfuls of boiling water. If not salt enough, add a little more seasoning. Return to the fire for three minutes; then serve.

Butter Beans.

These are cooked the same as string beans.

Fresh Lima Beans.

1 pint of shelled beans.
1 tablespoonful of butter.
1 level teaspoonful of salt.

Wash the beans and let them stand in cold water for an hour or more. On draining off the cold water, put them on to boil in three pints of boiling water. Cook for one hour; then drain off nearly all the water and add the seasonings. Serve hot.

Dried Lima Beans.

½ pint of beans.
1 tablespoonful of butter.
1 level teaspoonful of salt.

Put the beans to soak over night in one quart of cold water. Two hours before dinner time pour off the water, and, putting the beans in a stewpan with a quart of boiling water, let them simmer gently for an hour and fifty minutes. At the end of that time pour off the water, and add the salt and butter and a gill of boiling water. Let them stand in the saucepan on the back part of the stove until serving time.

Dried Lima Beans, No. 2.

½ pint of beans.
½ pint of milk.

1 teaspoonful of salt.
½ tablespooonful of butter.

Soak and cook the beans as in the recipe just given; then drain off all the water, and add the seasoning and milk, having the latter hot. Simmer for ten minutes and serve.

Succotash of Dried Lima Beans and Canned Corn.

½ pint of dried Lima beans.	⅛ teaspoonful of pepper.
½ can of sweet corn.	1 generous teaspoonful of salt.
½ pint of milk.	1 tablespoonful of butter.

Soak the beans over night, and then cook them in one quart of clear water for an hour and fifty minutes. Pour off the water, and, after adding the seasoning, milk, and corn, cook for three minutes after the mixture begins to boil. Serve very hot.

Shelled Kidney Beans.

Prepare the same as fresh Lima beans, but cook for one hour and a half.

Baked Beans.

1 pint of small white beans.	1 teaspoonful of molasses.
½ pound of salt pork.	¼ teaspoonful of pepper.
1 teaspoonful of mustard.	1 small onion.
1 teaspoonful of sugar.	1 level tablespoonful of salt.

Pick the beans free from stones and dirt. Wash them, and let them soak over night in three quarts of cold water. In the morning pour off the water and wash the beans in fresh water; then put them in a stewpan with cold water enough to cover them generously, and place on the fire.

Have the pork mixed lean and fat. Score the rind. Put the pork in the stewpan with the beans, and simmer until the beans begin to crack open, — not a minute longer. Drain all the water from them and rinse with cold water. Put the onion in the bottom of the bean pot. Put about half the beans in the pot, then put in the pork, having the scored side up. Next put in the remainder of the beans. Mix the mustard, salt, pepper, sugar, and molasses with a pint of boiling water and pour over the beans. Add just enough boiling water to cover the beans. Cover the pot and place in a slow oven. Bake for ten hours or more, adding boiling water whenever the beans look dry. The oven must never be hot enough to make the water on the beans bubble, and there should never be more water in the pot than will barely come to the top of the beans.

An earthen pot should be used in baking beans. The onion and molasses may be omitted.

Green Peas.

The time of cooking green peas depends upon the age and the length of time they have been picked. If they be young and freshly picked, they will cook in twenty minutes; but it may take forty or fifty if they have matured too much, or have been picked for a day or more. They should not be shelled many hours before they are cooked. Wash the pea pods and drain them, then shell them. Put them in a stewpan with just enough boiling water to cover them, and cook until tender. They must not boil rapidly, and as soon as they begin to boil the cover of the stewpan should be drawn a little to one side. Pour off a part of the water, and to every pint of peas add one tablespoonful of butter and half a teaspoonful of salt.

Canned Peas.

1 can of peas.
1 heaped teaspoonful of butter.
1 level teaspoonful of salt.
1 teaspoonful of sugar.
1 gill of hot water.

Turn the peas into a strainer, and pour cold water over them until they are thoroughly rinsed. Put them in a saucepan with the other ingredients, and simmer for ten minutes.

Asparagus on Toast.

1 bunch of asparagus.	1 tablespoonful of butter.
3 slices of toast.	1 tablespoonful of salt.

Cut off the tough white ends of a bunch of asparagus. Now cut the string that ties the bundles together, and put the asparagus in a colander. Let cold water run on it until it is perfectly free from sand. Tie again in a bundle, and put it in a stewpan with one tablespoonful of salt and enough boiling water to cover it. Cook gently for half an hour. Toast three slices of bread, and dip the edges in the water in which the asparagus was cooked. Arrange these on a warm platter, and spread the asparagus upon them. Now season the green part of the vegetable with the tablespoonful of butter, and serve.

The toast may be buttered also, if one like to have it rich.

Asparagus should be placed with the cut end in a little cold water until it is time to cook it.

Asparagus with Cream Sauce.

1 quart of asparagus.	½ tablespoonful of flour.
3 gills of milk.	2 teaspoonfuls of salt.
1 tablespoonful of butter.	

Cut up enough of the tender ends of asparagus to make one quart. Put these in the colander, and let cold water run on them until every particle of sand is removed. Put them in a saucepan with one quart of boiling water and one teaspoonful of salt, and cook gently for half an hour; then drain, and, after putting in a warm vegetable dish, pour the cream sauce over them.

To make the sauce, put the butter on the fire, in a pan, and when it is melted add the flour. Stir until smooth and frothy; then gradually add the milk, stirring all the while. Season with a scant teaspoonful of salt, and boil up once.

If you prefer, the asparagus may be seasoned with salt and butter, using a generous tablespoonful of butter and half a teaspoonful of salt; moistening with a gill of the water in which it is boiled.

Spinach.

½ peck of spinach.
1 generous tablespoonful of butter.
1 level tablespoonful of salt.

Pick over the spinach, removing all the roots and brown leaves. Have two pans filled with cold water. Put the spinach in one pan and wash it, a few leaves at a time, dropping it into the second pan of water. When all is done, turn the water from the first pan, which should at once be rinsed and filled again with clean water. Continue washing the spinach in this way until there is not a grain of sand left in it. This you learn by passing the hand over the bottom of the pan. Put the cleaned spinach in a stewpan with a pint of boiling water and the salt, and cook for half an hour. Turn into the colander and cut with a knife. Put into a hot vegetable dish and add the butter.

Greens.

Greens of all kinds are cooked in about the same way that spinach is, but they all require boiling water enough to cover them, and most of them require a much longer time to boil.

A small piece of salt pork or smoked bacon, or a shank of ham, is often boiled in the water for two or more hours before the greens are put in to cook. This meat is served with the greens, which require no seasoning except salt.

Hashed Cabbage.

1 small head of cabbage.
1 tablespoonful of salt.
2 tablespoonfuls of butter.

Take all the green and broken leaves from a small head of cabbage. Then divide the cabbage into eight parts, cutting from the top down to the stalk. Wash it and let it stand in cold water for an hour or more. Put it in a large kettle of boiling water and boil rapidly for forty-five minutes. The kettle must not be covered. When the cabbage is done, drain, and put in a chopping bowl. Mince rather fine and season with the salt and butter. If the cabbage be fresh from the garden, half an hour's cooking will be sufficient.

Creamed Cabbage.

1 quart of raw white cabbage, sliced.	1 teaspoonful of flour.
1 tablespoonful of butter.	½ teaspoonful of salt.
	1 gill of milk.

Let the cabbage stand in cold water for an hour or more; then drain off the water and put the cabbage in a stewpan with two quarts of boiling water. Cover, and cook for ten minutes. At the end of that time pour off the water and put in two quarts of fresh boiling water. Cook rapidly, with the cover off, for about three quarters of an hour. When that time has passed, put the cabbage in a colander and press out all the water; then cut it with a sharp knife. Put the butter in a frying-pan and set on the range. When it becomes hot, add the cabbage, as well as the salt and pepper. Cook for five minutes, stirring all the time; then cover, and set back where it will cook gently for ten minutes. Mix the milk with the flour, and pour the mixture over the cabbage. Stir gently, and again cover the pan. Cook for ten minutes more and serve.

Baked Cabbage.

1 pint of boiled and hashed cabbage.	1 teaspoonful of salt.
2 ounces of salt pork.	¼ teaspoonful of pepper.

Boil and hash the cabbage, as directed for hashed cabbage. Sprinkle with the salt and pepper, and mix lightly with a fork. Turn into a baking dish and spread over it the pork cut in thin slices. Bake for half an hour in a moderate oven. Serve in the dish in which it is cooked.

Fried Cabbage.

1 quart of boiled cabbage.	1 teaspoonful of salt.
3 tablespoonfuls of butter or beef drippings.	¼ teaspoonful of pepper.

Boil the cabbage as for hashed cabbage, and mince rather fine. Add the seasoning. Put the butter or drippings in a frying-pan and set on the fire. As soon as the butter is melted, put in the cabbage and cook one hour, stirring often, and having the pan covered. Serve very hot.

Squash.

Pare the squash and remove the seeds and the stringy substance from the inside. Cut it into small pieces, and place in a stewpan with enough boiling water to cover it. Cook for thirty-five minutes; then drain off the water, and mash fine. Season with salt, pepper, and butter. For a pint of mashed squash use a teaspoonful of salt and one tablespoonful of butter. Serve very hot.

The squash may be steamed instead of boiled; in which case cook it for fifty minutes.

Summer Squash.

Get a tender fresh squash. If the rind be very tender do not pare it. Cut up the squash and steam for one hour; then rub it through a colander into a saucepan. Place the saucepan on the fire, and to each pint of the strained squash add one tablespoonful of butter and one teaspoonful of salt. Cook for five minutes, and serve hot.

Fried Egg Plant.

1 small egg plant.	Dry crumbs.
1 egg.	Fat for frying.
1 teaspoonful of salt.	

Pare the egg plant and cut it in slices about half an inch thick. Season with the salt. Beat the egg in a soup plate, and dip a slice of egg plant in it, covering every part of it; then dip the slice in fine dry crumbs. Continue this until all the egg plant is breaded. Have the frying fat three or four inches deep, and when it is so hot that blue smoke rises from the centre put two slices of the vegetable in, and cook for about three minutes. Take up and drain on brown paper; then serve.

Boiled Macaroni.

Macaroni varies as to the time it will take to cook. Half an hour is the usual time, but it often requires forty-five minutes. Break it into pieces two or three inches long, and drop it into a saucepan of boiling water. Boil rapidly until tender, having the saucepan uncovered. When it has been cooking for fifteen minutes, add a teaspoonful of salt for every two ounces of macaroni. When done turn it into a colander to drain; then put it into a hot dish, and pour half a pint of sauce over it. The sauce may be cream, Bechamel, tomato, or brown sauce. A little grated cheese may be added to the cream sauce, if that be the kind used. Serve at once.

Macaroni with Cheese.

2 ounces of macaroni.
½ pint of cream sauce.

1 teaspoonful of salt.
1 gill of grated cheese.

Boil and drain the macaroni. Add the sauce to it, and put into an escalop dish. Cover with the cheese, and bake for half an hour.

Baked Hominy.

1 gill of fine breakfast hominy.
1 pint of boiling water.
½ pint of milk.

1 egg.
⅓ teaspoonful of salt.
1 teaspoonful of butter.

Wash the hominy in three waters, and stir it into the boiling water, into which the salt should be sprinkled. Boil gently for one hour, having the cover on the stewpan, and stirring often. Now add the butter, cold milk, and the egg, well beaten, and bake in a moderate oven for one hour. Three gills of cold boiled hominy may be substituted for the fresh article.

This is to be served with meat or eggs for breakfast, luncheon, or dinner.

Boiled Rice.

1 gill of rice.
3 pints of boiling water.
1 teaspoonful of salt.

Wash the rice by putting it in cold water and rubbing it hard between the hands. Do this three times. Drain off all the water, and put the rice in a large stewpan with the boiling water. Place it where it will boil all the time with the stewpan uncovered. When it has been cooking for fifteen minutes add the salt; but do not stir it, for rice is spoiled if stirred during the cooking. When it has boiled for twenty-five minutes, turn it into a colander and drain off all the water. Place the colander on a plate, and set it on the hearth or the back part of the range. Cover the rice with a coarse towel. In this way it can be kept hot and dry for a long time.

Baked Rice.

½ pint of boiled rice.
½ pint of milk.
1 teaspoonful of salt.

1 teaspoonful of butter.
1 egg.

Add the egg, well beaten, to all the other ingredients, and bake slowly for half an hour.

Rice Croquettes.

½ pint of boiled rice.
1 gill of milk.
2 eggs.
1 tablespoonful of butter.

1 tablespoonful of sugar.
½ teaspoonful of salt.
The grated yellow rind of a lemon.
Bread crumbs.

Put the milk, rice, butter, and seasoning on to boil. Beat one egg till light, and stir it into the boiling mixture. Cook for one minute, stirring all the time. Turn the mixture out on a plate, and set away to cool. When cold shape into small cylinders. Beat the second egg in a soup plate. Cover the croquettes, one at a time, with the beaten egg, then roll in dried bread crumbs. Fry in deep fat for one minute and a half. Drain on brown paper, and serve at once.

Vegetable Hash.

1 pint of hashed cabbage.
1 pint of hashed potatoes.
½ pint of hashed turnips.

½ pint of hashed beets.
2 tablespoonfuls of corned beef fat.

When the above-named vegetables, or any other kinds, such as parsnips and carrots, are left over from a boiled dinner, chop them separately and rather coarse. Season them with salt and pepper, the amount depending upon how well the vegetables were seasoned when served hot.

Mix them together. Put the corned beef fat in a frying-pan and set on the fire, and when it is melted add the vegetables and cover the pan. Place on a moderately hot part of the range, and cook for half an hour, stirring frequently with a fork.

Just before serving draw the pan forward to a hotter part of the fire, and stir for three minutes. Serve very hot.

Two tablespoonfuls of butter may be used instead of the beef fat.

Celery.

Celery should be kept in a cool place, but it must not be wrapped in wet paper or kept in water. Break the blades from the stalks, and scrape off any brown spots that may be found; next wash the celery, and let it stand in ice-water for ten or twenty minutes to become crisp. Put it in a celery dish with some bits of ice, and serve at once.

How to Keep Lettuce Crisp.

Lettuce can be kept crisp and fresh for several days, if necessary, by placing the roots in water. Do not let the water come up as high as the leaves. When ready to serve the lettuce, wash it leaf by leaf in a pan of cold water, and drop it into another pan of ice-water. It will become crisp in a few minutes. Shake the water from the leaves before serving.

CHAPTER XIV.

MISCELLANEOUS DISHES.

Boiled Eggs.

THE white and yolk should be equally well cooked in a boiled egg, the white being soft and creamy. Put the eggs in a deep saucepan, and pour over them a generous amount of boiling water, — one quart or more of water for four eggs. Cover the saucepan, and set on a part of the range where it is so cool that the hand can rest on it comfortably. At the end of ten minutes the eggs will be cooked to a soft creamy consistency. If the eggs be liked medium well done, cook for five minutes longer; if to be hard, they may remain in the water for twenty minutes.

Poached Eggs.

Put in a frying-pan boiling water to the depth of two or three inches. To each pint of water add a teaspoonful of salt and a teaspoonful of vinegar. Have the water just bubbling at one side of the pan. Break an egg close to the pan, and drop it gently into the water. Continue putting in eggs until you have the required number. When the white of the egg is set, slide a cake-turner under the egg, and lift it from the water. Slide it upon a slice of buttered toast.

In most parts of New England eggs cooked in this way are called dropped.

Muffin rings may be placed in the pan of water, and the eggs be dropped into them. This gives a better shape.

There are several inventions in the market by the use of which eggs can be poached easily and successfully.

Fried Eggs.

These are usually served with ham, but they may be served separately. Put into a pan any kind of clean sweet fat; ham or bacon fat is generally considered as the best. Have the fat about a quarter of an inch deep in the pan. Break the eggs separately, and slide them gently, one at a time, into the hot fat. With a long spoon dip up the fat and pour over the eggs. As soon as the whites are set, slide a cake-turner under the eggs and place them on a warm dish. They may be arranged on slices of ham, or the ham may be put in the centre of the dish, and the eggs arranged around it.

Scrambled Eggs.

> 4 eggs.
> 1 tablespoonful of butter.
> ⅙ teaspoonful of salt.

Beat the eggs with a spoon. Add the salt. Put the butter on the fire, in a frying-pan, and when hot stir in the eggs. Continue stirring until the eggs begin to set. Instantly turn them into a warm dish and serve.

Eggs au Gratin.

> 4 eggs.
> ½ pint of grated bread crumbs.
> 1 teaspoonful of Parmesan cheese.
> ½ teaspoonful of salt.
> 1/16 teaspoonful of pepper.
> 3 generous teaspoonfuls of butter.

Mix the salt, pepper, cheese, and butter with the crumbs. Beat the white of one egg to a stiff froth; then add the yolk and beat for a moment longer. Stir this egg mixture into the other ingredients.

Butter a gratin dish — or a small pie plate will do — and make little nests in it with the preparation. Cook in rather a hot oven for ten minutes. Take from the oven, and then break a fresh egg into each nest. Return to the oven and cook for three minutes longer. If there be objection to cheese, a teaspoonful of chopped parsley and a few drops of onion juice may be substituted for it.

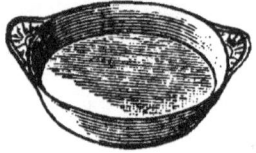

GRATIN DISH.

Baked Eggs.

Butter a gratin dish, or a deep pie plate, and break the required number of eggs into it. Put the plate in a moderate oven, and cook until the white is set. It will take from five to eight minutes to bake the eggs.

Pretty round and oval dishes come for this purpose. They are made of French china, and are fireproof.

Breaded Eggs.

5 eggs.	⅕ teaspoonful of pepper.
½ pint of dried bread crumbs.	Fat for frying.
1 teaspoonful of salt.	½ pint of bisque sauce.

Boil four of the eggs for ten minutes. Drop them into cold water and remove the shells. Cut the eggs in halves, lengthwise, and season them with the salt and pepper. Beat the uncooked egg in a soup plate. Dip the halves of eggs in this, and then roll in the bread crumbs. At serving time put the breaded eggs in the frying basket, and plunge into hot fat. Cook for about two minutes; then drain, and serve on a hot dish with the bisque sauce poured around them.

Creamed Eggs.

4 slices of toast.	1 teaspoonful of salt.
4 hard-boiled eggs.	1 tablespoonful of flour.
2 tablespoonfuls of butter.	3 gills of milk.
¼ teaspoonful of pepper.	

Cut the eggs into thin slices. Cut the slices of toast in halves, and lay them in a warm platter. Put the butter on the fire, in a frying-pan, and when it becomes hot add the flour. Stir until the mixture is smooth and frothy. Gradually add the cold milk, stirring all the time. When this boils up, add the salt and pepper.

Mix the eggs with the sauce and spread on the toast. Bake in a moderate oven for six minutes and serve immediately.

Egg Cutlets.

5 eggs.	⅛ teaspoonful of pepper.
1 tablespoonful of butter.	Crumbs for breading.
¾ teaspoonful of salt.	Fat for frying.

Put four of the eggs in a deep saucepan, and fill up with boiling water. Cover, and let them stand on the hearth or the coolest part of the range for twenty minutes. At the end of this time pour off the hot water and cover with cold water. Remove the shells and cut the eggs in two, lengthwise, using a plated knife.

Let a soup plate stand in hot water until heated through. Put the butter, salt, and pepper in this plate, and stir until the butter is melted. Beat the fifth egg in another soup plate, and have a third plate filled with dry and sifted bread crumbs. Drop the eggs, one at a time, in the melted butter, then in the beaten egg, and finally roll them in the crumbs. Lay them on a platter and set in a cold place until it is time to cook them; then put them in the frying basket and cook in hot fat for one minute. Serve with a bisque or curry sauce.

This dish is suitable for luncheon or supper.

Plain Omelet.

2 eggs.	1 tablespoonful of cold water.
¼ teaspoonful of salt.	1 heaped teaspoonful of butter.

Beat the egg enough to break it well, but not to make it light. Have the omelet pan warmed, and put the butter in it. Place over a very hot fire. As soon as the butter becomes so hot that it turns slightly brown, pour the eggs into the pan. With the left hand lift the pan a little at the handle side, tipping it forward slightly, so that the liquid egg shall flow to the other side. As soon as the egg begins to

ROLLING AN OMELET.

set, draw it up to the raised side of the pan. While the egg is yet quite soft, begin to roll the omelet. Begin at the left hand, and turn over in small folds until the lower part of the pan is reached. Let the omelet rest a few seconds, and then turn out on a hot dish.

The work of making an omelet is very simple, but there must be intense heat, and the work of folding and removing

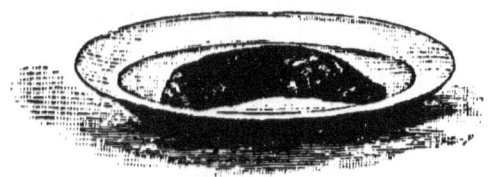

THE OMELET WHEN FINISHED.

from the pan must be done rapidly. Practice is essential to perfect omelet making. The great mistake which beginners usually make is, that they work too slowly, and cook the omelet too much. It should be a soft, creamy mass when done.

One can make a great variety of omelets by adding a few spoonfuls of any kind of delicate meat, fish, or vegetable, hashed fine and heated in a sauce. Spread the heated mixture on the omelet before you begin to fold it.

Baked Omelet.

3 eggs.	1½ gills of milk.
1 heaped tablespoonful of corn starch.	1 teaspoonful of salt.
	1 tablespoonful of butter.

Heat one gill of the milk to the boiling point. Mix the corn starch with the half-gill of cold milk and stir into the boiling milk. Cook for one minute, stirring all the time. Add the salt and butter, and take from the fire. Beat the yolks and whites of the eggs separately; then stir them into the cooked ingredients. Turn the mixture into a buttered baking dish and cook in a moderate oven for about twelve minutes. Serve at once.

Bread Omelet.

2 ounces of stale bread (one large slice).	1 level teaspoonful of salt.
1 gill of boiling water.	2 eggs.
1 gill of cold milk.	1 tablespoonful of butter.

Have the bread free from crust. Pour the boiling water over it. When soft, add the salt and milk, and break up with a spoon. Beat the yolks and whites of the eggs separately, and stir into the bread mixture. Put the butter in a frying-pan of good size, and set on the fire. When hot, turn in the omelet, and cook until it begins to set; drawing it back a little, as you would a plain omelet. Fold, and brown slightly. Turn out on a hot dish, and serve at once.

Welsh Rare-bit.

½ pint of soft mild cheese.
½ gill of milk.
1 egg.
½ tablespoonful of butter.
¼ teaspoonful of salt.
½ teaspoonful of mustard.
A grain of cayenne.
3 slices of toast.

Break the cheese into small bits. Beat the egg, and add the other ingredients to it. Put the mixture in a small saucepan, which place in another of boiling water. Stir over the fire until the mixture becomes a smooth, creamy mass. Immediately spread this on the hot toast, and serve. The rare-bit can be made on the table in the chafing dish.

Roasted Oyster Crackers.

1 tablespoonful of butter.
1 gill of boiling water.
3 gills of oyster crackers.

Melt the butter in the water; then stir the crackers into the mixture, that they may all get a slight coating of butter and water. Spread them in a shallow pan and put in a hot oven for ten or twelve minutes. They should be brown and glossy at the end of that time. Serve in a deep dish with oyster soup or oyster stew.

Fried Bread.

Cut slices of stale bread into half-inch squares. Put into a small frying-pan or granite-ware saucepan six tablespoonfuls of lard, and set on the fire. When the lard is so hot that it smokes all over, put in one square of the bread. If this becomes browned in one minute and a half, the lard is hot enough; if it is not hot enough, make another test very soon. Now put in the rest of the squares of bread, — there should be about half a pint. Fry until brown, which will be in about a minute and a half. While the bread is frying, stir it with a fork, in order that all parts may be equally browned. Take from the fat with a skimmer and drain on brown paper. When the fat has become slightly cooled, strain it through a piece of cheese-cloth and it will be ready to use again.

This bread is to serve with tomato, pea, and other soups.

Maple Syrup from Sugar.

Break up a pound of maple sugar and put it in a saucepan with half a pint of hot water. Boil for ten minutes. Pour into a pitcher, and when cold, cover, and put in a cool place. It is well to buy maple sugar in the spring and keep it in a cool, dry place for use in making syrup until the fresh syrup comes the next year.

Batter for Fruit Fritters.

1 gill of flour.
½ gill of milk.
1 egg.

¼ teaspoonful of salt.
1 teaspoonful of sugar.
½ tablespoonful of melted butter.

Mix the dry ingredients together. Add the milk, and beat the batter until light and smooth. Add the butter, and beat again. Finally add the egg, well beaten. This batter will answer for any kind of fruit.

Apple Fritters.

Core and pare large tart apples. Cut them in slices about one third of an inch thick. Season the slices with nutmeg, then dip them in the batter. Lift them, one by one, from the batter and drop gently into hot fat. Cook for three minutes; then lift from the fat, drain, and serve immediately. Powdered sugar may be sprinkled on the fritters when they are arranged on the dish.

Peaches, bananas, oranges, grapes, pears, etc., may be cooked in the form of fritters.

Milk Toast.

1 pint of milk.
1 tablespoonful of flour.
1 tablespoonful of butter.

½ teaspoonful of salt.
5 slices of toasted bread.

Mix the flour with one gill of cold milk. Put the remainder of the milk in the double-boiler and set on the fire. When the milk boils, stir in the flour mixture, and cook for ten minutes. Toast the bread till it is nicely and evenly browned. Stir the salt and butter into the cooking mixture; then dip the slices of toast in it. Lay the toast in a deep warm dish and pour the remainder of the cream over it. Cover the dish and serve.

Indian, brown, or graham bread may be used for this toast.

Baked Toast.

For this toast use a flat dish, such as comes for baking eggs, or a meat platter of stone china. Toast the bread and spread it, one slice deep, in the platter. Cover it with cold milk, and put in a moderately hot oven. When the milk is boiling hot, add bits of butter, and let the toast cook for one minute longer. Serve in the dish in which it was cooked. If salt be liked, sprinkle a little on the toast before the milk is added.

Allow one pint of milk and one teaspoonful of butter to five slices of toast.

If cream be plentiful, use that, and omit the butter.

Soft Butter Toast.

Toast stale bread till nicely browned. Dip it quickly into hot salted water, spread it with soft butter, and serve.

The butter must be only soft enough to spread easily. It will spoil it to melt it.

Use one teaspoonful of salt to a quart of boiling water.

Cracker Cream Toast.

Toast crackers and drop them into a cream, made as for milk toast. Let them soak in this for ten minutes; then dish and serve.

The crackers will be more delicate if they be soaked in cold water and toasted as for butter toast before being put in the cream.

Cracker Butter Toast.

Split Boston butter crackers and soak them in cold water until they begin to swell. Remove them from the water and drain on a plate. Arrange in the double-broiler and toast brown on both sides. Butter, and serve at once on a hot dish.

Mush.

Time was when the housekeeper was limited to three or four kinds of material for mush; but that is all changed, and the market is filled with many different preparations of wheat, oats, corn, etc. Each new article is pronounced by its makers to be the best. One of the principal recommendations which each manufacturer claims for his product is that it can be cooked in a short time. Many good articles that are prepared for the table by the printed directions on the package, calling for about ten minutes' cooking, are discarded because of unsatisfactory results, whereas if the cooking were continued for half an hour or more the dish would be delicious. It must be remembered that all cereals require thorough cooking, because of the starch in them. No matter what the cereal product may be, it should be cooked not less than half an hour.

Be sure to have the full quantity of water called for in the receipt, and to have it boiling when the meal is stirred into it. When dry meal is to be sprinkled into boiling water, stir the water briskly for a few moments before adding the meal, and stir constantly while the meal is being sprinkled in. Rules can be given here for only a few kinds of cereals, but these rules can be followed in cooking almost any one of the breakfast cereals.

Oatmeal Mush.

1 gill of oatmeal.
1 pint of boiling water.
½ teaspoonful of salt.

Stir the boiling water; then sprinkle in the oatmeal, stirring all the time. After adding the salt, cover the stewpan, and set back where the contents will cook gently for half an hour or longer. Do not stir the mush after the first five minutes.

Corn Meal Mush.

1 gill of yellow corn meal.
1 generous pint of boiling water.
½ teaspoonful of salt.

Put the meal in a stewpan and gradually pour the boiling water upon it, stirring all the time. Add the salt, and put the stewpan where the mush will cook gently for an hour or more. Stir frequently, and keep the stewpan covered.

Fried Mush.

½ pint of corn meal.
2 tablespoonfuls of flour.

1 teaspoonful of salt.
1 quart of boiling water.

Mix the dry ingredients well in a stewpan and pour the boiling water on them, stirring all the time. Beat vigorously and cook slowly for three hours, keeping the stewpan covered. At the end of that time dip a small bread-pan in cold water, and pour the mush into it, packing smoothly. Set away to cool.

In the morning turn the mush out on a board and cut in slices about half an inch thick. Roll these in dry flour and fry in hot fat until brown. Drain on sheets of brown paper, and serve very hot.

Boiled Hominy.

1 gill of hominy.
1 pint of boiling water.
½ teaspoonful of salt.

Wash the hominy in two or three waters, and stir into the boiling water. Add the salt. Cover the stewpan, and set where the hominy will cook gently for half an hour or more. Stir frequently. Use the fine breakfast hominy. This mush may be served with sugar and milk, or as a vegetable, with meat.

Fried Hominy.

Cook the hominy as directed in the rule for boiled hominy. Wet a deep dish and pour the hot hominy into it. When cold, cut in slices about half an inch thick. Roll the sliced hominy in flour.

Put two tablespoonfuls of sweet drippings in the frying-pan and place on the fire. When the fat is hot, lay in the slices of hominy. Cover the pan, and cook until brown on one side; then turn, and brown on the other. It will take about twenty minutes' time to brown the hominy. Serve very hot. Bacon or ham fat is the best for this dish.

Hominy Cakes.

½ a pint of cold hominy.
1 egg.
½ teaspoonful of salt.

⅛ teaspoonful of pepper.
1 tablespoonful of drippings.

Beat the hominy well with a fork, and add the seasonings and the egg, well beaten. Shape with the hands into small, flat cakes, and, after sprinkling these lightly with flour, fry them until brown on one side, and then turn and brown on the other side. Beef, pork, ham, bacon, or sausage fat may be used for frying. Do not use more than the tablespoonful.

These cakes are good for breakfast, luncheon, or tea.

Fruit Sauces.

All kinds of fruit may be used for sauces. The juicy fruits will require but little water, whereas the dry ones will need a great deal. The amount of sugar used in these fruit sauces depends upon the acidity of the fruit and the taste of the family. If the fruit is to be kept whole, add the sugar when the fruit is put on to stew, and cook slowly.

Never cook fruit in tin.

Fruit sauces that are to be served with meats should have very little sugar added to them.

Baked Sweet Apples.

Wash and wipe the apples. Put them in a deep earthen dish, with water enough to come up about an inch. Sprinkle sugar over the apples and bake in a moderate oven for two hours. Baste them twice with the water in the dish. Six apples will require two tablespoonfuls of sugar and a scant half-pint of water.

Baked Sour Apples.

Wash, wipe, and core six large apples, and place them in a deep earthen dish. Fill the holes with sugar, and sprinkle two extra tablespoonfuls over the apples. Pour a gill of hot water into the dish. Bake in a moderately hot oven until tender. It will take about an hour's time to cook them.

Broiled Apples.

Pare, core, and cut tart apples in slices about half an inch thick. Dip the slices into melted butter, and broil them over rather a bright fire. When soft, put them on a warm dish and sprinkle with sugar. Serve at once.

Fried Apples.

1 quart of tart apples.
2 tablespoonfuls of drippings.
1 tablepoonful of sugar.

Pare and slice the apples. Put the drippings in a frying-pan and set on the fire. When hot, add the apples. Cover the pan and cook until the apples are tender, turning them often. Add the sugar, and cook ten minutes longer.

These are particularly good when served hot with fresh pork.

Green Apple Sauce.

Pare, quarter, and core some tart apples and put them in a granite-ware or porcelain stewpan. Nearly cover them with water; then cover the stewpan and place on the fire. Cook until the apples are tender, and season with sugar. The exact time of cooking and the amount of sugar cannot be stated for any given measure of apples, because some apples cook so much more quickly than others, and some require more sugar.

Should you wish to have the pieces of apple kept whole in the cooking, add the sugar when the fruit is put on to stew, and cook slowly. If, on the other hand, the apple be liked all broken up and of light color, boil rapidly, and sweeten after the fruit is stewed.

Evaporated Apple Sauce.

1 pint of evaporated apples.
1 gill of sugar.
About one quart of water.

Wash the apples and let them soak over night in the quart of cold water. In the morning put the apples and water in a granite-ware or porcelain stewpan; cover, and place on rather a cool part of the range. Cook gently for one hour; then add the sugar, and cook for half an hour longer. There should be water enough to cover the apples generously when they are put on to stew. Do not stir this sauce. The juice of a lemon may be added if you choose.

Evaporated Peaches.

Cook this fruit the same as the evaporated apples.

Evaporated Apricots.

This fruit is to be cooked the same as evaporated apples.

Baked Pears.

9 pears.
1 gill of sugar.
1 pint of water.

Wash the pears and put them, with the water and sugar, in a deep earthen dish. Cover the dish and bake the pears in a slow oven for three hours.

Stewed Prunes.

Put the prunes in a bowl of cold water. Wash them one by one by rubbing them between the hands, and drop them into a bowl of cold water. Wash them in this second water and put them in a stewpan. To half a pound of prunes add one quart of cold water. Place the stewpan on the range and cook the prunes slowly for two hours or more. When done, they will be plump and tender. Turn them into a bowl and put in a cool place.

Cranberry Sauce.

1 pint of cranberries.
½ pint of granulated sugar.
½ pint of water.

Pick over the cranberries. Wash them, and put in a granite-ware or porcelain stewpan; then add the water and the sugar. Cook the sauce rapidly for ten or fifteen minutes; then turn into a bowl and set away to harden. This gives a sauce that will jelly. If liked softer, use a little more water.

Cranberry Jelly.

Make the same as cranberry sauce, but cook five minutes longer; then rub through a strainer fine enough to keep back the seeds.

Rhubarb Sauce.

Rhubarb may be stewed or baked. Pare and wash the stalks and cut them in pieces about an inch long; then put in a granite-ware stewpan. To a quart of the rhubarb add one gill of sugar and one gill of water, and stew gently until done; then turn into an earthen bowl. Another way is to put the rhubarb, water, and sugar in an earthen dish, cover the dish, and bake in a moderate oven for an hour and a half.

If the sauce be liked sweet more sugar may be used.

Dumplings.

½ pint of unsifted flour.
1 teaspoonful of baking powder.
¼ teaspoonful of salt.

½ teaspoonful of sugar.
⅓ cupful of milk.

Mix the dry ingredients and rub through a sieve. Wet with the milk, and stir quickly into the form of a smooth ball. Sprinkle the bread board with flour and roll the dough into a sheet about three quarters of an inch thick, which should then be cut into small cakes. If the dumplings are to be cooked with the stew, set the stewpan where the contents will cook rapidly, and arrange the dumplings on top of the stew. Cover the pan, and cook for exactly ten minutes. If they are to be steamed, place them on a plate in the steamer and cook for twelve minutes.

CHAPTER XV.

BREAD IN VARIOUS FORMS.

PERFECT bread will be light and sweet, and with a rich, nutty flavor of the wheat. To get this result good yeast and flour must be used; the dough, while rising, must be kept at a proper temperature, about 75° F., and the heat of the oven, when baking the dough, must be high enough to raise the inside of the loaf to about 220° F. This is necessary to cook the starch, expand the carbonic acid gas, air, and steam, and drive off the alcohol.

A good way to test the heat is to put in a piece of white paper. If it turn a dark brown in five minutes, the oven will be of the right temperature; but if it burn, the oven will be too hot, and must be cooled a little before the loaf is put in; or if the paper be only a light brown at the end of the five minutes, the oven must be made hotter.

When the bread is baked it should be cooled in such a way that the pure air shall circulate freely around it. The best way is to put the loaf across the pan, or to let it lean against the pan, having it rest on its edge. In this way the gases, alcohol, and steam pass off, making the loaf much sweeter and crisper than when it is wrapped in a cloth. The loaf should be perfectly cold before being put in the bread box.

When you are baking bread the heat should be greatest when the loaf is first put in the oven; then, after cooking for twenty-five minutes, the heat should be reduced a little. White bread made with water should get the greater part of its browning the first half-hour. If made with milk it will brown in twenty minutes; but it must be remembered that being brown does not mean that the bread is baked.

A piece of woollen blanket is of great value in making bread. Wrap it around the bowl in which the dough is rising, and it will keep the temperature even. Nothing is more injurious than chilling the dough before it is risen. It does not hurt it after it is well risen.

Bread can be made with either milk or water; simply substitute milk where water is called for. The milk should first be boiled and cooled.

Hop Yeast.

Put a tablespoonful of hops in one quart of cold water and place on the fire. Now pare and grate into a tin pan three large uncooked potatoes. When the hops and water begin to boil, strain the boiling water on the grated potatoes. Place the pan with the potatoes and hop-water on the stove, and stir until the mixture boils up. Take from the fire, and add one tablespoonful of salt and two of granulated sugar. Let this mixture stand until it is blood warm; then add half a cupful of liquid yeast, or half a cake of compressed yeast dissolved in one fourth of a cupful of water. Pour the mixture into a large earthen bowl which has been thoroughly heated. Cover, and set in a warm place for six hours. In that time the yeast should be so well risen that it is foamy all through. Now pour this into a stone jar, or into two preserve jars (the jars should be not more than half full), and put in a cold place, but not where the yeast will freeze. This yeast will keep three or four weeks. Made in this way it is called liquid yeast.

Liquid, compressed, or dry yeast, if sweet and good, will all make excellent bread. In very hot countries the dry yeast is by far the best, unless one have an ice chest to keep the liquid yeast in. As the method of making bread with the dry yeast is different from that of making with liquid yeast, a separate rule may be valuable.

Bread Made with Dry Yeast.

For three Loaves.

2 quarts of flour.
1¼ pints (2½ cupfuls) of blood-warm water.
2 tablespoonfuls of butter or lard.
1 yeast cake.
1 tablespoonful of sugar.
1 teaspoonful of salt.

For three small loaves there will be required two quarts of flour, one pint and a gill of blood-warm water, one yeast cake, one tablespoonful of sugar, two tablespoonfuls of butter or lard, and one teaspoonful of salt.

Sift the flour in the bread pan. Break up the yeast cake and put it in a quart bowl; then add a gill of the water, and mash with a spoon until the yeast and water are well mixed. Beat in one gill of the flour. Cover the bowl and set in a warm place for two hours. At the end of that time the batter should be a perfect sponge. Add to the sponge the pint of warm water, half the butter or lard, and the salt and sugar. Stir this mixture into the flour and mix well with a spoon. Sprinkle the moulding board thickly with flour, and, turning the dough upon it, knead for twenty minutes, using as little flour as possible. At the end of this time the ball of dough should be soft, smooth, and elastic. Place the dough in the bowl and rub the second spoonful of butter or lard over it. Cover with a clean towel and then with a tin or wood cover. Set the bowl in a warm place and let it rise over night. In the morning the dough will have increased to three times its original volume, and will be a perfect sponge. Knead it in the bowl for five minutes — do not use flour — and then shape into three small loaves. Put these in deep pans, and with a sharp knife cut lengthwise through the centre of each loaf. Put the pans in a warm place and cover with clean towels. Let the loaves rise to twice their size, and then bake in a moderately hot oven for fifty minutes.

Water Bread.

1 quart of flour.	¼ cake of compressed yeast, or
½ pint of water,—generous measure.	½ gill of liquid yeast.
	½ teaspoonful of salt.
1 tablespoonful of butter or lard.	1 teaspoonful of sugar.

Sift the flour into the bread bowl. Take out half a cupful to use in kneading. Put the salt, sugar, and half the butter in the flour. Dissolve the yeast and mix with the flour. Beat well with a strong spoon.

Sprinkle flour on the board and knead the dough for twenty minutes or half an hour. Return to the bowl, and rub the remainder of the butter or lard over it. Cover with a clean towel; then put a tin or wooden cover on the bowl and raise and finish as directed in the rule for bread made with dry yeast. This will make two small loaves or one large one.

Potato Bread.

1 quart of flour.	1 potato.
½ pint of boiling water, generous measure.	½ teaspoonful of salt.
	1 tablespoonful of sugar.
¼ cake of compressed yeast, or ½ gill of liquid yeast.	1 tablespoonful of butter or lard.

Cover the potato with boiling water and cook for thirty minutes. Take it up and mash fine and light; then pour the boiling water on it. Let this stand until it is blood-warm; then beat into it the yeast, sugar, and a pint and a half of flour. Beat well for ten minutes; then cover the dough and set it in a warm place to rise. It will take between four and five hours. When the dough has risen to a light sponge, add the salt and butter or lard to it, and beat well.

Sprinkle the board with flour, turn the dough out on it and knead for fifteen or twenty minutes. Return the dough to the bowl; cover, and set in a warm place to rise. When it has risen to more than double the original size, shape it into two small loaves, or a loaf of medium size and a small pan of rolls. Cover the bread with a clean towel and raise to double the original size.

If all the dough be put into one loaf, it must be baked for one hour; if two small loaves be made, bake them for forty-five minutes. This is delicious bread. Milk may be substituted for water.

Entire-wheat Bread.

3 gills of water.
3 pints of entire wheat flour.
½ teaspoonful of salt.
1 level tablespoonful of sugar.

½ tablespoonful of butter or lard.
¼ cake of compressed yeast, or
¼ cupful of liquid yeast.

Sift the flour into the mixing bowl, but take out a gill to use in kneading. Dissolve the yeast in the water. Mix the salt, sugar, and butter with the flour, and stir in the yeast and water. Beat well; then knead for twenty minutes or half an hour. Cover, and set to rise. Finish the same as water bread.

This bread must be mixed as soft as possible and should be baked thoroughly. Bake a loaf of medium size one hour and a quarter.

Graham Bread.

1 pint of graham meal.
1 pint of white flour.
3 gills of water, generous measure.

¼ cake of compressed yeast, or
¼ cup of liquid yeast.
1 level teaspoonful of salt.
½ gill of molasses.

Sift the meal and flour into the mixing bowl, turning in the bran also. Dissolve the yeast in the water, and add the salt and molasses to it. Turn this mixture out on the flour, and beat the dough vigorously for twenty minutes or longer. Cover the bowl and let the dough rise over night. In the morning wet the hand in cold water and beat the dough for five or ten minutes; then shape, and put in a well buttered pan. Let it rise to nearly double the original size, and bake for an hour and a half, having the oven quite hot the first half-hour, and very moderate the last hour.

Success in making this bread depends upon the thorough beating and baking. Flours vary so much that it is impossible to give the exact amount of liquid, but the dough should be as thick as you can mix and beat it with the hand. It must, however, never be kneaded stiff, like bread made with white flour.

Rye Bread.

Substitute rye meal for graham, and proceed exactly as directed for graham bread.

Rye Bread, No. 2.

Make this bread as directed for entire-wheat bread, substituting fine rye flour for the entire-wheat flour.

Boston Brown Bread.

3 gills of corn meal.	1 level teaspoonful of salt.
3 gills of rye meal.	1 level teaspoonful of soda.
5 gills of sweet milk.	2 tablespoonfuls of cold water.
1 gill of molasses.	

Sift all the meal into a bowl. Put the milk, molasses, and salt into a bowl. Dissolve the soda in the cold water and add to the liquid ingredients. Stir this into the meal and beat vigorously for five minutes or more; then put into a well buttered brown-bread tin and steam for five hours; or the batter may be put into three one-pound baking-powder cans. They will steam in less time than if in the large loaf. Whatever sort of tin the loaf be steamed in, it must have a cover. It will do no harm to cook this bread more than five hours, but if in the large loaf it must not cook less. Graham meal may be substituted for the rye.

Steamed Indian Bread.

½ pint of corn meal.
½ pint of flour.
1 pint of sour milk or buttermilk.
3 tablespoonfuls of cold water.
1 teaspoonful of butter.

½ teaspoonful of salt.
½ teaspoonful of soda.
2 tablespoonfuls of molasses, generous measure.

Sift the meal and flour into the mixing bowl, and add the salt. Mix the milk and molasses together. Dissolve the soda in the water and stir into the milk and molasses. Add this to the flour and meal, and beat well. Now add the butter, melted, and turn the batter into a well buttered bread pan. Cover the pan and place in the steamer. Cook for four hours and a half. Take the pan from the steamer, and cook in a moderate oven for half an hour longer.

This bread is delicious served hot from the oven, or toasted and buttered, or toasted and served with hot cream poured over it.

Pulled Bread.

Tear the crust from a part of a loaf of baker's bread. Now tear the crumb of the loaf into long, thin pieces. Spread the torn bread in a pan and put in a hot oven to become brown and crisp. It will take about fifteen minutes. Serve hot with cheese. Pulled bread is also nice with chocolate or coffee.

Rolls from Bread Dough.

It is almost impossible to shape and raise rolls for an early breakfast, but if one have a cold room or a refrigerator the rolls can be put in the pan the night before, and they will then be ready to bake for breakfast. Reserve about a pint and a half of the risen bread dough and work into it a tablespoonful of butter or lard. Put the dough in a bowl; cover it with a plate and place the bowl in the refrigerator or in a cold room. In the evening shape the dough into rolls and rub a little soft butter over them. Cover the pan closely, but leave ample room for the rolls to rise; then put in the refrigerator or cold room. Bake in the morning in a moderately hot oven for half an hour.

Sponge Rolls.

1 pint of flour.	½ teaspoonful of salt.
½ pint of warm water.	1 tablespoonful of butter.
1 teaspoonful of sugar.	⅛ cupful of yeast.

Sift the flour into a bowl; then add the salt and sugar. Melt the butter in the warm water (be sure it is not above 100°), and add the yeast. Put this mixture with the flour, and beat thoroughly with a strong spoon. Cover the bowl and let the dough rise over night. In the morning butter a French-roll pan and half fill each compartment with the sponge, being careful not to break it down unnecessarily. Let the rolls rise for an hour and bake them in a moderately hot oven for half an hour.

Parker House Rolls.

1½ pints of flour.	1 tablespoonful of butter or lard.
½ pint of milk, scant measure.	¼ cake of compressed yeast, or
1 teaspoonful of sugar.	¼ cupful of liquid yeast.

Boil the milk, and let it cool. Sift the flour into the mixing bowl. Mix the salt and sugar with the flour. Make a hole in the middle of the flour, by drawing it back to the sides of the pan. Pour the milk very gently into this place, being careful not to wet the flour above the point where the milk will come when it is all poured in. Now add the dissolved yeast, stirring gently at the bottom of the pan. Cover the bowl and set in a warm place for four hours; then stir the mixture until a dough is formed. Add the butter or lard, and knead on the board for twenty minutes. Do not use any flour in kneading. Put the dough back in the bowl; cover, and set in a warm place to rise to nearly three times the original size (it will take about three hours for this). Next put the dough on the board and roll down to the thickness of half an inch. Cut the dough with an oval cutter. Place a small round stick on the roll, about one third of the distance from the end. Press with the stick until the dough is half as thick here as in other parts. Fold the short end of the dough over, and the roll will be shaped. A little soft butter may be placed between the folds. Place the rolls in a buttered pan, having them a little way apart. Cover, and set in rather a cool place — say seventy degrees — until the rolls are risen to a little more than double the original size. Bake them in a moderately hot oven for twenty minutes.

Caution. Do not use any flour in kneading the dough, and when it has risen put no flour on the board when it is to be rolled out. The risen dough must not be kneaded, merely turned on the board and rolled thin. If the rolls be required for luncheon begin them at half past seven or eight o'clock in the morning, and double the amount of yeast. The raising time will then be only half that given. This dough can be used for luncheon rolls and pin wheels.

Milk Rolls.

1 pint of flour.	1 tablespoonful of butter.
1½ gills of milk.	¼ teaspoonful of salt.
⅛ cupful of yeast.	1 teaspoonful of sugar.

Boil the milk, and add the butter, sugar, and salt to it. Let the mixture stand until it becomes blood-warm; then add the yeast. Pour this new mixture on the flour, and beat well with a strong spoon; then knead on the board for twenty minutes. Return the dough to the bowl, and cover closely, — first with a towel, then with a tin or wooden cover. Set in a warm place over night. In the morning shape in either long or cleft rolls, and let these rise in the pans for an hour and a quarter, or until they have doubled in size. Bake in a moderately hot oven for half an hour, if the rolls be placed close together; but if they be detached, as would be the case with cleft rolls, bake for only fifteen or twenty minutes.

Luncheon Rolls.

Make the dough for milk rolls. In the morning work it well in the bowl; then sprinkle the board lightly with flour, and roll the dough down to the thickness of a quarter of an inch. Spread this with soft butter and roll up as for a jelly roll. Cut from this slices about an inch thick, and set them on end in a buttered baking-pan. Have the rolls a little way apart and let them rise to double the original size. Bake them in a moderately hot oven for twenty-five minutes.

Baking Powder Biscuit.

1 pint of flour, measured before sifting.
½ pint of milk, scant measure.
1½ teaspoonfuls of baking powder.
½ teaspoonful of salt.
½ tablespoonful of butter.
½ tablespoonful of lard.
½ teaspoonful of sugar.

Mix thoroughly in a sieve the flour, sugar, salt, and baking powder, and then rub through the sieve. Rub the butter and lard into this mixture. Have the oven very hot, the pans buttered, the board, cutter, and rolling pin ready. Now add the milk to the mixture, stirring quickly and vigorously with a strong spoon. Sprinkle the board with flour and turn out the dough upon it. Roll down to the thickness of about half an inch and cut with a small cutter. Bake in a quick oven. Do not crowd the biscuit in the pan. If they be cut small, and the oven be very hot, they will bake in ten or twelve minutes. They should not stand in the oven after they are done.

It is impossible to give in this receipt the exact quantity of milk to use, flour varies so much; but the dough should be mixed as soft as it is possible to handle.

Quick Luncheon Rolls.

Follow the rule for baking powder biscuit; then roll the dough thin, spread it with soft butter and roll up like jelly roll. Cut the roll into slices about three quarters of an inch thick and set them on end in a baking-pan, having them a little way apart. Bake them in a quick oven for about fifteen minutes.

Pin Wheels.

Make the dough for milk rolls, and when it has risen, roll it as thin as possible. Spread it with soft butter and sprinkle over this half a cupful of sugar and one tablespoonful of cinnamon mixed together. Roll up like a jelly roll and cut into slices about half an inch thick. Place these slices in a well buttered pan and let them rise to double the original size. Bake in a moderately hot oven for twenty-five minutes.

If you prefer, a baking powder biscuit dough may be used and the pin wheels be baked in a quick oven for fifteen minutes.

Crumpets.

1 pint of flour, generous measure.	½ teaspoonful of salt.
1 pint of warm water.	½ teaspoonful of sugar.
⅛ cupful of yeast.	2 tablespoonfuls of butter.

Put the flour, salt, and sugar in a bowl. Add the water and yeast, and beat vigorously for fifteen minutes. Cover the bowl, and set in a warm place over night. In the morning beat in the melted butter and pour the batter into buttered muffin pans. Let the crumpets rise for an hour, and bake them for half an hour in a moderate oven.

If you choose you may add the butter to the mixture at night. In that case the risen sponge may be taken out by spoonfuls, being careful not to break it down, and the crumpets will then require only half an hour to rise.

Crumpets may be baked on a griddle instead of in muffin pans. If they are baked on a griddle, measure the quart of flour lightly. When ready to fry them, butter the muffin rings and also a griddle, which should not be so hot as for common griddle-cakes. Place the buttered rings on the griddle and put a spoonful of the batter in each one. When the crumpets get done on one side, turn them, and brown the other side. It will take about twelve minutes to cook them.

Sally Lunn.

1 pint of flour.	1½ tablespoonfuls of butter.
½ pint of milk.	¼ cake of compressed yeast, or
1 tablespoonful of sugar.	¼ cupful of liquid yeast.
½ teaspoonful of salt.	1 egg.

Sift the flour and mix with it the sugar and salt. Heat the milk to about a hundred degrees, and dissolve the butter in it. Dissolve the compressed yeast in two tablespoonfuls of tepid water, and stir into the milk and butter. Separate the parts of the egg, and beat the white until light; then beat the yolk well. Add the milk mixture and the egg to the flour, and beat well. Pour this batter into a well buttered cake pan. Cover, and let it rise in a warm place for two hours. Bake for half an hour in a moderately hot oven, and serve on a hot dish. This is suitable for luncheon or supper. If any of the cake be left, split, toast, and butter it.

Flour Pop-overs.

1 pint of flour.	1 teaspoonful of salt.
1 pint of milk.	1 teaspoonful of sugar.
3 eggs.	

BREAD IN VARIOUS FORMS.

Pop-overs should always be baked in stone or earthenware cups that come for the purpose, the former being by far the better. Have a dozen cups buttered and arranged in an old dripping-pan. Put the sifted flour, sugar, and salt in a mixing bowl. Beat the eggs until very light; then add the milk to them. Pour this mixture on the flour, only half of it at first, and beat until the batter is smooth and light, say for about five minutes. Pour the batter into the cups and bake in a moderately hot oven for fifty minutes. They should, when done, have increased to four times their original size.

MUFFIN CUP.

If only half a dozen pop-overs be wanted, use half of all the other materials, and take two small eggs or a very large one.

Rye Pop-overs.

½ pint of wheat flour.
3 gills of rye meal.
1 pint of milk.

3 eggs.
1 teaspoonful of salt.
2 tablespoonfuls of sugar.

Make these the same as flour pop-overs, only bake them one hour.

Graham Pop-overs.

Made the same as the rye, substituting graham for rye.

Wheat Gems.

½ pint of flour.
½ pint of milk.
1 large egg.

1 teaspoonful of sugar.
½ teaspoonful of salt.

Beat the egg till it is light, and add the milk to it. Add half of this mixture to the flour, salt, and sugar. Beat well, and add the remainder of the milk and eggs; then beat for five minutes longer. Pour the batter into hot buttered gem-pans and bake in a quick oven for twenty-five minutes.

Raised Wheat Muffins.

1 generous pint of flour.
½ pint of milk.
1 tablespoonful of butter.
½ tablespoonful of sugar.

½ teaspoonful of salt.
1 egg.
⅛ cupful of yeast, or ⅛ of a yeast cake.

Put the flour, salt, and sugar in a deep earthen bowl. Boil the milk and add the butter to it. Let this mixture stand until only tepid; then add the milk, butter, and yeast to the flour, and beat well. Cover the bowl and let it stand in rather a cool part of the kitchen, unless the weather be very cold; in which case it will be necessary to keep the bowl in a warm place. When morning comes, the batter will be found to have risen to a light sponge. Beat the egg till very light and add it to this sponge, beating in well. Half fill well buttered muffin pans with the batter; cover, and let the muffins rise in a warm place for one hour. Bake for half an hour in a moderately quick oven.

MUFFIN PANS.

These muffins should not be set to rise before nine o'clock at night. They are nice for luncheon or tea, but when they are intended for luncheon put them to rise in the morning and use almost twice as much yeast as you otherwise would. With the quantity of materials stated above, a dozen muf- can be made.

Sour Milk or Buttermilk Muffins.

3 gills of flour.
½ pint of sour milk.
1 egg.
1 teaspoonful of sugar.

½ teaspoonful of soda.
½ teaspoonful of salt.
1 tablespoonful of cold water.
2 level tablespoonfuls of butter.

Melt the butter in a hot cup. Put the dry ingredients in a mixing bowl. Beat the egg till it is light. Dissolve the soda in the water and add it to the milk. Stir well, and add to the dry mixture; then add the egg, and finally the melted butter. Beat well and pour into hot buttered gem-pans. Bake for twenty minutes.

Graham Muffins.

1 gill of cold water.
1 gill of sweet milk.
½ pint of graham.
½ pint of wheat flour.
½ teaspoonful of salt.

2 even teaspoonfuls of baking powder.
2 tablespoonfuls of molasses.
1 egg.

Mix the graham, flour, salt, and baking powder together, and rub through a sieve. Beat the egg till very light, and add the milk and molasses to it. Turn this mixture on the dry ingredients, and beat vigorously for about a minute. Fill a dozen well buttered muffin cups with the batter, and bake in a moderately hot oven for half an hour.

Sugar may be substituted for the molasses. These muffins, when cold, are good for luncheon or dinner.

Rye Muffins.

Make them the same as graham muffins.

Graham Muffins with Sour Milk.

½ pint of sour milk.
½ pint of graham.
1 gill of flour.
2 tablespoonfuls of sugar.

½ teaspoonful of soda.
½ teaspoonful of salt.
1 tablespoonful of water.
1 egg.

Make in the same way flour muffins are made, and bake for half an hour.

Rye Muffins with Sour Milk.

Make these the same as graham with sour milk, substituting rye meal for graham.

Cream of Tartar Muffins.

1 pint of flour, measured before sifting.	½ teaspoonful of salt.
3 scant gills of milk.	1 teaspoonful of sugar.
1 teaspoonful of cream of tartar.	½ tablespoonful of butter.
½ teaspoonful of soda.	½ tablespoonful of lard.

Mix all the dry ingredients and rub them through a sieve and into a bowl. Add the milk, and then the butter and lard, melted. Beat quickly, and put into heated and buttered iron gem-pans. Bake for fifteen minutes in a quick oven. If more convenient, two scant teaspoonfuls of baking powder may be substituted for the soda and cream of tartar.

With these ingredients a dozen muffins can be made.

Blueberry Muffins.

Make these the same as cream of tartar muffins, using, however, two tablespoonfuls of sugar, and lightly stirring into the batter half a pint of blueberries.

Yellow Corn Meal Muffins.

½ pint of yellow corn meal.	2 tablespoonfuls of sugar.
½ pint of flour.	½ teaspoonful of salt.
2½ gills of milk.	1½ teaspoonfuls baking powder.
2 tablespoonfuls of butter.	1 egg.

Mix all the dry ingredients and rub them through a sieve and into a bowl. Melt the butter in a hot cup. Beat the egg till light. Add the milk to it and turn this mixture into the bowl containing the dry ingredients. Add the melted butter, and beat quickly and vigorously. Pour into buttered muffin pans and bake for half an hour in a moderate oven.

White Corn Meal Muffins.

½ pint of white corn meal.
½ pint of sifted flour.
½ pint of milk, generous measure.
2 tablespoonfuls of butter.

1½ teaspoonfuls baking powder.
4 tablespoonfuls of boiling water.
2 tablespoonfuls of sugar.
½ teaspoonful of salt.
1 egg.

Put the butter in a hot cup and pour the boiling water over it. Set on the back part of the stove. Mix all the dry ingredients and rub through a sieve and into a bowl. Beat the egg till light, and add the milk to it. Stir this mixture into the dry ingredients. Add the melted butter and water. Pour into buttered muffin pans and bake for half an hour in a moderate oven.

With these ingredients a dozen muffins can be made.

Corn Bread.

½ pint of flour.
1 gill of corn meal.
½ pint of milk.
2 tablespoonfuls of sugar.
1 generous tablespoonful of butter.

1½ teaspoonfuls baking powder.
⅓ teaspoonful of salt.
2 tablespoonfuls of boiling water.
1 egg.

Mix all the dry ingredients together and rub through a sieve. Beat the egg till light, and add the milk to it; then pour this mixture on the dry ingredients, which should be beaten well. Now add the butter, first melting it in the hot water. Pour the batter into a well buttered pan and bake for half an hour in a moderately hot oven.

Spider Corn Cake.

¾ cupful of corn meal.
¼ cupful of flour.
½ teaspoonful of salt.
1 tablespoonful of sugar.
⅓ teaspoonful of soda.

1 cupful of sweet milk.
½ cupful of sour milk.
1 tablespoonful of butter.
1 egg.

Have a small short-handled, cast-iron frying-pan heating on the top of the stove. Put all the dry ingredients, except the soda, in a sieve and rub through into a bowl. Dissolve the soda in half a cupful of the sweet milk, and add it to the sour. Stir this mixture and the well beaten egg into the dry ingredients. Butter the hot frying-pan with the one tablespoonful of butter, and pour the batter into the pan. Now pour the other half cupful of milk, slowly and gently, over the mixture in the pan (it must not be stirred). Put the pan in a moderately hot oven, and cook the cake for half an hour. Slip out on a hot plate and serve at once.

FRYING-PAN.

Corn Dodgers.

3 gills of corn meal.	½ pint of boiling water, — generous.
½ teaspoonful of salt.	
1 tablespoonful of sugar.	Sausage or pork fat, or any good drippings for frying.
1 teaspoonful of butter.	

Put the meal, salt, sugar, and butter in a bowl and pour the boiling water on the mixture. Beat the batter vigorously for two or three minutes; then shape it with the hands into small, flat cakes. Have in the frying-pan hot fat to the depth of half an inch. When it is smoking hot, put in the cakes and fry on one side until brown, then turn and brown on the other side. Serve very hot.

Baltimore Hominy Bread.

1 gill of fine breakfast hominy.	1 level teaspoonful of salt.
1 gill of milk.	1 tablespoonful of butter.
1 pint of water.	2 eggs.

Wash the hominy, and stir it into the pint of boiling water. Add the salt, and boil gently for one hour, stirring often; or half an hour will do, if you can afford no more time. Take the cooked hominy from the fire and beat the butter into it; then add the milk, and beat for four or five minutes. Beat the eggs till light, and add them to the other ingredients. Butter a deep earthen plate and pour the mixture into it. Bake in rather a hot oven for half an hour. Serve in the dish in which it is baked.

This bread is nice with any kind of meat, but particularly with broiled or fried bacon.

Buckwheat Cakes.

1 pint of buckwheat.	½ teaspoonful of soda.
1 gill of white corn meal.	1 gill of yeast.
1 teaspoonful of salt.	1 generous pint of warm water.
1 tablespoonful of molasses.	2 tablespoonfuls of cold water.

Put the buckwheat, meal, and salt in a deep pail, and add to the mixture the water, yeast, and molasses. Beat vigorously for twenty minutes. Cover the pail and set in a warm place until morning. In the morning rub the soda through a fine sieve, letting it fall on the batter. Beat well. Fry on a griddle, serving as soon as cooked. Reserve one pint of the batter for raising the next batch of cakes. It should be kept in the refrigerator or the cellar.

Remember that success in making buckwheat cakes depends largely upon a thorough beating and careful raising.

Sour Milk Griddle Cakes.

1 pint of sour milk.	1 teaspoonful of sugar.
1 generous pint of sifted flour.	1 tablespoonful of butter.
1 teaspoonful of salt.	1 tablespoonful of water.
1 rounded teaspoonful of soda.	1 egg.

Dissolve the soda in the water and stir into the sour milk. Add the flour, salt, and sugar, and beat well; then add the egg, well beaten, and the butter, melted. If there be plenty of sour cream, use a gill, and omit the butter. Put the cream in the measure and then fill up with the sour milk.

Baking Powder Griddle Cakes.

½ pint of sweet milk.	1 teaspoonful of sugar.
½ pint of flour.	1 teaspoonful of baking powder.
⅓ teaspoonful of salt.	2 tablespoonfuls of melted butter.

Mix all the dry ingredients and rub through a sieve. Pour the milk upon them, and beat well. Add the butter, and beat a minute longer. Fry in small cakes on a griddle.

Sour Milk Indian Griddle Cakes.

Make these the same as flour griddle cakes, using half flour and half corn meal.

Sour Milk Graham Griddle Cakes.

Make these the same as the Indian, substituting an equal quantity of graham for corn meal.

Hominy Griddle Cakes.

1 pint of boiling water.	½ pint of milk.
1 gill of fine breakfast hominy.	1 teaspoonful of salt.
½ pint of flour.	1 egg, — two would be better.

Put the hominy and half the salt in the boiling water, and cook for half an hour, stirring frequently. At the end of that time take from the fire and add to it the milk, flour, and remainder of the salt, and beat vigorously for fifteen minutes; then add the eggs, whites and yolks beaten separately. Fry in very small cakes on a hot griddle.

Hominy Griddle Cakes with Sour Milk.

½ pint of cooked hominy.
½ pint of sour milk.
½ pint of flour.
½ teaspoonful of salt.

½ teaspoonful of soda.
1 tablespoonful of water.
1 egg.

Have the hominy freshly cooked or warmed over. Dissolve the soda in the cold water and stir into the sour milk. Add the flour, salt, and hominy, and beat well; then put in the egg, also well beaten. Fry in small cakes.

Ground Rice Griddle Cakes.

1 pint of milk.
1½ gills of water.
3 gills of wheat flour.
2 tablespoonfuls of rice flour.

1 tablespoonful of sugar.
½ teaspoonful of salt.
¼ teaspoonful of soda.
2 eggs.

Put the milk on to heat in the double-boiler. Mix the rice flour with one gill of the water and stir into the boiling milk. Cook for twenty minutes, stirring often. Turn the cooked mixture into a large bowl and stir occasionally while cooling. This is to prevent the forming of a crust on the batter. When cold, add the salt and sugar, and the soda, dissolved in half a gill of cold water. Now beat in the flour. Finally add the eggs, whites and yolks beaten separately. Fry in small cakes on a hot griddle, and serve immediately.

Blueberry Griddle Cakes.

½ pint of sour milk.
½ pint of flour.
¼ pint of blueberries.

½ teaspoonful of soda.
½ teaspoonful of salt.
1 tablespoonful of water.

Dissolve the soda in the cold water. Stir this into the sour milk. Now add the flour and salt, and beat well. Stir the berries in very gently. Fry the same as any other griddle cakes.

Bread Griddle Cakes.

1 pint of stale bread.
3 gills of milk.
1 gill of flour.
½ teaspoonful of salt.

¼ nutmeg, grated.
¼ teaspoonful of soda.
2 eggs.
2 tablespoonfuls of sugar.

Soak the bread in the milk for several hours, then rub it through a colander. Add the seasonings, the soda, dissolved in a tablespoonful of cold water, and then the flour. Beat well, and add the eggs, well beaten. Fry on a moderately hot griddle.

These cakes take longer to cook than the ordinary batter cake. If eggs be dear, use two more tablespoonfuls of flour, and omit one egg.

Raised Flannel Cakes.

½ pint of flour.
1 gill of corn meal.
2½ gills of milk.
1 teaspoonful of sugar.

½ teaspoonful of salt.
1 tablespoonful of yeast.
1 egg.
1 tablespoonful of butter.

Boil the milk and pour it on the corn meal. Let this stand until it becomes tepid. Add the yeast, and pour the liquid mixture on the dry ingredients. Beat well; then cover the bowl and let it stand in a warm place over night. In the morning add the egg, white and yolk beaten separately. Fry the cakes on a griddle.

Waffles.

½ pint of milk.
½ pint of flour.
2 tablespoonfuls of butter.

2 eggs.
¼ teaspoonful of salt.

Warm the milk, and melt the butter in it. Let the mixture cool to about blood-heat. Beat the yolks of the eggs till light, and add the milk and butter to them. Pour this

BREAD IN VARIOUS FORMS.

mixture on the flour and beat well. Beat the whites of the eggs to a froth, and stir them into the batter. Add the salt.

WAFFLE-IRON.

Have the waffle-iron hot and well greased, and fry the waffles at once. Serve them the moment they are taken from the irons.

If eggs be scarce, use one egg and half a teaspoonful of baking powder.

In cooking waffles it is important to have both halves of the iron equally hot; and to insure this the iron must be turned frequently, both before and after the batter is poured in.

Hominy Waffles.

½ pint of hot boiled hominy.
½ pint of milk.
1 pint of flour, generous measure.
2 tablespoonfuls of butter.

2 eggs.
1 teaspoonful of baking powder.
½ teaspoonful of salt.

Stir the butter and salt into the hot hominy. Gradually beat in the milk; then let the mixture cool. Mix the baking powder with the flour, and sift into the hominy mixture. Beat well; then add the eggs, well beaten, and cook in hot irons. Serve the waffles the instant they come from the irons.

Raised Wheat Waffles.

1 pint of flour.
3 gills of milk.
⅛ cupful of yeast.
1 tablespoonful of sugar.

2 tablespoonfuls of butter.
½ teaspoonful of salt.
1 egg.

Boil the milk, and, after adding the butter to it, let the mixture stand until cool. Put the flour, sugar, and salt in a bowl. Add the milk and yeast, and beat well for fifteen minutes, or even twenty. Let this batter rise over night. In the morning add the egg, well beaten. Have the waffle-irons hot and well greased, and cook the cakes quickly. They should be served the moment they come from the irons. They will be sufficiently cooked as soon as they are browned on both sides.

CHAPTER XVI.

CAKE.

Raised Fruit Cake.

3 gills of raised dough.
1 gill of butter.
½ gill of wine.
1 gill of flour.
2 gills of sugar.

½ teaspoonful of soda.
3 tablespoonfuls of water.
½ of a nutmeg, grated.
2 eggs.
¾ pound of raisins.

Dissolve the soda in the cold water and work into the dough. Now add the butter, sugar, nutmeg, wine, and the eggs, well beaten. Mix all thoroughly, and then beat in the flour. Stir in the raisins, and put into a deep well buttered bread-pan to rise for one hour. Bake for an hour and a half in a moderately hot oven.

Spice Cake.

¼ cupful of butter.
½ cupful of sugar.
½ cupful of molasses.
2 cupfuls of flour, scant measure.
½ cupful of sour milk.
½ teaspoonful of ginger.

⅛ teaspoonful of salt.
1 teaspoonful of cinnamon.
½ teaspoonful of soda.
¼ of a nutmeg, grated.
The juice and rind of half a lemon.
1 egg

Beat the butter to a cream. Gradually beat into it the sugar, then the spice and lemon, and next the molasses. Now dissolve the soda in one tablespoonful of cold water, and stir it into the sour milk. Add this and the egg, well beaten, to the other ingredients. Lastly, add the flour, and beat briskly for half a minute. Pour into a well buttered pan, and bake in a moderate oven for about fifty minutes.

This cake will keep moist for a week or ten days. If one like fruit, half a cupful of stoned raisins and half a cupful of currants may be stirred lightly into the batter just before it is put in the pan.

Blackberry Jam Cake.

½ cupful of butter.
⅔ cupful of sugar.
1 generous cupful of flour.
⅔ cupful of stoned raisins.
⅔ cupful of blackberry jam.

2 tablespoonfuls of sour cream or milk.
½ teaspoonful of soda.
½ of a nutmeg, grated.
2 eggs.

Beat the butter to a cream, then beat in the sugar. When very light, beat in the jam and nutmeg. Dissolve the soda in one tablespoonful of cold water, and add it to the sour cream. Add this and the egg, well beaten, to the other ingredients. Now add the flour, and beat for half a minute. Sprinkle a tablespoonful of flour over the raisins, and stir them in lightly. Pour the batter into a well buttered pan, and bake for fifty minutes. This makes one small loaf.

This cake may be put away to be used as a pudding when convenient. Steam it for one hour, and serve with a wine sauce. It is almost as good as a plum pudding.

Rich Sponge Cake.

6 large eggs.
3 gills of sugar.

3 gills of flour.
1 lemon.

Grate a little of the lemon rind into a deep saucer. Squeeze the juice on this. Beat the yolks of the eggs and the sugar together until the mixture is a light, spongy mass. Add the lemon juice and rind, and beat a little longer. Beat the whites of the eggs with a whisk until a thick white froth is formed. Cut the flour and whites of eggs into the sugar and yolks, adding only a little at a time, and doing the work lightly and gently, so as not to break down the frothy egg. Pour the mixture into a well buttered pan, and bake in a moderate oven, the time of baking depending upon the thickness of the loaf. If it be three inches deep when put in the pan, it will take one hour to bake. It is essential that the oven should be very slow at first. This will cause the sponge to rise evenly, making the cake tender, rich, and moist.

Plain Sponge Cake.

3 eggs.
3 gills of sugar.
1 pint of flour.
1 gill of cold water.

1 lemon.
1 teaspoonful of cream of tartar.
½ teaspoonful of soda.
¼ teaspoonful of salt.

Beat the eggs together until light. Add the sugar, and beat with a spoon for ten minutes or longer. The sugar and eggs must be beaten until they form a light, spongy mass. Add the juice of the lemon, and beat a little longer. Dissolve the soda in the cold water. Mix the cream of tartar with the flour. Stir the water and soda into the egg mixture; then add the flour. Beat well, and pour into the pans and bake.

These materials will make two sheets, or one sheet and a small, round loaf, or one sheet and one cake, baked in a deep round tin. The round cake can be used for a cream, Washington, or chocolate pie. A part of the batter may be baked in a pudding dish, and served with a liquid sauce; or a part of the batter may be baked in tin muffin cups, putting a teaspoonful in each cup.

This sponge cake is one of the most useful and satisfactory when made properly. Great care must be taken to have the sugar and eggs beaten together thoroughly.

Corn Starch Cake.

1 gill of butter.
1½ gills of sugar.
1½ gills of flour.
½ gill of corn starch.
½ gill of milk.

½ teaspoonful of cream of tartar.
¼ teaspoonful of soda.
2 eggs.
Flavor.

Beat the butter to a cream, and gradually beat the sugar into it. Beat the eggs separately, and stir them into the creamed sugar and butter. Dissolve the soda in the milk, and add this. Mix together the flour, corn starch, and cream of tartar, and add to the other ingredients. Flavor the batter, and beat vigorously for a few seconds; then turn into a well buttered shallow cake pan. Bake for thirty minutes in a moderate oven.

A good flavor for this cake is one tablespoonful of lemon juice and a light grating of the rind of a fresh lemon.

Angel Cake.

5 whites of eggs.
1 scant gill of pastry flour, measured after sifting.

1½ gills of powdered sugar.
½ teaspoonful of cream of tartar.
½ teaspoonful of vanilla.

Mix the cream of tartar with the flour, and sift four times. Beat the whites of the eggs to a stiff, dry froth. Sift the powdered sugar on the eggs, and beat for three minutes. Add the vanilla. Gradually add the flour, and beat it in quickly. Pour the batter into an ungreased pan, and put into rather a cool oven. Bake for about forty minutes.

When the cake is baked, take the pan from the oven and invert it, letting it rest on a sieve or rack, so that there shall be a current of air under and over the pan while the cake is cooling.

Success in making angel cake depends upon the proper beating of the eggs and a slow oven.

Rich Cup Cake.

½ pint of sugar.
⅓ cupful of butter.
3 gills of flour.
½ gill of milk.

2 large eggs.
½ teaspoonful of cream of tartar.
¼ teaspoonful of soda.
Flavor.

Beat the butter to a cream, and gradually beat the sugar into it. Beat the eggs separately, and add to the sugar and butter. Dissolve the soda in the milk, and stir into the mixture. Now add the flour, in which the cream of tartar should be mixed. Flavor with any spice or extract you like, or with the grated yellow rind of a lemon and one tablespoonful of the juice. Pour the batter into a buttered pan, and bake in a moderate oven for forty-five minutes, if in a deep loaf; but if in a sheet, thirty minutes' time will be enough.

Plain Cup Cake.

1 gill of sugar.
2 tablespoonfuls of butter.
1 gill of milk.
3 gills of flour, scant measure.

1 large egg.
½ teaspoonful of soda.
1 teaspoonful of cream of tartar.
Flavor.

Beat the butter to a cream, and gradually beat the sugar into it. Add the egg, unbeaten, and beat the mixture vigorously for three or four minutes. Add the flavor and milk, and lastly the flour, in which the soda and cream of tartar should be thoroughly mixed. Pour the batter into a shallow cake pan, and sift powdered sugar over it. Bake in a moderate oven for twenty-five minutes.

Cold Water Cake.

½ pint of sugar.
1 gill of cold water.
1 scant gill of butter.
2 small eggs.
3 gills of flour.
½ teaspoonful of soda.

½ pint of citron, currants, and raisins, in equal parts; the raisins to be stoned and chopped.
½ teaspoonful of cinnamon.
½ teaspoonful of grated nutmeg.

Beat the butter to a cream, and gradually beat into it the sugar. Add the yolks of the eggs, and beat well. Dissolve the soda in the water, and add to the mixture. Beat vigorously until the water will not separate from the other ingredients. Now beat in the spice. Beat the whites of the eggs to a stiff froth, and add them to the mixture. Now add the flour, and finally stir the fruit in lightly. Bake in one deep loaf, or in a thick sheet. If in a loaf, cook for one hour; if in a sheet, about thirty-five minutes.

Swiss Cake.

2 tablespoonfuls of butter.	½ pint of flour.
3 gills of sugar.	1½ teaspoonfuls baking powder.
½ pint of milk.	Flavor to taste.

Measure the butter scantily, and make it soft in a warm bowl. Beat the sugar into it. Have the eggs well beaten, and then beat them with the sugar and butter for five minutes. Add the flavor, then the milk, and finally the flour, in which the baking powder should be mixed. Bake for about twenty-five minutes in a buttered, shallow pan. The cake is to be eaten fresh.

Tea Cake.

1 gill of sugar.	1 egg.
1 gill of milk.	1½ teaspoonfuls baking powder.
½ pint of flour, scant measure.	⅙ of a nutmeg, grated.
1 tablespoonful of butter.	

Beat the butter until soft. Beat the sugar into it. Add the unbeaten egg, and beat vigorously for five minutes. Add the nutmeg and milk, then the flour, in which the baking powder should be mixed. Beat vigorously for a few seconds, and pour into a buttered cake-pan. Bake in a moderately hot oven for twenty minutes, and serve warm.

Blueberry Cake.

1 generous pint of flour.	2 tablespoonfuls of butter.
½ pint of milk.	½ teaspoonful of salt.
1 gill of sugar.	1 egg.
2 heaped teaspoonfuls of baking powder.	½ pint of blueberries.

Mix the baking powder, sugar, and salt with the flour, and rub through a sieve. Rub the butter into this mixture. Beat the egg till light, and add the milk to it. Add this to the dry ingredients, and beat well. Now add the berries, stirring as little as possible. Spread the mixture in a well buttered shallow baking pan, having it about an inch and a half thick. Bake in a moderately hot oven for about twenty-five minutes. Serve hot.

The batter may be put in buttered muffin tins, and baked for about twenty minutes. This will fill twelve muffin cups.

Hermits.

1½ gills (¾ of a cupful) of maple sugar.	1 tablespoonful of milk.
1 gill of butter.	¼ teaspoonful of clove.
1 pint and a gill (2½ cupfuls) of flour.	1 teaspoonful of cinnamon.
1 egg.	½ teaspoonful of soda.
	1 gill of currants.

Beat the butter to a cream, and gradually beat in the sugar and spice. Dissolve the soda in the milk, and beat this into the sugar and butter. Add the egg, well beaten, and finally the flour and currants. Roll out about an inch thick, and cut in squares. Bake in rather a quick oven for about twelve minutes.

The sugar should be the soft maple. The clove may be omitted. If maple sugar is not to be had, white sugar may be used.

Beat the butter to a cream, and gradually beat into it the sugar. Add the yolks of the eggs, and beat well. Dissolve the soda in the water, and add to the mixture. Beat vigorously until the water will not separate from the other ingredients. Now beat in the spice. Beat the whites of the eggs to a stiff froth, and add them to the mixture. Now add the flour, and finally stir the fruit in lightly. Bake in one deep loaf, or in a thick sheet. If in a loaf, cook for one hour; if in a sheet, about thirty-five minutes.

Swiss Cake.

2 tablespoonfuls of butter.
3 gills of sugar.
½ pint of milk.

½ pint of flour.
1½ teaspoonfuls baking powder.
Flavor to taste.

Measure the butter scantily, and make it soft in a warm bowl. Beat the sugar into it. Have the eggs well beaten, and then beat them with the sugar and butter for five minutes. Add the flavor, then the milk, and finally the flour, in which the baking powder should be mixed. Bake for about twenty-five minutes in a buttered, shallow pan. The cake is to be eaten fresh.

Tea Cake.

1 gill of sugar.
1 gill of milk.
½ pint of flour, scant measure.
1 tablespoonful of butter.

1 egg.
1½ teaspoonfuls baking powder.
⅙ of a nutmeg, grated.

Beat the butter until soft. Beat the sugar into it. Add the unbeaten egg, and beat vigorously for five minutes. Add the nutmeg and milk, then the flour, in which the baking powder should be mixed. Beat vigorously for a few seconds, and pour into a buttered cake-pan. Bake in a moderately hot oven for twenty minutes, and serve warm.

Blueberry Cake.

1 generous pint of flour.	2 tablespoonfuls of butter.
½ pint of milk.	½ teaspoonful of salt.
1 gill of sugar.	1 egg.
2 heaped teaspoonfuls of baking powder.	½ pint of blueberries.

Mix the baking powder, sugar, and salt with the flour, and rub through a sieve. Rub the butter into this mixture. Beat the egg till light, and add the milk to it. Add this to the dry ingredients, and beat well. Now add the berries, stirring as little as possible. Spread the mixture in a well buttered shallow baking pan, having it about an inch and a half thick. Bake in a moderately hot oven for about twenty-five minutes. Serve hot.

The batter may be put in buttered muffin tins, and baked for about twenty minutes. This will fill twelve muffin cups.

Hermits.

1½ gills (¾ of a cupful) of maple sugar.	1 tablespoonful of milk.
1 gill of butter.	¼ teaspoonful of clove.
1 pint and a gill (2½ cupfuls) of flour.	1 teaspoonful of cinnamon.
	½ teaspoonful of soda.
1 egg.	1 gill of currants.

Beat the butter to a cream, and gradually beat in the sugar and spice. Dissolve the soda in the milk, and beat this into the sugar and butter. Add the egg, well beaten, and finally the flour and currants. Roll out about an inch thick, and cut in squares. Bake in rather a quick oven for about twelve minutes.

The sugar should be the soft maple. The clove may be omitted. If maple sugar is not to be had, white sugar may be used.

into the mixture of butter and sugar. Dissolve the soda in half a tablespoonful of cold water. Stir this mixture into the sour milk and add all to the sugar, butter, and eggs. Now stir in the flour. Cover the mixture and set it away in a cold place until morning. In the morning sprinkle the moulding board with flour and put about one fourth of the dough on it. Roll this down to the thickness of half an inch and cut into round cakes with a hole in the centre. If you do not possess a regular doughnut cutter, a biscuit cutter will do, as a piece can be cut from the centre with a thimble. Fry in lard for about three minutes.

It is supposed that pastry flour will be used. If, however, the "new process" flour be taken, omit one eighth of the measure.

Dropped Doughnuts.

1 gill of milk.
1 gill of sugar.
3 gills of flour.
⅓ teaspoonful of salt.
⅓ of a nutmeg, grated.

The grated yellow rind of a lemon.
1 heaped teaspoonful of baking powder.
1 egg.

Beat the white of the egg to a stiff froth and beat the yolk and sugar with it for three minutes. Add the seasonings, next the milk, and finally the flour, in which the baking powder should be mixed. Beat well. Drop a teaspoonful of this mixture into hot fat and cook for about four minutes, turning the doughnuts frequently. Lift them from the fat with a wire spoon or a fork. Do not stick the fork into them. When they are drained, sprinkle them with powdered sugar. Be careful not to have the fat too hot and to hold the teaspoonful of batter close to the fat, and the doughnuts will come up in round balls. These are very delicate.

Strawberry Short Cake.

For the Cake.

3 gills of flour.	2 heaped tablespoonfuls of butter.
1 gill of milk — generous measure.	
1 tablespoonful of sugar.	1 heaped teaspoonful of baking powder.
¼ teaspoonful of salt.	

Mix the dry ingredients together and rub twice through a sieve. Rub the butter through this mixture; then wet with the milk. Butter a large, deep tin pie plate. Divide the dough into two parts and roll them out the size of the plate. Lay them in the plate, one on top of the other, and bake in a quick oven for twenty minutes. On taking the two cakes from the oven, tear them apart. Place the under one on a warm plate and butter well; upon this spread one pint of strawberries, slightly crushed, and mixed with a generous gill of sugar; put on the top part of the cake, and serve immediately.

This is the old-fashioned strawberry short cake. Currants, blackberries, peaches, etc., may be substituted for the strawberries when that fruit is out of season.

Strawberry Short Cake, No. 2.

For the Cake.

½ pint of flour.	3 tablespoonfuls of milk.
1 gill of sugar.	1 teaspoonful of baking powder.
1 heaped tablespoonful of butter.	1 egg.

Beat the butter to a cream; then gradually beat in the sugar. Now add the unbeaten egg, and beat the mixture vigorously for three or four minutes. Beat in the milk and then the flour, in which the baking powder should be mixed. Bake this batter in two well buttered deep tin plates. They will require about twenty minutes' time in a moderate oven. When baked, put them on plates to cool.

Filling.

1 pint of stemmed strawberries.
1½ pints of whipped cream.
1 gill of sugar.

1 tablespoonful of gelatine.
½ gill of water.

Measure the gelatine generously and put it in a cup with the cold water. Let it soak for an hour or more; then place the cup in a pan of boiling water and stir until the gelatine is dissolved. Have the whipped cream in a bowl and set it in a pan of ice water. Stir the sugar and dissolved gelatine into it. Continue stirring this mixture until it thickens. Spread half of this cream on one of the cakes, and on this spread about two thirds of the strawberries. Put the second cake on top of this. Spread the remainder of the cream and strawberries on this, and serve at once.

The gelatine may be omitted. In that case, crush the strawberries and sugar together. Put a layer of strawberries on the cakes, then a layer of whipped cream.

Icing.

1 egg white.
½ pint of powdered sugar.
1 teaspoonful of water.

1 teaspoonful of lemon juice, or
½ teaspoonful of vanilla.

Put the unbeaten white of the egg into a bowl, and gradually beat into it the powdered sugar. When smooth and light, add the water and sugar. Spread smoothly on the cake and let it stand in a cool place until it hardens. If in a hurry to have it harden, omit the water.

Chocolate Icing.

Make the white icing. Shave one ounce of plain chocolate and put it into a small pan with three tablespoonfuls of powdered sugar and one of boiling water. Stir over a hot fire until smooth and glossy, and then stir this into the icing. If it seems too thick, add a few drops of water.

Do not use the lemon in the white icing when the chocolate is to be added.

CHAPTER XVII.

PASTRY.

Delicate Paste.

1 pint of sifted flour.	1 tablespoonful of sugar.
1 gill of butter.	1½ teaspoonfuls baking powder.
½ gill of lard.	1 teaspoonful of salt.

Mix all the dry ingredients together and rub through a sieve into a bowl. Add the butter and lard, and cut and mix with a knife until the shortening is in fine bits. Now add the cold water, still stirring with a knife. Sprinkle the board lightly with flour, and turn the paste out upon it. Roll down into a square sheet about one fourth of an inch thick. Fold up and roll down again. Do this four times; then put away to chill. This paste is suitable for meat and fruit pies, baked dumplings, tarts, etc.

Plain Paste.

1 pint of sifted flour.	1 teaspoonful of sugar.
2 tablespoonfuls of butter.	2 teaspoonfuls of salt.
3 tablespoonfuls of lard.	1 generous gill of cold water.
2 teaspoonfuls of baking powder.	

Make this the same as delicate paste, except that it is to be rolled but twice. This paste answers for meat and fruit pies when one does not wish to use pastry as rich as the delicate paste.

Mince Meat.

2½ pounds of the round of beef.
2 quarts of chopped apples.
½ pint of chopped suet.
1½ pints of stoned raisins.
1 pint of currants.
¼ pound of citron.
1 quart of sugar.
½ pint of molasses.

3 pints of cider.
2 tablespoonfuls of salt.
4 tablespoonfuls of cinnamon.
1 tablespoonful of allspice.
1 tablespoonful of mace.
1 level teaspoonful of clove.
4 nutmegs, grated.
4 lemons.

Put the beef in a small stewpan and just cover with boiling water. Cook for three hours, having the water only bubble at one side of the stewpan. Take from the fire and let the meat cool in the water, with the cover off the stewpan. When cold, remove all fat and gristle, and chop the meat rather fine. Put it in a large bowl with all the other ingredients except the cider, and mix thoroughly. Now add the cider, and let the mixture stand in a cold place over night. In the morning turn the mince meat into a porcelain kettle and heat slowly to the boiling point; then simmer gently for one hour. Put the mixture into stone jars and set away in a cold place; or it may be put in glass jars and sealed. It will keep for years in this way. If one wish to add brandy or wine, it may be done now or at the time that the pies are made. If economy be necessary, half the amount of currants and raisins given will answer. On the other hand, if one can afford it, when the pies are being made, one tumbler of jelly or marmalade to three or four pies will be found a great improvement.

Apple Pie, Sliced.

3 pints of pared and sliced apples.
⅙ of a nutmeg, grated, or 1 teaspoonful of cinnamon.

½ pint of sugar.
4 tablespoonfuls of cold water.
Half the rule for delicate paste.

Pare the apples and cut into thick slices. Line a large plate with paste and then fill with the apples, being careful not to break the paste. Sprinkle with the sugar and nutmeg, and then with the water. Roll the remainder of the paste a little larger than the pie plate. Make a slight opening in the centre. Cover the pie with this, tucking the edges under the lower crust. Bake in a moderately hot oven for one hour. Reduce the heat after the first half-hour.

Stewed Apple Pie.

1 pint of stewed apple.
½ pint of sugar.

1/; of a nutmeg, grated.
Half the rule for delicate paste.

Cover with a thin crust a pie plate of medium size. Roll a piece of the paste into a narrow strip about one fourth of an inch thick, and long enough to go around the edge of the plate. Wet the edge of the undercrust with cold water and lay the narrow strip of paste over it. Now fill the plate with the seasoned apple. Roll the remainder of the paste a little larger than the pie plate. Place a larger plate on this, upside down, and cut around it. Remove the plate, cut a slit in the centre of the paste, and cover the pie, fulling the crust on a little. Bake in a moderately hot oven for forty-five minutes. Less sugar may be used, and any flavor may be substituted for the nutmeg. It must be remembered, however, that nutmeg, cinnamon, and lemon are the best flavors for apple.

Mince Pies.

Make mince pies in the same way as directed for stewed apple, but bake them for one hour.

Peach Pie.

Make this in the same way as sliced apple, but use only half as much sugar.

Berry Pies.

1½ pints of blueberries or black- | 1 tablespoonful of flour.
berries. | 2 tablespoonfuls of water.
2 tablespoonfuls of sugar. | Half the rule for delicate paste.

Make this in the same way as sliced apple pie, and bake in a moderate oven for fifty minutes.

Sour and juicy berries will require more sugar and no water.

Lemon Pie.

1 tablespoonful of corn starch. | ½ pint of water.
2 tablespoonfuls powdered sugar. | ½ pint of granulated sugar.
½ saltspoonful of salt. | 2 eggs.
1 lemon. | ¼ the rule for delicate paste.

Mix the corn starch with one third of the water, and put the remainder on to boil. Stir the sugar, salt, and corn starch into the boiling water, and cook for one minute, stirring all the time. Take from the fire, and add the juice and the grated yellow rind of the lemon. When cool, add the yolks of the eggs, well beaten. Line a deep plate with the paste and fill with the mixture. Bake in a moderate oven for half an hour. Take from the oven and cool for fifteen minutes.

Beat the whites of the eggs to a stiff dry froth, and then beat the powdered sugar into them. Spread this meringue over the pie, and place in the oven. Cook for twelve minutes with the oven door open; then put away to get icy cold.

Squash Pie.

1 pint of milk. | ⅙ of a nutmeg, grated.
1 pint of stewed squash. | 2 eggs.
1 level tablespoonful of butter. | A piece of stick cinnamon about
1 level teaspoonful of salt. | two inches long, or,
1 gill of sugar. | 1 teaspoonful of ground cinnamon.

Put the milk and cinnamon on the fire in the double-boiler, and cook for twenty minutes. Rub the squash through a fine strainer, and add the salt, sugar, butter, and nutmeg to it. Pour the boiling milk on this mixture. Remove the cinnamon, and beat well; then set away to cool. When cool, add the eggs, which should have been thoroughly beaten with a spoon. Line a deep piate with pastry and pour the squash mixture into it. Bake for forty-five minutes in a moderate oven.

Sweet Potato Pie.

Make these the same as squash pies; using, however, a scant measure of sugar.

Cream Pie.

1 gill of sugar.	4 tablespoonfuls of milk.
½ pint of sifted flour, scant measure.	1 egg.
	1 teaspoonful of baking powder.
3 tablespoonfuls of butter.	Flavor.

Make this the same as cup cake and bake in a deep tin plate, in a moderate oven, for about twenty minutes. When the cake is cool, split it with a sharp knife, and fill with a mixture made as follows: —

Filling.

½ pint of milk.	½ saltspoonful of salt.
3 tablespoonfuls of sugar.	1 egg.
1 level tablespoonful of flour.	Flavor.

Put the milk in the double-boiler and set on the fire. Mix the flour and sugar together and add the unbeaten egg to these ingredients. Beat with a spoon until light; then stir into the boiling milk and cook for fifteen minutes, stirring often. Now add the salt, and take from the fire. When cool, add the flavor, which may be anything you choose. If orange, lemon, or vanilla extract, use half a teaspoonful. Use the same flavor for the cake.

Washington Pie.

Make the cake the same as for cream pie, but bake it in two deep tin plates for about twelve minutes. Spread one sheet with any kind of jelly or marmalade. Lay the second sheet on top of this and dredge with powdered sugar.

Chocolate Pie.

Make the same as cream pie, but add to the cream one tablespoonful of chocolate dissolved with one tablespoonful of sugar in half a tablepoonful of boiling water. Cover the cake with a chocolate icing.

Berry Tart.

1½ pints of berries.	3 tablespoonfuls of water.
1 gill of sugar.	Half the rule for delicate paste.
1 tablespoonful of flour.	

Put the berries in an oval vegetable dish that has a broad rim. Mix the sugar and flour together and sprinkle over the berries. Pour the water over the mixture. Roll the paste to the shape of the top of the dish, but a little larger. Prick with a fork, and cover the top of the dish, turning in the edges. Bake in a moderate oven for about fifty minutes. When cold, sprinkle powdered sugar over the crust, and serve.

The sugar is for blackberries, blueberries, strawberries, raspberries, and cherries. Currants and gooseberries will require twice as much sweetening.

The dish may be filled with apples or peaches, cut in quarters, instead of the berries. In that case use twice as much water, and flavor with a little nutmeg.

These tarts are much more healthful than pies, the under-crust of which is apt to be soggy.

Apple Turnovers.

½ pint of flour.	¼ teaspoonful of salt.
1 gill of milk.	1 tablespoonful of butter.
1 teaspoonful of baking powder.	1 egg.
1½ tablespoonfuls of sugar.	10 tablespoonfuls of apple sauce.

Mix the flour, salt, baking powder, and sugar. Rub this mixture through a sieve and then rub into it the butter. Now beat the egg till light, and add to it the milk. Stir this liquid into the dry ingredients. Sprinkle the moulding board with flour, and roll down the dough to the thickness of about one fourth of an inch. Cut this dough into cakes the size of a saucer. It is a good way to lay a saucer upside down on the dough and cut around it with a jagging-iron or knife.

Put two tablespoonfuls of stewed, sweetened, and seasoned apples on each piece of dough; fold over, and roll up, pinching the edges together. Have on the fire a kettle containing hot fat about five or six inches deep. When the fat begins to smoke, put in a few turnovers and cook for eight minutes. Drain on brown paper. They are good hot or cold.

The apple used in turnovers may be flavored with either cinnamon or nutmeg.

CHAPTER XVIII.

PUDDINGS.

Steamed Apple Pudding.

1 pint of flour.	½ teaspoonful of salt.
½ pint of milk, scant.	½ cupful of sugar.
1 heaping teaspoonful of baking powder.	½ tablespoonful of butter.
	3 pints of apples.

Pare and core the apples and cut them into eighths. Mix the flour, salt, baking powder, and half a tablespoonful of sugar together, and rub through a sieve. Warm a little of the milk, and dissolve the butter in it. Add the remainder of the milk to this, and pour upon the flour. Stir into a smooth ball, and, putting it on a board that has been well sprinkled with flour, roll very thin. Line a buttered melon mould with it, having the sheet of dough large enough to

MELON MOULD.

STEAMER.

hang over the sides of the mould. Now fill the mould with the apples and sprinkle the sugar over them. Bring the edges of the paste together and put the cover on the mould. Steam for two hours and a half. At serving time turn out on a flat dish, and serve with wine or nutmeg sauce.

This makes rather a large pudding for three people, if the first part of the dinner has been substantial. If one prefer, half the quantity may be made.

Quick Steamed Apple Pudding.

3 pints of pared and quartered apples.	½ pint of water.
1 tablespoonful of butter.	1 gill of milk.
½ pint of flour.	¼ teaspoonful of salt.
1 gill of sugar.	1 teaspoonful of baking powder.
	¼ of a nutmeg, grated.

Put the apples, water, sugar, and nutmeg into a broad porcelain or granite-ware saucepan, and set on the fire. When the apples begin to boil, set back where they will cook gently. Now mix the flour, salt, and baking powder together and rub through a sieve. Rub the butter into this dry mixture and then wet with the milk, stirring rapidly into a soft dough. Sprinkle the bread board with flour, and roll the dough into a round piece about the size of the top of the saucepan. Lay this on the apples; then put on the cover, and continue the gentle cooking for thirty minutes. Now lift the crust to a plate for a moment, and turn the apple into a pudding dish. Place the crust over it, and serve with nutmeg sauce or creamy sauce.

Baked Apple Dumplings.

½ pint of flour.	3 tablespoonfuls of sugar.
2 tablespoonfuls of butter.	½ gill of cold water.
1 tablespoonful of lard.	5 apples.
½ teaspoonful of baking powder.	A little nutmeg.
½ teaspoonful of salt.	

Make the paste the same as directed for delicate paste. (See Pastry, page 253.) Pare and core the apples. Cut the paste in five equal parts, and roll one piece at a time until large enough to cover the apple. Place an apple in the centre and fill the hole with sugar. Grate a little nutmeg over it. Now draw the paste over the fruit, pressing the edges together, and place in a baking pan, the rough side down. Bake in a moderately hot oven for half an hour. Serve with a hot liquid sauce.

Steamed Apple Dumplings.

Make these the same as baked dumplings, using, however, only half as much shortening; and steam for forty-five minutes.

Apple Tapioca Pudding.

1 gill of tapioca.	½ teaspoonful of salt.
1¼ pints of cold water.	A heaping quart of pared, cored, and quartered apples.
1 gill of sugar.	
1 tablespoonful of lemon juice.	

Wash the tapioca and let it soak over night in the water. In the morning put the tapioca and water in the double-boiler and cook for one hour. Now stir into the cooked tapioca the salt, sugar, lemon, and apples. Pour the mixture into a pudding dish, and bake in a moderate oven for an hour and a quarter. Let it stand in a warm place for an hour before it is served. Powdered sugar and cream should be served with it.

Apple and Indian Pudding.

1 gill of molasses.	½ teaspoonful of salt.
1 quart of milk.	1 pint of pared and quartered apples.
1 gill of Indian meal.	
1 tablespoonful of butter.	¼ of a nutmeg, grated.

Have the milk boiling, and pour it gradually upon the meal, stirring all the while. Turn into the double-boiler, and cook for an hour, stirring often. Now add the molasses, butter, salt, and nutmeg, and beat well. Stir in the apples, turn into a buttered pudding dish, and cook in a slow oven for two hours and a half. The apples may be sour or sweet, but sweet are the better. Serve with cream or with hard sauce.

Peach Tapioca Pudding.

Make this the same as apple tapioca, but use fresh, canned, or evaporated peaches. If the last named be used, soak them over night in water enough to cover them, and in the morning simmer them for ten or twenty minutes.

Sponge Apple Pudding.

4 large apples.	1 egg.
½ pint of flour.	1 teaspoonful of baking powder.
1 gill of sugar.	¼ teaspoonful of salt.
1 gill of milk.	

Have the apples pared and sliced. Beat the egg until light; then add the sugar, and beat five minutes longer. Now add the milk, and finally the flour, with which should be mixed the baking powder. Beat the batter, and pour it into a well buttered pudding dish that will hold about a quart. Cover with the apples, and bake in a moderately hot oven for about forty minutes. Serve with a hot liquid sauce.

Prune Pudding.

2 dozen prunes.	1 lemon.
⅓ package of gelatine.	1 gill of sugar.
1 quart of water.	Liquid cochineal.

Soak the gelatine in half a pint of cold water. Wash the prunes thoroughly, and put them in a stewpan with a pint and a half of water. Cook them slowly for two hours. Take the prunes from the liquid, and remove the stones. Measure the liquid, and if there be more than half a pint, boil it rapidly until reduced to that amount. If, however, there be less than half a pint, add enough water to make the full measure. Return the liquid and prunes to the fire. Color with a few drops of cochineal. Add the lemon juice, soaked gelatine, and sugar. Stir the mixture until the gelatine is dissolved;

then turn it into a mould, and set away to harden. Serve this pudding with either whipped cream or soft custard.

If the flavor of wine be liked, the water in which the prunes were cooked may be reduced to a gill, and a gill of wine be added to the mixture.

Prune Tapioca Pudding.

½ cupful of tapioca.
3 cupfuls of cold water.
1 cupful of prunes.

½ teaspoonful of salt.
1 tablespoonful of lemon juice.
½ cupful of sugar.

Wash the tapioca and soak it over night in the three cupfuls of cold water. In the morning put the tapioca and water in the double-boiler and cook for one hour. Before putting the tapioca on to cook, wash the prunes, and, putting them in a saucepan with cold water enough to cover them, place on the fire. Let them simmer gently until they absorb all the water; then turn out on a plate to cool, and remove the stones.

When the tapioca has been cooking for an hour, stir all the seasonings into it. Spread a layer of the tapioca in a small pudding dish; then sprinkle with prunes, next with another layer of tapioca, and finally with the remainder of the prunes. Cover with the tapioca and bake in a moderate oven for one hour. Take the pudding from the oven and let it partially cool; then serve with sugar and cream, or with soft custard.

Raspberry Tapioca Pudding.

½ gill of flaked tapioca.
1½ gills of water.
½ gill of sugar.

1 pint of raspberries.
½ tablespoonful of lemon juice.
¼ teaspoonful of salt.

After measuring the tapioca, turn it out on the moulding board and crush it as fine as possible with the rolling pin. Now wash it, and soak it in the cold water for three hours or longer, — better over night, if there be time. Put the soaked tapioca in a double-boiler and cook it until it is perfectly clear. If it has been soaked over night it will cook in half an hour, but if soaked for only three hours it will require cooking for an hour and a half. When the tapioca is clear, add the sugar, salt, and lemon; then take the dish from the fire and stir in the raspberries. Rinse a bowl with cold water and pour the pudding into it. Set away to cool. At serving time turn out the pudding on a flat dish and surround it with whipped cream; or it may be served with plain cream.

Little Fruit Puddings.

½ pint of unsifted flour.	1 teaspoonful of baking powder.
1 gill of sweet milk.	¼ teaspoonful of salt.
1 tablespoonful of sugar.	18 tablespoonfuls of stewed and sweetened fruit.
1 tablespoonful of butter.	

Put the flour, sugar, salt, and baking powder together. Mix well, and rub through the sieve. Rub the butter into these ingredients. Pour the milk on this mixture, and beat well. Have six little earthen cups well buttered. Put a tablespoonful of the batter in each cup, and draw it to the sides of the cups, making a well in the batter. Put three tablespoonfuls of stewed and sweetened fruit in these wells, and cover with half a tablespoonful of the batter. Bake the puddings in a moderately hot oven for half an hour. Turn out on a warm dish and serve with a hot sauce.

Blueberry Pudding.

2 tablespoonfuls of butter.	⅓ of a nutmeg.
½ cupful of sugar.	⅓ teaspoonful of soda.
¾ cupful of flour.	1 tablespoonful of sour milk.
1½ cupfuls of blueberries.	1 teaspoonful of cold water.
1 egg.	

Beat the butter to a cream, and add the sugar gradually, beating well. Now add the egg, well beaten, and beat vigorously for three minutes. Grate in the nutmeg. Dissolve the soda in the teaspoonful of cold water; add the sour milk to this, and stir all into the butter and sugar mixture. Now stir in the flour, and lastly add the berries, stirring lightly. Turn into a well buttered mould and steam for two hours. Serve with a hot sauce. Foaming sauce is particularly good with this pudding.

Blueberry Pudding, No. 2.

½ a five-cent loaf of baker's bread.	2 tablespoonfuls of butter.
3 gills of milk.	3 tablespoonfuls of sugar.
2 eggs.	½ teaspoonful of salt.
1 pint of blueberries.	¼ of a nutmeg, grated.

Cut the bread in thin slices and spread the butter on it. Line a pudding dish with the bread, and sprinkle thickly with berries. Put in another layer of bread, then the remainder of the berries, and finish with bread. Beat the eggs, sugar, salt, and nutmeg together, and add the milk to them. Pour this custard over the bread and berries and put away in a cool place for two or three hours. Steam for one hour and a quarter, and serve with hot sauce.

The pudding may be covered with a plate and baked in a slow oven for forty-five minutes, if it be inconvenient to steam it.

Berry Pudding.

½ pint of flour, generous measure.	1 tablespoonful of butter.
1 gill of milk.	1 heaping teaspoonful of baking powder.
1 gill of sugar.	
3 gills blueberries or blackberries.	1 egg.

Beat the butter and sugar together. Add the egg, well beaten, then the milk, and finally the flour and baking powder, mixed together. Beat well, and then stir the berries in lightly. Turn into a buttered pudding dish, and bake in a moderately hot oven for forty-five minutes. Serve with a hot sauce.

PUDDINGS. 267

This pudding may be steamed. It will require two hours' time for that mode of cooking.

Blackberry Pudding.

Make this in the same manner as the first blueberry pudding, substituting blackberries for the blueberries.

Steamed Black Pudding.

1 pint of blueberries or blackberries.	½ pint of water.
	⅛ of a nutmeg, grated.
1 quart of stale bread.	2 tablespoonfuls of butter.
1 gill of sugar.	

Cut the bread in thin slices and butter them. Simmer the berries, sugar, water, and nutmeg together for ten minutes. Butter a mould or a large bowl and spread a layer of the buttered bread in it. Cover this with berries and juice; then put in another layer of bread. Continue this until all the materials are used, having the last layer one of fruit. Let the pudding stand for two hours, and then steam for one hour and half. At the end of that time turn into a pudding dish and serve with a hot sauce.

Baker's bread is the best for this dish.

Rhubarb Pudding.

½ a five-cent loaf of baker's bread.	1½ gills of sugar.
½ pint of rhubarb, generous measure.	3 tablespoonfuls of butter.

Have the butter soft. Cut the bread in thin slices, and spread the butter on it; then dip it in cold water. Have the rhubarb peeled and cut in thin slices before measuring. Put a layer of bread in a pudding dish, then a layer of rhubarb. Sprinkle half the sugar over this; then put in another layer of bread, rhubarb, and sugar. Finish with a layer of bread. Cover the dish and steam for one hour;

then take the dish from the steamer, remove the cover, and bake the pudding until it turns a delicate brown,— about twenty minutes. Serve with a hot sauce.

Jam Pudding.

Use the same materials as are given in the first rule for blueberry pudding; omitting, of course, the berries, and stirring into the butter, sugar, and egg mixture one gill of any kind of jam.

Steamed Batter Pudding.

| ½ pint of milk. | 2 eggs. |
| 1 gill of flour. | ¼ teaspoonful of salt. |

Have a covered mould well buttered. Beat the eggs till light, and add the milk and salt to them. Pour half this mixture on the flour, and beat well. When the batter is smooth, beat in the remainder of the liquid mixture and pour the batter into the mould. Cover closely and steam for one hour. Serve with a hot sauce. This pudding should be turned out of the mould very carefully, and served on a hot dish.

Quiver Pudding.

3 gills of stale bread.	1 tablespoonful of sugar.
3 gills of milk.	¼ teaspoonful of salt.
2 eggs.	A slight grating of nutmeg.
1 gill of stoned raisins.	

Beat together the eggs, sugar, salt, and nutmeg. Use a spoon and beat very thoroughly. Butter a quart mould. Cut the bread in thin slices and put a layer in the mould. Sprinkle some of the raisins over this, then put in another layer of bread. Continue until all the bread and fruit have been used. Pour the custard on this, one spoonful at a time. Cover, and stand in a cool place for three or four hours. Steam for one hour, and turn out on a warm dish. Serve with either vanilla, creamy, or golden sauce.

Plum Pudding.

3 gills of boiling milk.	1 tablespoonful of shredded citron.
½ pint of fine cracker crumbs.	¼ teaspoonful of salt.
2 tablespoonfuls of butter.	¼ teaspoonful of grated nutmeg.
2 tablespoonfuls of sugar.	½ teaspoonful of cinnamon.
1 gill of stoned raisins.	2 eggs.
1 gill of currants.	

Pour the milk on the cracker crumbs and spice. Add the butter, and set away to cool. Beat together the yolks of the eggs and the sugar. Add this and the fruit to the cooled mixture. Beat the whites of the eggs to a stiff froth and stir them into the pudding. Turn the batter into a well buttered mould; then cover closely and steam for five hours. Serve with a hot sauce.

This rule may be doubled, making two small puddings, one of which can be kept in a cool place for a couple of weeks. Steam it at least an hour when it is warmed up.

Chester Pudding.

1 gill of molasses.	½ teaspoonful of soda.
1 gill of milk.	1 teaspoonful of cinnamon.
1 gill of beef suet, chopped fine.	⅛ teaspoonful of mace.
3 gills of flour.	½ teaspoonful of salt.
1 gill of raisins.	Juice and grated rind of a lemon.

Put into a large bowl the suet, molasses, spice, lemon, and raisins, and beat together for one minute. Dissolve the soda in the milk, and add the milk to the ingredients in the bowl. Beat well, and then add the flour. Beat for three minutes, and turn into a buttered pudding dish. Steam for five hours, and serve hot with wine sauce or any rich sauce.

Wayne Pudding.

½ pint of flour.
1 gill of molasses.
1 gill of milk.
2 tablespoonfuls of butter.
½ teaspoonful of salt.
½ teaspoonful of soda.

¼ of a nutmeg, grated.
1 teaspoonful of cinnamon.
1 gill of stoned raisins.
1 gill of stoned currants.
1 egg.

Beat the butter to a cream, and beat into it the molasses, spice, and salt. Dissolve the soda in the milk. Beat the egg till light, and beat it into the butter and molasses. Now add the milk and soda. Add the flour next, and finally the fruit, beating the mixture well. Turn into a buttered mould and steam for three hours. Serve with a hot liquid sauce.

Turkish Pudding.

This is made the same as Wayne pudding, substituting prunes, dates, and figs for the currants and raisins. These fruits must be washed, and cut into small pieces. Use half a pint of the mixed fruit.

Graham Pudding.

3 gills of graham.
1 gill of sweet milk.
1 gill of stoned and chopped raisins.

½ gill of molasses.
½ teaspoonful of soda.
¼ teaspoonful of salt.

Sift the graham into a bowl. Dissolve the soda in one tablespoonful of the milk. Add to this the remainder of the milk, and the molasses and salt. Stir well, and pour upon the graham. Beat the butter vigorously for five minutes; then stir in the raisins. Turn the mixture into a buttered mould, which should then be covered and placed in the steamer. Cook for four hours. Serve with golden or creamy sauce.

Steamed Indian Pudding.

1 cupful of granulated corn meal.	½ cupful of molasses.
½ cupful of sour milk.	1 teaspoonful of salt.
½ cupful of chopped suet.	1 level teaspoonful of soda.

Mix the suet, molasses, and salt together. Dissolve the soda in a tablespoonful of cold water. Add to the sour milk, and stir into the other ingredients. Now add the meal, and beat well. Pour the batter into a well buttered mould, and steam for four hours. Serve with molasses sauce.

Steamed Indian Berry Pudding.

When blueberries and blackberries are in season add half a pint of either kind of berries to the batter for steamed Indian pudding, and steam and serve as directed above.

Steamed Indian and Apple Pudding.

Make the batter as directed for steamed Indian pudding, and add to it a cupful and a half of pared and sliced apples. Steam and serve the same as the plain Indian pudding.

Baked Indian Pudding.

3 pints of milk.	1 tablespoonful of butter.
2 tablespoonfuls of corn meal.	⅓ teaspoonful of salt.
1 gill of molasses.	

Boil one pint of the milk, and pour gradually upon the meal, stirring all the time. Turn the mixture into the double-boiler and cook for half an hour, stirring frequently. At the end of that time take from the fire and add the molasses, butter, salt, and the quart of cold milk. Add the milk gradually, beating well. Pour the mixture into an earthen pudding dish that will just hold it, and bake in a very slow oven for four hours. When it has been cooking for one hour, set the dish in a pan of hot water and cover with an earthen plate. This would not be essential in a large pudding, but a small one dries up in the long cooking unless these precautions be taken. The pudding will be spoiled if the oven be hot enough to make it bubble.

Mock Indian Pudding.

1 pint of milk.	1 tablespoonful of butter.
2 tablespoonfuls of rice.	½ teaspoonful of cinnamon.
1 gill of molasses.	¼ teaspoonful of salt.

Wash the rice and mix it with the other ingredients; using, however, only half the butter. Turn into an earthen dish and bake slowly for two hours. At the end of the first hour add the second half tablespoonful of butter, and stir well. Serve with cream.

Bread Pudding.

½ pint of stale bread.	¼ teaspoonful of salt.
1 pint of milk.	1 egg.
1 tablespoonful of sugar.	

Break the bread into small bits and measure it lightly. Let it soak in the milk, in a cool place, for two or three hours; then mash it with a spoon. Beat the sugar, salt, and egg together, and stir into the bread and milk. Pour into a small pudding dish and place the dish in a larger tin dish in which there is warm water enough to come within one inch of the top of the pudding dish. Place in a moderate oven and bake for about thirty-five minutes. Serve with vanilla or creamy sauce.

Cake Pudding.

Put any kind of stale cake on a plate and in the steamer, and steam for half an hour. Serve with a hot liquid sauce.

Sponge Pudding.

1 egg.	1 heaped teaspoonful of baking powder.
1 gill of sugar.	
1 generous gill of flour.	¼ teaspoonful of salt.
3 tablespoonfuls of water.	1 tablespoonful of lemon juice.

Beat the egg till light; add the sugar, and beat for five minutes; then add the water, salt, and flavor, and finally the flour, with which the baking powder should be mixed. Turn into a well buttered pudding dish and bake in a moderate oven for about twenty-five minutes.

Serve with a hot liquid sauce.

The lemon juice may be omitted.

Cottage Pudding.

½ pint of sifted flour.	¼ teaspoonful of salt.
1 gill of milk.	1 heaped teaspoonful of baking powder.
1 gill of sugar.	
1 tablespoonful of butter.	1 egg.

Beat the butter to a cream; then beat the sugar into it. Next add the unbeaten egg and beat vigorously for three or four minutes. Add the salt and milk, and then the flour, with which should be mixed the baking powder. Beat for a few seconds, and, turning the batter into a small, well buttered pudding dish, bake for about twenty-five minutes in a moderate oven. Serve with a hot liquid sauce.

The measure of flour is for pastry flour.

If the new-process flour be used, measure a very scant half-pint.

Lemon Pudding.

2 rounded tablespoonfuls of granulated sugar.	1 tablespoonful of butter.
	2 tablespoonfuls of milk.
1 tablespoonful of powdered sugar.	1 gill of water.
3 rounded teaspoonfuls of corn starch.	The juice and grated rind of half a lemon.
1 saltspoonful of salt.	1 egg.

Mix the corn starch with three tablespoonfuls of water. Put the remainder of the water in a saucepan and set on to boil. Stir the mixed corn starch into this and cook for five minutes. Take from the fire and add the salt and the lemon; reserving half a teaspoonful, however. Beat the butter to a cream, and gradually beat into it the granulated sugar, then the yolk of the egg, and finally the milk. Stir this mixture into the cooked ingredients, and, pouring all into a pudding dish that will hold about a pint, bake in a moderate oven for twenty minutes. Let it cool for ten minutes.

Beat the white of the egg to a stiff dry froth, and beat into it the tablespoonful of powdered sugar, and the reserved half teaspoonful of lemon juice. Spread this meringue on the pudding and bake for fifteen minutes with the oven door open. Serve this pudding very cold.

Cream Pudding.

1 pint of milk.
2 tablespoonfuls of flour.
3 tablespoonfuls of fruit juice, or 1 tablespoonful of wine.

⅓ teaspoonful of salt.
1 gill of granulated sugar.
2 eggs.

Reserve half a gill of milk and put the remainder on the fire, in the double-boiler. Mix the flour and salt to a smooth paste, with the cold milk. Add to this mixture the eggs, well beaten, and stir into the boiling milk. Cook for eight minutes, stirring three times. Turn the hot mixture into the pudding dish and spread the sugar over it. Wet the sugar with the wine or fruit juice, and set away to cool. The sugar and fruit juice make the sauce.

DOUBLE-BOILER.

Chocolate Pudding.

1 egg.
1 pint of milk.
2 tablespoonfuls of corn starch.
1 tablespoonful of boiling water.
3 tablespoonfuls of sugar.

½ teasponnful of salt.
½ teaspoonful of vanilla.
1 ounce of shaved chocolate (one of the squares in a half-pound cake of chocolate).

Reserve half a gill of milk and put the remainder on the fire, in the double-boiler. Mix the cold milk with the corn starch and salt. Beat the egg well and add to the corn starch mixture. Stir this into the boiling milk, and beat well. Put the shaved chocolate, sugar, and boiling water in a small frying-pan and set over a hot fire. Stir until the mixture is smooth and glossy; then beat this into the pudding, and cook for two minutes longer. Take from the fire and add the vanilla. Dip a mould in cold water and turn the pudding into it. Set away to cool. At serving time turn out on a flat dish and surround with whipped cream; or serve with plain cream and sugar. A soft custard, flavored with vanilla, makes a good sauce for this pudding.

Chocolate Pudding, No. 2.

1 pint of milk.
1 tablespoonful of corn starch.
1 gill of granulated sugar.
1 ounce of chocolate.
2 eggs.

2 tablespoonfuls of powdered sugar.
1 tablespoonful of boiling water.
1 teaspoonful of vanilla.
¼ teaspoonful of salt.

Reserve one gill of the milk and put the remainder on the fire, in the double-boiler. Beat the yolks of the eggs well, and add to them the sugar and salt. Mix the milk with the corn starch and add this to the sugar and yolks of eggs. Shave the chocolate and put it in a pan with two tablespoonfuls of sugar and one of boiling water. Stir over a hot fire until smooth and glossy, and stir this mixture into the hot milk. Now add the corn starch mixture and stir well.

Cook for eight minutes, stirring often. Add half the vanilla, and turn into a pudding dish. Let it stand in a cool place for ten minutes.

Beat the whites of the eggs to a stiff dry froth, and then gradually beat into them the powdered sugar and the remainder of the vanilla. Cover the pudding with this méringue and place in the oven. Cook for twelve minutes with the oven door open. Serve cold.

Caramel Pudding.

½ pint of brown sugar.
½ pint of water.
¼ of a box of gelatine.

4 egg whites.
½ teaspoonful of vanilla.

Soak the gelatine in one gill of cold water for two hours. Put the sugar and the other gill of water in a small saucepan and set on the fire. Boil until the mixture becomes a thick syrup. Now add the gelatine and vanilla, and heat again to boiling point.

Beat the whites of the eggs to a stiff, dry froth. Pour the hot syrup slowly on the eggs, beating briskly all the time. Turn the mixture into a mould, and set away to cool. When firm, turn out on a flat dish, and serve with a custard sauce.

Custard Sauce.

3 gills of milk.
4 egg yolks.
3 tablespoonfuls of sugar.

⅛ teaspoonful of salt.
½ teaspoonful of vanilla.

Make this sauce as directed for soft custard. (See Sweets, page 289.) Serve it cold.

Corn Starch Pudding.

2 heaped tablespoonfuls of corn starch.

1 pint of milk.
½ teaspoonful of salt.

Reserve one gill of milk and put the remainder on the fire, in the double-boiler. Mix the milk with the corn starch and salt, and stir into the milk when it boils. Beat well, and cook for ten minutes, stirring often; then turn into a pudding dish, and let it stand for ten minutes. Serve with sugar and cream, or with an egg or fruit sauce.

Custard Pudding.

1½ pints of milk.
3 eggs.
½ teaspoonful of salt.

3 tablespoonfuls of sugar.
⅙ of a nutmeg, grated.

Break the eggs into a bowl and add the sugar and salt. Beat well with a spoon, — never with an egg beater, as they must not be light. Add the milk to them and turn into a small pudding dish. Place the dish in a pan of warm water and set in a very moderate oven. Bake the pudding until firm in the centre. It should take not less than half an hour; better longer, as the slower the custard cooks the smoother and richer it will be. The oven must not be hot enough to have the water boil. Test the custard by running a knife down the centre. If it comes out clean the custard is done; but if a milky substance clings to it, cook the pudding a little longer. The flavor may be cinnamon, lemon, or anything else one chooses.

Cocoanut Pudding.

½ pint of milk.
½ pint of stale sponge cake.
1 gill of grated cocoanut.
1 gill of sugar.

¼ teaspoonful of salt.
2 eggs.
Grated yellow rind of half a lemon.

Soak the cake in the milk for one hour. Beat the whites of the eggs to a stiff froth, and beat into them the sugar and yolks of eggs. Stir this mixture into the cake and milk. Add the salt, lemon rind, and cocoanut. Turn the mixture into a buttered pudding dish, and bake slowly for about thirty-five minutes. Serve cold.

Tapioca Pudding.

1 gill of flake or pearl tapioca.
1½ pints of milk.
½ teaspoonful of salt.

Wash the tapioca and let it soak over night in one pint of cold water. In the morning pour off the water and add the milk. Cook for one hour in the double-boiler. Stir in the salt, and cook for half an hour longer. Serve with sugar and cream, or with preserved fruit.

The hot pudding may be turned into a mould which has been dipped in cold water. Let it stand in a cool place for several hours; then turn out on a flat dish, and pour preserved fruit around it.

Oatmeal Pudding.

| 1 gill of oatmeal. | 3 gills of water. |
| ½ gill of raisins. | ½ teaspoonful of salt. |

Put the water and raisins in a stewpan; cover, and simmer for half an hour. At the end of that time stir in the salt and oatmeal. Boil rapidly for one minute; then set the stewpan back where the contents will only simmer for one hour. Rinse a mould or bowl in cold water and turn the pudding into it. Set away to cool. Serve with sugar and cream.

Boiled Rice Pudding.

1 gill of rice.
1 pint of milk.
½ teaspoonful of salt.

Wash the rice in three waters, rubbing it well between the hands. Put it on the fire in one pint of cold water, and let it cook for ten minutes. Drain off the water and add the salt and milk; then cook in the double-boiler for two hours. Do not stir it while it is cooking. Serve hot with sugar and cream.

If raisins be liked mix a gill of them with the rice when the milk is added.

Rice Balls.

Cook the rice the same as for boiled rice pudding. Wet small custard cups or after-dinner coffee cups in cold water and fill them with the hot pudding. Let them stand where they will keep warm until serving time; then turn them out on a flat dish and put a bit of bright jelly on top of each ball. Serve with soft custard.

The rice ball must be hot and the custard cold.

Cold Rice Pudding.

2 tablespoonfuls of rice.
3 tablespoonfuls of sugar.
1 level tablespoonful of corn starch.

½ teaspoonful salt.
1½ pints of milk.
Flavor to taste.

Wash the rice and soak it in cold water for an hour. Pour off this water and put the rice on the fire in a pint of cold water. When this boils, drain off the water and add a pint of milk. Cook in the double-boiler for an hour. Mix the corn starch with a gill of cold milk and add to the rice mixture. Let this cook ten minutes longer; then add the sugar, salt, the remainder of the cold milk, and the flavor, which may be the grated yellow rind of an orange or lemon, a slight grating of nutmeg, or a teaspoonful of vanilla or lemon extract. If cinnamon be liked, a piece about four inches long may be cooked with the rice and milk, and be removed when the sugar and salt are added. Stir the mixture well, and turn into a pudding dish. Bake in a moderate oven for half an hour, and put away to cool. This pudding does not require a sauce.

English Rice Pudding.

1 gill of chopped suet.
1 gill of stoned raisins.
1 heaped gill of rice.

1 level teaspoonful of salt.
1 gill of sugar.
1 quart of milk.

Wash the rice, and mix it with the suet, sugar, raisins, and salt. Add one pint of the milk; then place in a very moderate oven and cook for half an hour. At the end of that time stir in the second pint of milk, and continue cooking slowly for two hours. Serve hot.

Baked Rice Pudding.

1 gill of rice.
1 quart of milk.
1 gill of raisins.

½ teaspoonful of salt.
3 tablespoonfuls of sugar.
1 tablespoonful of cinnamon.

Wash the rice and put it in a pudding dish with the sugar, salt, cinnamon, raisins, and a pint of the milk. Bake in a slow oven for one hour, stirring it twice in that time. Add the second pint of milk and cook an hour and a half longer. Serve hot. This pudding does not require a sauce.

Hot Farina Pudding.

1 pint of milk.
3 level tablespoonfuls of farina.
½ teaspoonful of salt.

Put the milk in the double-boiler. Measure the farina into a cup. When the milk boils, add the salt, and, with a tablespoon, stir the milk rapidly. When it is well in motion begin to sprinkle in the farina, stirring all the while. Beat the mixture well, and cook for thirty minutes. Serve with sugar and cream.

Cold Farina Pudding.

1 pint of milk.
2 level tablespoonfuls of farina.
½ teaspoonful of salt.

1 tablespoonful of sugar.
½ teaspoonful of vanilla.

Put the milk in the double-boiler and set on the fire. When it boils, stir rapidly until all parts are in motion. Continue the stirring, and sprinkle in the farina. Now add the salt, and cook for forty minutes; then beat in the sugar and flavor. Dip a mould in cold water and turn the hot mixture into it. Set away to cool. Serve with sugar and cream, or any kind of preserved fruit.

Farina Fruit Pudding.

Make the pudding the same as for cold farina, omitting the sugar and flavor. When it is cooked, add to it one gill of preserved jelly or marmalade. Turn into the mould and set away to cool. Serve with plain or whipped cream and sugar, or with soft custard.

Rose Pudding.

¼ package of pink gelatine, generous measure.
1 gill of sherry.
1 gill of boiling water.
1 gill of cold water, scant.
1 gill of sugar.
1 lemon.

Soak the gelatine in the cold water for two hours; then pour the boiling water on it, keeping it in the same bowl in which it has been soaked. Add the sugar, and stir until the sugar and gelatine are dissolved. Now put in the wine and lemon juice. Strain the liquid into a large bowl and let it stand until cold; then place the bowl in a pan and surround it with water and ice. As soon as the liquid begins to thicken, beat it with a beater or a whisk until it is light and spongy. It will then be of a rose-pink color. Rinse a mould in cold water and pour the pudding into it. Set in a cold place for an hour or more. At serving time dip the mould in tepid water, to loosen the pudding. Wipe the outside of the mould and see to it that the pudding comes away from the sides. Turn out on a flat dish and serve with a custard sauce in a separate dish;

or, this pudding may be served with whipped cream heaped around it; in which case the custard is, of course, omitted.

Uncolored gelatine may be used, if more convenient, and the pudding be colored with liquid cochineal.

Snow Pudding.

¼ box of gelatine.
⅛ gill of cold water.
½ pint (scant) of boiling water.

Juice of one lemon.
½ pint of sugar.
Whites of two eggs.

Soak the gelatine in the cold water for two hours. Pour upon this the boiling water, and stir until the gelatine is dissolved; then add the sugar and lemon juice, stirring until the sugar is dissolved. Set the bowl in a pan of cold water to cool; ice water is the best. Stir frequently; and when it begins to congeal, add the unbeaten whites of the eggs, and beat constantly until the mixture becomes a thick, white sponge that will just pour. Immediately pour it into a mould that has been dipped in cold water, and set away to become firm.

At serving time dip the mould in tepid water and turn the pudding out on a flat dish. Pour the sauce around it, or serve in a separate dish. Make the sauce by the rule for custard sauce for snow blancmange.

Snow Pudding, No. 2.

½ pint of boiling water.
½ gill of cold water.
2 tablespoonfuls of corn starch.

2 tablespoonfuls of sugar.
2 tablespoonfuls of lemon juice.
Whites of two eggs.

Put the sugar, lemon juice, and boiling water in a small saucepan, — not tin, — and set on the fire. Mix the cold water with the corn starch and stir into the boiling liquid. Put the saucepan in another pan of boiling water, and, after covering, cook the mixture for ten minutes. Beat the whites of the eggs to a stiff, dry froth, and stir them into

PUDDINGS. 283

the cooked corn starch. Wet a mould in cold water and turn the mixture into it. Set away to cool. Serve with a custard sauce made the same as for snow blancmange.

Orange Snow Pudding.

¼ box of gelatine.
½ gill of cold water.
1 gill of boiling water.

1½ gills of orange juice.
Whites of two eggs.

Make this pudding the same as snow pudding No. 1, and serve with the same kind of sauce.

Snow Blancmange.

1 pint of milk.
2 rounded tablespoonfuls of corn starch.
2 tablespoonfuls of sugar.

⅓ teaspoonful of salt.
Whites of two eggs.
⅔ teaspoonful of vanilla, or ¼ teaspoonful of almond.

Reserve one gill of the milk, and, putting the remainder in the double-boiler, set it on the fire. Mix the cold milk with the corn-starch. When the milk boils, stir in the corn starch and cold milk. Add the sugar and salt, and beat well. Replace the cover of the boiler and cook the pudding for ten minutes.

Beat the whites of the eggs to a stiff dry froth. Add the flavor and the whites of the eggs to the pudding, stirring gently, but mixing well. Dip a mould in cold water and turn the pudding into it. Set away to cool. Serve with custard sauce or with sugar and cream.

Custard Sauce.

1 pint of milk.
1 whole egg and two yolks.
3 tablespoonfuls of sugar.

½ saltspoonful of salt.
Flavor the same as used for pudding.

Beat the eggs, sugar, and salt together. Add the milk, and, putting the sauce in the double-boiler, set it on the fire. Stir all the time until the custard thickens. It will take about five minutes if the water in the lower boiler was boiling when the upper boiler with its contents was put on the fire. Cool, and add the flavor.

PUDDING SAUCES.

Wine Sauce.

1 gill of powdered sugar.	3 tablespoonfuls of wine.
2 tablespoonfuls of butter.	3 tablespoonfuls of hot milk.

Beat the butter to a cream and gradually beat into it the powdered sugar. When this mixture becomes light and frothy, beat in the wine, a tablespoonful at a time. When all the wine has been beaten in, place the bowl in a pan of boiling water. Add the hot milk slowly, beating all the time. Take the bowl from the hot water immediately, and the sauce will be ready to use.

Foaming Sauce.

2 tablespoonfuls of butter.	White of one egg.
1 gill of powdered sugar.	3 tablespoonfuls of sherry.

Beat the butter to a cream. Gradually beat into it the powdered sugar. Now add the well beaten white of the egg, and beat for two minutes longer. Add the wine, a spoonful at a time, and continue beating until the mixture is perfectly smooth. Place the bowl in a pan of boiling water and stir for three minutes. Serve in a hot bowl.

Creamy Sauce.

1 gill of powdered sugar.	2 tablespoonfuls of wine.
2 heaped tablespoonfuls of butter.	2 tablespoonfuls of milk.

Beat the butter to a cream, and gradually beat in the powdered sugar. Now beat in the wine, a little at a time.

PUDDINGS. 285

Next add the milk, half a spoonful at a time, beating until perfectly smooth. Place the bowl in a pan of boiling water, and stir the sauce for about two minutes.

Half a teaspoonful of vanilla may be substituted for the wine.

Fruit Sauce.

1 gill of jelly or preserves.
White of one egg.

Beat the white of the egg to a stiff dry froth, and gradually beat into it the jelly or fruit.

Egg Sauce.

1 gill of powdered sugar.
1 egg.
2 tablespoonfuls of milk.

½ a teaspoonful of vanilla, lemon, or orange extract.

Beat the white of the egg to a stiff dry froth, and gradually beat into it the powdered sugar. Now add the yolk of the egg, the flavor, and the milk. Serve at once.

Vinegar Sauce.

1 cupful of sugar.
1 level tablespoonful of flour.
1 cupful of boiling water.
1 tablespoonful of butter.

¼ teaspoonful of salt.
2 tablespoonfuls of vinegar.
¼ nutmeg, grated.

Mix the flour and sugar together, and pour the boiling water upon the mixture. Add the salt, butter, nutmeg, and vinegar, and simmer for ten minutes.

Molasses Sauce.

1 gill of molasses.
1 gill of sugar.
1 gill of water.
1 teaspoonful of flour.

1 tablespoonful of butter.
¼ teaspoonful of salt.
1 tablespoonful of lemon juice, or
½ tablespoonful of vinegar.

Mix the flour and sugar together. Pour the boiling water upon it. Add the molasses, and place on the range. Simmer for ten minutes; then add the other ingredients, boil up once and serve.

Clear Sauce.

1 gill of water.
1 gill of sugar.
Flavor.

Put the water and sugar in a small saucepan and set on the fire. Simmer for twelve minutes, and add any flavor you wish. If wine, three tablespoonfuls.

Clear Lemon Sauce.

Put into a saucepan one gill of sugar, a gill and a half of water, a thin slice of the yellow rind of lemon, and a slight grating of nutmeg. Cook gently for ten minutes; then add two tablespoonfuls of lemon juice, and serve.

Cinnamon Sauce.

1 level tablespoonful of flour.	1 cupful of boiling water.
½ tablespoonful of butter.	A piece of stick cinnamon about three inches long.
⅛ teaspoonful of salt.	
½ cupful of sugar.	

Mix the sugar and flour together and pour the boiling water upon the mixture, stirring all the while. Add the cinnamon, and place the saucepan on the fire. Simmer for ten minutes; then add the other ingredients and cook for two minutes longer. Strain and serve.

Nutmeg Sauce.

1 gill of sugar.	¼ of a nutmeg, grated.
1 gill of boiling water.	1 tablespoonful of butter.
1 teaspoonful of flour.	1 saltspoonful of salt.

Mix the flour, sugar, and nutmeg together, and pour the boiling water on them. Place on the fire, and stir until the mixture begins to boil. Simmer for ten minutes; then add the salt and butter. Boil up once and serve. Any flavor may be substituted for the nutmeg.

This is one of the simplest and most useful pudding sauces made.

Italian Sauce.

1 gill of sugar.	1 tablespoonful of lemon juice.
1 gill of water.	A slight grating of nutmeg.
A slight grating of the yellow rind of a lemon.	1 teaspoonful of butter. Whites of two eggs.

Boil the sugar, water, nutmeg, and the rind of lemon for fifteen minutes. When this mixture has been boiling for ten minutes, begin to beat the whites of the eggs to a stiff dry froth. Add the butter and lemon juice to the boiling syrup; then, when all boils up, pour the syrup in a thin stream on the whites of the egg, beating constantly. Beat for two minutes and the sauce will be ready to serve. It is particularly good for any kind of moist, steamed, or baked pudding.

Golden Sauce.

2 tablespoonfuls of butter.	1 egg.
1 gill of powdered sugar.	½ teaspoonful of vanilla extract.

Beat the butter to a cream. Gradually beat into it the powdered sugar. Next add the yolk of the egg, and beat well. Beat the white of the egg to a stiff froth and stir into the sauce. Add the flavor. Place the bowl in a pan of boiling water and cook for four minutes, stirring all the time.

Three tablespoonfuls of wine may be substituted for the vanilla.

Hot Cream Sauce.

1 egg.	1 teaspoonful of butter.
½ cupful of powdered sugar.	1 teaspoonful of vanilla extract.
1 teaspoonful of corn starch.	1 cupful of boiling milk or cream.

Beat the white of the egg to a stiff, dry froth; then gradually beat into it the powdered sugar and corn starch. Next add the yolk of the egg and beat well. Pour upon this the cupful of boiling milk, and place on the fire. Stir until it boils, then add the butter and vanilla, and serve. Any other flavor may be substituted for the vanilla.

CHAPTER XIX.

SWEETS.

Soft Custard.

1 pint of milk.	⅛ teaspoonful of salt.
2 large tablespoonfuls of sugar.	Flavor.
3 eggs.	

Beat the eggs and sugar together for six minutes, and add a gill of cold milk to them. Put the remainder of the milk in the double-boiler and set on the fire. When this milk comes to the boiling point, pour it over the ingredients in the bowl, and stir well. Turn the mixture into the double-boiler, and, placing it on the fire, cook, stirring all the while, until the custard will coat the spoon. It will take about five minutes. Take from the fire, and instantly turn into the cold bowl. Stir constantly until it begins to cool. Should it grow thin as it cools, you may know that it has not cooked enough; in which case it should be returned to the double-boiler and cooked a little longer. If, on the other hand, it begins to look slightly curdled on taking it from the fire, it has cooked too much. In that case, pour it back and forth from one bowl to another, holding the bowl from which it is poured quite high, and the custard will become smooth again, unless it be very much overdone.

Soft custard is one of the easiest dishes for dessert that one can make, and one of the most useful; but only experience will enable one to detect the changes in the cooking mixture. It is impossible to give exact time. When eggs are cheap allow four; for this dish is improved by the use of a generous number.

The yolks of the eggs make a richer custard than when the whole egg is used. If the whites be required for any other purpose, you may use even half a dozen yolks.

Baked Cup Custards.

Make these the same as the custard pudding, and pour into four custard cups. Place the cups in a pan of warm water and bake in a moderate oven until firm in the centre.

Steamed Cup Custards.

Make the same as the baked custards, but steam over boiling water until firm in the centre.

Tapioca Custard.

2 tablespoonfuls of tapioca.
1 cupful of cold water.
1 pint of milk.
1 large egg.

1 gill of sugar.
½ teaspoonful vanilla extract.
¼ teaspoonful of salt.

Wash the tapioca in cold water; then put it in a bowl with the cupful of cold water and soak it over night. In the morning put the milk in a double-boiler and set on the fire. Beat together the sugar, eggs, and salt. Drain off any water the tapioca may have absorbed. Add the tapioca to the eggs and sugar, and, as soon as the milk boils, stir in this mixture. Cook for five minutes, stirring all the time. Take from the fire and add the vanilla extract. Pour into a bowl and set away to cool. At serving time pour the pudding into a glass dish. It should be icy cold.

Rennet Custard.

1 pint of sweet milk.
2 tablespoonfuls of sugar.
⅛ of a nutmeg.

1 tablespoonful of rennet wine, or
½ tablespoonful of essence of rennet.

Make the milk blood-warm, and then add the sugar and rennet wine, stirring only enough to mix the ingredients. Pour this into glass custard cups, and grate the nutmeg over the custards. Let them stand in a warm room until the mixture becomes firm; then set in a cold place until serving time.

The prepared rennet, which can be bought in small bottles, may be substituted for the rennet wine.

Slip

1 pint of milk.	1 tablespoonful of rennet wine.
2 tablespoonfuls of sugar.	2 tablespoonfuls of sherry.

Have the milk blood-warm, — about one hundred degrees. Flavor it, and pour it into the dish in which it is to be served. Now add the rennet wine, and stir gently, to mix it. Let the dish stand in the warm room until the mixture has stiffened; then place it in the refrigerator, or in a cold room, until the time to serve. The slip must not be disturbed until you are ready to serve it on the table, as it may separate into curds and whey when once broken.

Strawberry Bavarian Cream.

1 pint of strawberries.	1 gill of cold water, scant measure.
1 gill of sugar.	¼ package of gelatine.
½ gill of boiling water.	1 quart of whipped cream.

Pick over the strawberries, put them in a bowl with the sugar, and crush well. Let them stand for two hours. Soak the gelatine in the cold water for two hours. Next whip the cream. Rub the strawberries and sugar through a strainer into a large bowl. Pour the boiling water on the gelatine, and when this is dissolved, add it to the strained strawberries. Place the bowl in a pan of ice-water and let it stand, stirring all the time, until it begins to thicken. Immediately add the whipped cream, stirring it in gently.

Pour the cream into a mould, which has been dipped in cold water, and set away to harden. At serving time dip the mould in tepid water, turn out the cream on a large flat dish, and heap whipped cream around it. One pint and a half of cream will give enough whipped cream to make the dish and to serve with it.

Sea Moss Farina Blancmange.

1 pint of milk.	1 saltspoonful of salt.
1 even teaspoonful of sea moss farina.	1 tablespoonful of sugar.
	½ teaspoonful of flavor.

Put the farina in a bowl, and gradually pour the milk over it, stirring until smooth. Turn into the double-boiler and cook, stirring frequently, until the mass looks white; then add the sugar, salt, and flavor. Rinse a mould in cold water, and turn the blancmange into it. Set away in a cool place to harden. It should have three or four hours for this. Serve with powdered sugar and cream.

Chocolate Blancmange.

Make as directed for the sea moss farina. While it is cooking put into a small pan two tablespoonfuls of shaved chocolate, two tablespoonfuls of sugar, and one of hot water. Stir over a hot fire until smooth and glossy; then stir into the hot blancmange. Pour into moulds and set away to harden.

Moss Blancmange.

1 gill of Irish moss.	1 saltspoonful of salt.
1 quart of milk.	1 teaspoonful of vanilla or lemon extract.
2 tablespoonfuls of sugar.	

Measure the moss loosely. Wash it and pick out all the pebbles and seaweed. Continue washing it until every particle of sand is removed. Put it in the double-boiler with the cold milk, and place on the fire. Cook for twenty minutes, stirring frequently; then add the salt, and strain into a bowl. Now add the sugar and flavor. Rinse a bowl in cold water, and, after turning the blancmange into it, set it away to harden. Serve with powdered sugar and cream.

Wine Jelly.

½ package of gelatine.
½ pint of wine.
1 pint of water.

2 lemons.
½ pint of sugar.

Soak the gelatine in a gill of cold water for two hours. Heat the remainder of the water to the boiling point, and pour it upon the soaked gelatine. Add the sugar, lemon juice, and wine. Place the bowl in a pan of boiling water and stir until the liquid is clear. Strain through a napkin and pour into moulds. Set away to harden.

Cider Jelly.

½ package of gelatine, scant measure.

½ pint of sugar.
1½ pints of cider.

Soak the gelatine in half a pint of the cider for two hours. Heat the rest of the cider to the boiling point and pour it on the soaked gelatine. Add the sugar, and place the bowl in a pan of boiling water. Stir until the liquid is clear; then strain, pour into a mould, and set away to harden.

Lemon Jelly.

½ package of gelatine.
1 gill of cold water.
1 gill of lemon juice.
1 pint of boiling water.

½ pint of sugar.
A few strips of the thin yellow rind of a lemon.

Soak the gelatine for two hours in the cold water. Pour the pint of boiling water on the lemon rind and let it stand for two hours. At the end of that time place on the fire; and when it boils pour it over the soaked gelatine. Now add the sugar, and, placing the bowl in a pan of boiling water, stir until the liquid is clear. Strain through a coarse napkin, and, turning into a mould, set away to harden.

In hot weather be generous in the measure of gelatine.

Orange Jelly.

½ a package of gelatine.
Enough oranges to yield ½ pint of juice.
½ pint of boiling water.

½ pint of sugar.
The juice of one lemon.
1 gill of cold water.

Soak the gelatine in the cold water for two hours. Squeeze the oranges, grating the thin yellow rind from one into the juice; but be careful not to grate off any of the white skin. Add the lemon juice. Pour the boiling water on the soaked gelatine. Add the sugar, and place the bowl in a pan of boiling water. Now add the fruit juice, and stir until the liquid is clear. Strain through a napkin and pour into moulds. Set away to harden.

Whipped cream is a desirable addition to this jelly when it is served.

Strawberry Jelly.

Make in the same way as the orange jelly, using half a pint of strawberry juice.

Raspberry Jelly.

Make in the same way as orange jelly, using raspberry juice.

Blackberry Jelly.

Use a pint of blackberry juice and half a pint of water, and proceed as for orange jelly.

Coffee Jelly.

½ package of gelatine.
1 gill of cold water.
1 gill of boiling water.

1 pint of hot coffee.
½ pint of sugar.
1 tablespoonful of lemon juice.

Soak the gelatine in the cold water for two hours or more. Pour the boiling water and hot coffee on this. Add the sugar and lemon juice. Set the bowl in a pan of boiling water and stir until all the sugar is dissolved; then strain through a coarse napkin and turn into a mould. Set away in a col l place for six or more hours. Serve with whipped cream, or with plain cream and sugar.

DIRECTIONS FOR FREEZING.

The mixture to be frozen should be icy cold. Put it in the freezing can, and place this in position in the wooden tub. See that every part of the freezer is properly fastened, and that the can and beater work with ease when the crank is turned. Pound the ice in a bag until it is almost as fine as snow. Put a layer of ice in the freezer, having it come about one third the height of the tin can. Now add a layer of salt, and, with a wooden paddle or a flat stick, pack the salt and ice as solid as possible. Continue this until the salt and ice come to the top of the tin can. Work the freezer occasionally, that the mixture may be more firmly packed. Now begin to turn the crank slowly for ten minutes; then turn rapidly for ten minutes longer, at the end of which time the mixture should be frozen into a light, thick mass. Take off the cross-piece; next wipe the top of the tin can; take out the beater, scrape off all the frozen mixture, and return it to the freezer. Work a strong iron spoon up and down in the cream until the mass becomes compact and light. Place a piece of white or brown paper over the can, and then put on the cover and replace the cross-

MALLET AND ICE-BAG.

piece. Put a piece of woollen carpet over the tub and set away in a cold place.

In warm weather it will be necessary to repack the cream. To do this, place the freezer on the edge of the sink and take the stopper from the lower part of the tub. This will allow the water to pass off. Now put back the stopper and pack with enough salt and ice to come over the cover of the tin can.

For a two-quart freezer allow for the first packing one pint and a half of salt and enough ice to pack *hard* to the top of the wooden tub. Snow may be used in winter. If the snow should be very dry, sprinkle a little water over each layer before it is packed down. Never let the water off while freezing, unless there be danger of its coming up to the cover of the tin can. In that case take out the stopper and let off only enough water to be assured that the rest cannot get into the tin can. The water is essential to the freezing of the cream.

When the frozen mixture has been used, and the ice has melted, pour the water into a strainer, and save the salt to use when freezing again.

Vanilla Ice Cream.

3 gills of milk.
1 pint of cream, generous measure.
½ pint of sugar.

1 tablespoonful of flour.
1 egg.
1 tablespoonful of vanilla.

Set the milk on the fire, in the double-boiler. Put the flour, half the sugar, and the unbeaten egg in a bowl, and beat until light. Stir this into the boiling milk, and cook for fifteen minutes, beating frequently. On taking from the fire, add the remainder of the sugar and the cream. Beat well, and set away to cool. When cold, add the flavor, and freeze.

Any other flavor may be substituted for vanilla. For

SWEETS. 297

coffee ice cream use three tablespoonfuls of the extract of coffee ; for lemon, three fourths of a tablespoonful of lemon extract.

Chocolate Ice Cream.

Make the foundation the same as for vanilla cream. Shave one ounce of plain chocolate and put it in a small pan with two tablespoonfuls of sugar and one tablespoonful of boiling water. Stir this over a hot fire until smooth and glossy; then stir it into the cooking mixture. Finish with the cream and sugar, the same as when making the vanilla cream, and freeze.

Pistachio Ice Cream.

Make the cream the same as for vanilla ice cream, but flavor with a teaspoonful of pistachio extract and half a teaspoonful of almond. Color with one eighth of a teaspoonful of the green coloring that can be bought of first-class grocers. This is a delicious cream.

Be sure to get the flavor and coloring of a reputable manufacturer.

Peach Ice Cream.

1½ pints of cream.	3 gills of sugar.
1 pint of fresh, ripe peaches.	⅕ teaspoonful of almond extract.

After paring and stoning the peaches, mash them in a bowl with the sugar and let them stand for an hour or more; then rub them through a fine strainer, and add the cream and almond to them. Freeze. A little liquid cochineal may be added to the cream to give it color.

Strawberry Ice Cream.

1 quart of strawberries.
3 gills of sugar.
1½ pints of cream.

Hull the strawberries and mash them in a bowl with the sugar. Let them stand for two or more hours; then rub through a strainer fine enough to keep back the seeds. Add the cream, and freeze.

Lemon Sherbet.

3 gills of sugar.
1½ pints of water.
5 lemons.

Boil the sugar and water together for twenty minutes. Cool the syrup, add the lemon juice, and freeze.

Orange Sherbet.

| 3 gills of sugar. | 1 lemon. |
| 10 oranges. | 1½ pints of water. |

Grate the thin yellow rind of three oranges into a bowl. Squeeze the juice of two oranges on this and let the mixture stand for an hour or more. Boil the sugar and water together for thirty minutes. Add the orange and lemon juice to this. Strain the juice in which the rind has been soaking, and add to the mixture. Freeze.

In grating the orange rind great care must be taken not to go beyond the thin yellow surface. If the grating be deep, the sherbet will be bitter.

The juices of any acid fruit may be made very sweet, diluted with water, and frozen.

Milk Sherbet.

1 pint of milk.	2 lemons.
½ gill of boiling water.	1 gill granulated sugar.
3 tablespoonfuls of powdered sugar.	½ tablespoonful of corn starch.

Cut the thin yellow rind from the lemon and put it in a bowl. Pour the water on the rind. Cover the bowl and set it on the back part of the range for half an hour. Mix the lemon juice and powdered sugar together. When the rind has steeped for half an hour, strain the water on the lemon juice and sugar.

Mix the corn starch with three tablespoonfuls of milk. Put the remainder of the milk on to boil in the double-boiler. Stir the corn starch mixture into the boiling milk, and, after adding the sugar, cook for ten minutes. Cool this mixture, and then freeze for ten minutes. Take the cover from the freezer and stir the lemon mixture into the cream. Put on the cover and finish freezing.

Peach Ice.

1 quart of sliced ripe peaches.
1½ gills of sugar.
1½ pints of water.

Boil the sugar and water until the syrup is reduced to one pint. Mash the peaches fine, and rub through a strainer. Add the syrup to the strained fruit, and freeze.

Apricot Ice.

½ can of apricots.
½ pint of water.
½ pint of sugar.

Rub the apricots through a sieve. Add the water and sugar to the strained fruit, and freeze.

The sugar and water may be boiled together for fifteen minutes, and, when cold, added to the strained apricot. This will give a smoother and richer ice.

CHAPTER XX.

BEVERAGES.

Tea.

THE making of a good cup of tea is one of the simplest things in the world. Use an earthenware or china teapot. Fill it with boiling water and let stand for four or five minutes; then pour out the water, leaving not a drop in the pot. Put the dry tea into the warm pot and after putting on the cover, set back where it will keep warm for a few minutes; then pour the boiling water on the tea and send to the table. This is for all the light kinds of tea, such as Oolong or black tea. English breakfast tea should steep on the fire for a few minutes, to suit most tastes. If made without this steeping, it has a much brighter and fresher flavor, but it lacks the body so much prized by lovers of this beverage.

The proportions of tea and water vary with the taste of the family or individual. The old rule of a teaspoonful for each person and a teaspoonful for the pot, makes rather strong tea, if three gills of water be allowed for each person.

The water must be boiling when it is poured on the dry tea. Many people seem to think that, if it has boiled some time in the past, it will suffice simply to have it hot when the tea is made. But if water boil a long time all the gases will be driven off, and the water become flat and flavorless. Such water is unfit for the making of tea and coffee.

Keep the teakettle clean, by washing it out every day, and always fill the kettle with fresh water when preparing to make tea or coffee.

The Oolong and all light teas deteriorate with age, whereas English breakfast tea improves.

Coffee.

Much of the quality of a cup of coffee depends upon the berry, and the process of making. There are two classes of berries: the strong and the mild. To the strong belong the Rio and Santas; to the mild, the Java, Mocha, Maracaibo, and others. The last named kinds are usually the highest priced.

Coffee should not be roasted a long time before it is ground. Few housekeepers roast their own coffee. Only a small amount of the roasted article should be bought at a time. It should be kept in an air-tight jar and in a dry place. Do not buy the coffee already ground, for it loses its fine flavor more rapidly when in the ground form than when whole. Have a small mill, that can be regulated to grind coarse or fine.

A mixture of two or more kinds of coffee gives the most satisfactory results. Two thirds Java or Maracaibo with one third Mocha will give a rich, smooth coffee. If the flavor be desired strong, one part Java, one part Mocha, and one part Rio may be used. If economy must be practised, all Rio may be taken. If the roasted coffee be thoroughly heated just before or after it has been ground, and if, after being taken from the fire, but while still hot, a little butter be stirred into it, the beverage will be much richer and smoother; or the entire purchase may be thoroughly heated at one time, and the butter be stirred into it then. Allow a generous tablespoonful of butter to a pound of coffee.

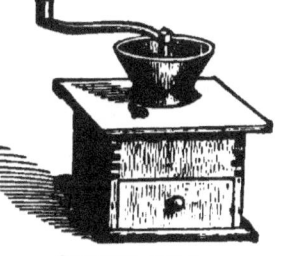

COFFEE-MILL.

There are many methods of making coffee. Two of the best are given below.

Boiled Coffee.

2 tablespoonfuls of coarsely ground coffee.	2 tablespoonfuls of cold water.
1 pint of boiling water.	⅛ saltspoonful of salt.

Scald the coffee-pot with boiling water. Put the dry coffee into it and pour the boiling water upon it. Place on the fire, and, when it begins to boil, draw the pot back where the coffee will just bubble for five minutes. At the end of that time add the salt and cold water. Set the pot back where the coffee cannot boil, and let it stand for two or three minutes; then serve.

There is a coffee settler in the market which can be used instead of the salt and water.

An egg makes the coffee richer in flavor, and clears it perfectly. One small egg will answer for six or eight tablespoonfuls of coffee. The egg, shell and all, should be broken into a cup and beaten. After using what is required, cover the cup and put it in a cold place. This will keep for two or three days.

When an egg is used for clearing the coffee it should be stirred into the dry grounds, and be cooked with the coffee.

If one wish the beverage stronger or weaker, increase or diminish the amount of the ground berry.

Filtered Coffee.

Coffee biggins come expressly for making filtered, or "drip" coffee. There are two compartments to this pot. In the upper one there is a double strainer, on which is placed the coffee. Above the coffee there is placed another rather coarse strainer. This upper compartment is placed on the lower one; boiling water is poured through the upper strainer and it falls like rain upon the coffee below. The points to remember when making

BEVERAGES.

coffee in this way are to have the pot hot, the coffee ground to a fine powder, the water poured on gradually while boiling, and not to have the beverage boil.

COFFEE BIGGIN.

Use two tablespoonfuls of finely ground coffee to one pint of boiling water. After putting the coffee in the pot, and fitting every part into its proper place, set the coffee-pot in a pan of hot water and on the range. Pour half a gill of boiling water into the upper strainer, and put on the cover. Let this stand for three or four minutes, that the powder may become wet and swell. Now add half the remaining boiling water; and after two or three minutes add the remainder. At the end of five minutes all the water will have filtered through, and the coffee be ready to serve.

A small quantity of coffee cannot be made in a large pot, because the water will pass through the thin layer of powder before it has had time to extract the strength of the berry. If all the water were poured on the powder at once, it would dislodge the dry grains and pass through without extracting the flavor from the coffee.

A flannel bag is often hung in a coffee-pot, the fine powder being put in it and the boiling water poured directly on the dry coffee. There are many inventions in the line of coffee-pots which are very satisfactory, but the housekeeper should investigate and test them for herself.

Coffee-pots must be kept absolutely clean, if you would have a satisfactory cup of coffee. A few old grounds, lodged in a groove in the pot, may spoil the flavor of the finest berry.

If you cannot have cream for your cup of coffee, at least have hot milk.

Cocoa.

Several preparations are made from the cocoa bean. We find the product in the market in the form of chocolate, plain, and also sweetened and flavored. This is the roasted bean ground to a smooth, fine substance, which retains the oily substance known as cocoa butter. This makes a rich beverage which few people can use daily. The chocolate is valuable in the preparation of various kinds of food and confections, and to use occasionally as a beverage. In its sweetened form it can be taken in the pocket when going on long tramps; an ounce of it will allay the feeling of faintness and hunger which comes with long fasting.

Breakfast cocoa is made by pressing nearly all the cocoa butter from the roasted and finely ground bean. This gives a delicate dry powder, which makes a digestible, nutritious, and pleasant drink. Because it in part takes the place of animal food, it is very economical.

The cocoa shells and nibs, when prepared as a beverage, are not very valuable as a food, because only a small part of the cocoa is extracted in the boiling. The process of preparing the cocoa bean for the market is almost wholly mechanical, so that when you get your cocoa and chocolate from a trustworthy manufacturer you may be sure that you are using a perfectly pure article and one absolutely clean.

Chocolate.

1 pint of milk.	1½ tablespoonfuls of sugar.
1 ounce of good chocolate.	1 tablespoonful of hot water.

Put the milk on the fire, in the double-boiler. Shave the chocolate, and, putting it into a small pan with the sugar and water, stir over a hot fire until smooth and glossy. Stir this into the boiling milk; then beat the chocolate with a whisk, to make it froth. Pour into a hot pot, and serve at once.

Long cooking separates the oil from the chocolate and spoils the beverage.

Breakfast Cocoa.

1 pint of milk
2 level teaspoonfuls of breakfast cocoa.
3 tablespoonfuls of water.

Put the milk in the double-boiler and set on the fire. Mix the cocoa to a smooth paste, with the cold water. When the milk boils, add the cocoa, and boil for one minute. Serve hot.

The flavor of this cocoa is always finer when the milk actually bubbles up after the cocoa is added. If water or part water be used, measure the cocoa more generously.

Nothing is much more delicious than a good cup of cocoa, and nothing is more disappointing than the slops one so often gets under this name, because many people prepare it by pouring hot water on the powder and then adding sugar and milk. This will do when it is impossible to boil it, but it is only a makeshift. It should be remembered that the cocoa bean contains a considerable amount of starch, and this starch will be improved by boiling.

Broma.

Broma is prepared the same as cocoa, but requires a few minutes' longer cooking, because of the addition of a starchy substance to the powder.

Cocoa Shells and Nibs.

The thin shells that are removed from the roasted cocoa bean, and a part of the nut in a roughly broken state, are used for a beverage. The shells are sometimes used alone, but this makes rather a poor drink. The shells and nibs are put into a cocoa pot with boiling water and simmered for four hours or more. Use a gill of the shells, one tablespoonful of the nibs, and a quart of water. This will give a generous pint of the beverage. Serve it with hot milk and sugar.

Lemonade.

1 lemon.
½ pint of water.
2 tablespoonfuls of sugar.

Squeeze the lemon and strain the juice. Add the sugar and water to it and use at once. It should be very cold or very hot. Add ice in warm weather.

When the water is not good, or in case of sickness, boiling water may be poured on the sugar and fruit juice ; then cool the lemonade.

When making a lemonade for a company of people, it may be mixed in a large handsome bowl. Add to it all or any one of the following named fruits :—

For one gallon of lemonade use four quarts of water, twenty lemons, one quart of sugar, one banana, half a pineapple, six oranges, one pint of strawberries.

Use the juice of the lemons and oranges ; have the pineapple and banana cut in thin slices ; the strawberries should be whole. Raspberries, as well as strawberries, may be used

CHAPTER XXI.

PRESERVES AND PICKLES.

Quality of the Fruit.

IT is a waste of time and strength to preserve unripe, over-ripe or inferior fruits. One should select sound, ripe, well flavored fruits for this purpose.

What to do with Fruit Pulp.

When making jellies with crab apples, quinces, peaches, etc., there is always a great deal of pulp left. The thrifty housekeeper does not like to throw this away, although all the fine flavor of the fruit has been extracted with the juice. If fruit be plentiful and cheap, it will be economy to throw this impoverished pulp away; if, on the other hand, fruit be high and scarce, add some fresh fruit, sugar, and water to the cooked pulp, and boil until a smooth marmalade is formed.

Cooked quince may be combined with fresh tart apples, sugar, and a little water. While the mixture is hot, can it, and it will be found good for pies and other uses when the fresh fruit is scarce.

Preserved Peaches.

The peaches should be sound and ripe. Weigh the fruit, and for every nine pounds make a syrup with three pounds of sugar and one pint of water; skimming the syrup as soon as it boils up.

Have ready a kettle of boiling water and a bowl of cold water. Fill a wire basket with peaches and plunge into the boiling water for two minutes. Lift the basket from the water and turn the peaches into a bowl. Pare them, and drop them into the cold water. This is to preserve the color.

Drop the peaches, a few at a time, into the boiling syrup. Cook them until they are heated through, and are tender; then put in a hot jar as many as will go in without crowding, and fill up with syrup. Cover the jar at once.

If many peaches are to be preserved it is best to make the syrup in several lots, as otherwise the long cooking, together with the fruit juice, will make it dark.

Preserved Pears.

Make a syrup like that for the peaches, allowing one quart of water to three pounds of sugar and nine pounds of pears.

Pare the pears with a silver knife and drop them in a bowl of cold water to preserve the color. On taking them from the water drop them into the boiling syrup. Cook them gently until they can be easily pierced with a silver fork. The time depends upon the ripeness of the fruit. The pears may be preserved whole or in halves. Put the cooked fruit into hot jars, and, after filling up with boiling syrup, seal.

Crab Apples.

Make the syrup as for peaches; allowing, however, half a pound of sugar to a pound of fruit. Clean the blossom end of the apples by rubbing, and drop them into water. Wash and drain them. Drop them, a few at a time, into the hot syrup, and cook until they can be pierced with a silver fork. Fill the jars with the fruit, and, after filling up with hot syrup, seal the jars.

The stems are left on crab apples.

Preserved Plums.

Make the syrup for the large white plums the same as for crab apples. Peel the plums by plunging in boiling water, like peaches. Cook and finish the same as crab apples.

Preserved Damson Plums.

These are preserved the same as the white plums, except that they are not peeled. They will cook in about three minutes.

Grape Preserve.

This preserve should be made with a tender-skinned grape. The Concord grape is too tough-skinned to make a satisfactory preserve.

Squeeze the pulp out of the skin, and, after putting it in the preserving kettle, set on the fire. Stir frequently, and cook until the pulp will break up readily. This will require only a few minutes' boiling. Rub the pulp through a sieve, rejecting the seeds. Measure the skins and pulp, and put them in the preserving kettle. For every quart of the fruit add one pint and a half of sugar, and one gill of water. Cook for twenty minutes after the preserve begins to boil; then put in jars and seal. If you choose, use less sugar; or, if you prefer to have the preserve sweeter, allow a pound of sugar for each pound of fruit.

Preserved Quinces.

Have a kettle of boiling water on the fire. Pare the fruit and remove the cores; then weigh it. Drop the pared fruit into the boiling water, and cook gently until so tender that it can be pierced with a straw. Take it from the water and drain it. Make a syrup the same as for peaches, and put the cooked fruit into it. Simmer for about half an hour; then put up in jars. This amount of sugar — one pound to three pounds of fruit — makes a fairly rich preserve. Less may be used if one prefer to have the quinces less rich.

Preserved Pineapple.

Pare the pineapple, remove the eyes, and cut the fruit into thin slices, cutting down the sides until the heart is reached. Weigh the sliced fruit and put it in a bowl, with half a pound of granulated sugar to every pound of fruit. Mix the fruit and sugar well, and put it in a cold place over night. In the morning put the fruit and sugar in the preserving kettle, and place on the range. When the syrup begins to boil, skim carefully; then fill the hot jars with the preserve and seal them.

The pineapple may be shredded with a silver fork, instead of being sliced. Be careful to keep out all the woody fibres of the heart of the fruit.

Preserved Uncooked Pineapple.

Pare the pineapple and take out all the eyes. With a sharp knife, cut the fruit in thin slices, cutting down the sides until the heart is reached (this is to be discarded). Weigh the sliced pineapple and put it in an earthen dish. Add to it as many pounds of granulated sugar as there are pounds of fruit. Stir this gently; then pack the fruit and sugar in pint jars, leaving space for two tablespoonfuls of Jamaica rum in each jar. Add the liquor; then put on the covers and tighten them. Set away in a cool, dark place.

Wine or brandy may be substituted for the rum; or, the jars may be packed solidly to the top, and sealed, without using any spirit. This fruit will keep well, and is so tender that it will melt in the mouth. It is, of course, very rich.

Sun Cooked Strawberries.

Pick over the berries and weigh them; then put them in the preserving kettle. Add to them as many pounds of granulated sugar as there are of strawberries. Do not have the fruit and sugar more than three or four inches deep in the preserving kettle. Place on the fire and heat slowly to the boiling point. Let the preserve cook for just ten minutes from the time it begins to boil, skimming well. Take up and pour into meat platters, having the preserve not much more than an inch and a half deep. Set the platters on tables at sunny windows. They should stand in the sun for twenty-four full hours. If the sun does not shine one day, let the fruit remain until it does. Put up cold in preserve jars. This preserve is perfect.

CANNING FRUITS.

The destruction of germs and the exclusion of air are the principles upon which canning is based. The article to be preserved is cooked for a short time, and then put in jars from which the air has been expelled by heating them to the boiling point. They are then sealed, and when cold are set in a cool, dark place. If all the conditions be right, the fruit will keep for an unlimited number of years, and when opened will be found to have nearly all the freshness and aroma of newly gathered fruit.

Now this is true of the majority of fruits, but not of all. The strawberry subjected to this process will come out a pale, spongy, insipid thing, whereas the raspberry seems to have its color, flavor, and odor intensified. If, however, a generous amount of sugar be added to the strawberry in the cooking, the fruit will retain its shape, color, and flavor. It is an error to attempt to can this berry without sugar, or with only a small amount.

Filling the Jars.

To fill the jars, have on the stove two pans partially filled with water. Let the water in one be boiling, but in the other not so hot that the hand cannot be held in it with comfort. Put a few jars and covers in the cooler water, turning them now and then until all parts become warm; then put them in the boiling water. This does away with all danger of breaking. When the jars have been heated in boiling water, drain, fill, and seal them one at a time.

In filling the jars be sure that they stand level, that the syrup has filled all the interstices between the fruit, and that it also runs over the top of the jars. Even with this overflowing of the syrup it will be found that, after cooling, the can is not quite full; but if the work has been properly done, the fruit will keep all right.

Different Fruits Need Different Treatment.

Now, as to the different modes of treating various kinds of fruit. We know that, when the germs are killed and the air is excluded, sugar is not necessary for the preservation of the fruit. But there are few kinds of fruit that are not improved by some sugar, because it fixes the color and flavor, and gives much finer results. Some kinds of fruit require but little sugar for this purpose, while others are poor indeed without a generous amount. One has only to contrast the flavor and quality of the canned peaches that are put up with and without sugar to realize the great superiority of those with which saccharine matter has been used. Where fruits are too dry to give out enough juice to cover them generously, a light syrup should be used. But with juicy fruits, avoid water if possible. A good rule in the case of small berries is to allow one third of a pound of sugar to each pound of fruit.

For fruit like peaches, pears, plums, etc., make a light

syrup. Quinces must first be cooked in clear water until tender.

In paring fruit use silver-plated knives, and drop each piece as soon as pared into a bowl of cold water, which has been made acid by the addition of lemon juice. This prevents the fruit from turning dark. Use earthen bowls, and wooden or silver-plated spoons. Avoid any delay while doing this work.

To Can Small Fruits.

Any fruit, if boiled long enough to have all the germs killed and the air expelled, will keep indefinitely if sealed while boiling hot. Sugar helps to preserve the fruit, but it is not absolutely essential to its preservation. Sugar, however, preserves the fine flavor and color of the fruit. Some fruits are not good when canned, unless a great deal of sugar be used, whereas just the contrary is true of other kinds. Tastes differ as to the amount of sugar to be employed; each housekeeper must study her own tastes and those of her family. Blueberries need no sugar, but are richer if a little be used. Blackberries and raspberries are better for some sugar, — say a pound of sugar to four or six pounds of fruit. More may be used, if liked. Strawberries require a great deal to preserve the color and texture. All small fruits are richer if preserved in their own juice.

Here is a rule for preserving raspberries, and the same general principles apply to other fruits: — Take twelve quarts of raspberries and two of sugar. Heat and crush three quarts of the fruit; then turn it, together with the juice, into a piece of cheese-cloth which has been placed over a bowl. Squeeze as much juice as possible from the hot fruit. Put the juice and sugar in the preserving kettle. and set on the fire. When the mixture begins to boil, skim well, and add the whole berries. Simmer for fifteen minutes, skimming well. Put the hot fruit in heated jars, and seal.

If the combined flavor of raspberry and currant be liked,

use a quart of currant juice for the syrup. In that case use an extra pint of sugar. The twelve quarts of raspberries are then preserved whole.

Canned Rhubarb.

Get tender rhubarb. Pare it, and cut in pieces about two inches long. Wash, and then pack it in glass jars. Fill the jars with cold water, and let them stand for ten or fifteen minutes. Pour off the water and fill the jars to overflowing with fresh cold water. Seal the jars and put them in a cool, dark place. This will keep for a year or more, and should be treated the same as fresh uncooked rhubarb when required for use.

Blackberry Jam.

After picking over the berries, put them in the preserving kettle and set on the range. Stir the fruit frequently. Let it boil for twenty minutes, counting from the time it begins to bubble. Take it from the fire and rub it through a sieve fine enough to keep back the seeds. Measure the strained mixture and put it back in the preserving kettle with a pint and a half of granulated sugar for every quart of strained fruit. Heat the preserve slowly and stir frequently. Let it simmer for forty-five minutes; then put up the jelly in tumblers.

If the fruit be of the large, soft kind that has few seeds, it need not be strained.

Raspberry Jam.

> 12 quarts of raspberries.
> 3 quarts of sugar

Pick the fruit free from leaves, stems, and imperfect berries. Put it in a preserving kettle and set on the fire. Stir frequently. Simmer for half an hour after it begins to boil; then add the sugar, and simmer for one hour longer. Put the jam in hot jars, and seal while hot.

Currant and Raisin Jam.

3 pounds of sugar.
1 pound of raisins.
3½ pounds of currants.

1 orange.
1 pint of water.

Cut the raisins in two and seed them; then cook them for one hour or more in the pint of water. Pick over the currants and put them on to cook in the preserving kettle. Add the orange juice, and cook for fifteen minutes after the fruit begins to boil.

Remove the seeds from the orange, and, after chopping the pulp and peel very fine, rub through the sugar. When the currants have been boiling for fifteen minutes, add the other ingredients to them, and cook for fifteen minutes longer. Put into jelly glasses, and when cold cover. This quantity will fill twelve glasses.

Pear Marmalade.

8 pounds of sugar.
8 pounds of Seckel pears.

½ pound of crystallized ginger.
4 small lemons.

Boil the lemons in clear water until the peel can be pierced with a broom splint; then cut it into small pieces. Peel and chip the pears, and cut the ginger in thin slices. Put all the ingredients into the preserving kettle and simmer for two hours. Pour the marmalade into jelly glasses. This quantity will fill eighteen.

The water in which the lemons are cooked is to be thrown away.

Jellies.

In no department of preserving does the housekeeper feel less sure of the results than in jelly making, so much depends upon the condition of the fruit. This is more pronounced in the case of small fruits than with the larger kinds.

When currants are over-ripe, or have been picked after a rain, the result of using them will be uncertain. Perhaps we notice it more with this fruit than with any other, because it is so generally used for jelly. An understanding of the properties of fruit which forms the basis of jellies may help the housekeepers to a better knowledge of the conditions and methods essential to success.

Pectin, which forms the basis of vegetable jellies, is a substance which, in its composition, resembles starch and gum. It gives to the juices of fruits the property of gelatinizing. This property is at its best when the fruit is just ripe; better a little under-ripe than over-ripe. When boiled for a long time fruit loses its gelatinous property and becomes of a gummy nature.

These facts show the importance of using fruit that is but just ripe and freshly picked, as well as the need of care not to overcook the juice.

Covering Jellies.

There are several methods of covering jellies. Pasting paper over the top of the glass is one of the oldest. Thin sheets of cotton batting, tied over the top, make a good covering. A piece of white tissue paper cut to fit into the glass, and simply laid on top of the jelly, is all that some people use. It is stated that the jelly will not mould or shrink so much when covered in this way as when the paper is pasted over the glass.

Currant Jelly.

After freeing the currants from leaves and stems, put them in the preserving kettle and set on the range. Crush the fruit with a wooden vegetable masher, and stir frequently until heated to the boiling point. Have a large square of cheese-cloth in a strainer which is set over a bowl. Turn the crushed fruit and juice into this and let it stand long enough to drain thoroughly. Do not use any pressure to extract the juice. Have a flannel bag suspended over a bowl, and pour the strained juice into this. Now measure the liquid, and put it into a clean preserving kettle. When it boils up, add a scant quart of sugar for every generous quart of fruit juice. Stir until the sugar is all dissolved and the liquid begins to bubble; then strain through a clean piece of cheese-cloth into a bowl. Immediately fill the tumblers, which must be dry and warm. Let them stand uncovered until the jelly is set, then cover with a round of paper, and over this tie a thin sheet of cotton batting; or paper may be pasted over the glasses. If you use the glasses that come with covers, nothing else will be required except the first sheet of paper. Many housekeepers prefer to use even less sugar than the amount given, allowing only a pint and a half of sugar to each quart of fruit juice.

Currant Jelly, No. 2.

Pick the currants free from stems and leaves, and put them, a few quarts at a time, in a large earthen or graniteware dish, and crush them with a vegetable masher. Put the crushed fruit into a square of cheese-cloth, and press out the juice. Put the strained juice into the preserving kettle and set on the fire. When it boils, skim it well; then turn it into a flannel bag and let it drain into an earthen bowl. Do not press the juice through the bag. Measure this strained juice, and put it on the fire in a clean preserving kettle. Let it boil for five minutes. Now add a pint of granulated sugar for every pint of currant juice. Stir the mixture until it begins to boil. Boil for just one minute; then fill the glasses, which must be warm, and set them in a sunny window until the jelly is firm. It may require only a few hours' time for this, and it may take even a day or two; all depends upon the condition of the currants.

A much clearer and handsomer jelly is made by putting the currant juice, when it has been strained the second time, into the clean kettle, and adding, when it comes to the boiling point, the sugar; then stirring until the sugar is dissolved, and filling the glasses immediately. Set in the sun until the jelly becomes firm. It will take two or three days. This is called sun-cooked jelly. The currants must be in perfect condition for this kind of jelly; just ripe, and freshly picked.

Crab Apple Jelly.

Wash the fruit and put it in a preserving kettle with just enough water to cover it. Let it simmer for one hour. Have a piece of cheese-cloth in a strainer that is set over a bowl, and turn the cooked fruit and liquid into it. Let this drain well; then strain the liquid through a clean flannel bag. Measure it, and place on the fire, in the preserving kettle. Boil for ten minutes, counting from the time it begins to boil; then add the sugar, using a pint and a half for every quart of juice. When this boils up, strain through clean cheese-cloth, and fill warm tumblers. Cover when the jelly is set.

Peach, apple, and quince jellies may be made in this way.

Other Jellies.

Jelly can be made from any of the small juicy fruits in the same manner as currant jelly.

Cucumber Pickles.

100 small green cucumbers.
2 quarts of small silver-skin onions.
Six small green peppers.
1 gallon of vinegar.

1 pint of rock salt.
¼ ounce of alum.
1 tablespoonful of mustard seed.
1 tablespoonful of whole clove.
1 tablespoonful of allspice.

Have a part of the stems left on the cucumbers. Wash the cucumbers in cold water; then lay them in a tub or jar, sprinkle the salt over them, and cover with ice water. Lay a large piece of ice on top of the cucumbers, and set away in a cold place for thirty-six hours. At the end of that time take the cucumbers from the salt and water, and place in a stone jar, mixing the onions and peppers among them.

Tie the whole spice in a thin muslin bag and after putting it, with the vinegar and alum, in a porcelain or graniteware saucepan, set the pan on the fire. When the vinegar boils, pour it on the pickles, putting the spice on top. When the contents of the jar are cold, set away in a cool, dark place. The pickles will be ready for use in twenty-four hours.

Sweet Cucumber Pickles.

100 small green cucumbers.	¼ teaspoonful of celery seed.
1 gallon of vinegar.	½ tablespoonful of allspice.
1 pint of coarse salt.	½ of a nutmeg.
1 pint of sugar.	A small piece of mace.
1 stick of cinnamon.	1 small green pepper.
½ tablespoonful of white mustard seed.	1 gill of grated horseradish.
	1 ounce of green ginger.
½ tablespoonful of black mustard seed.	1 ounce of alum.

Have the cucumbers picked with a part of the stems on. Wash them, and put in a tub or stone jar. Make a brine with the salt and six quarts of water. Pour this on the cucumbers while boiling hot. On the second and third days pour off the brine. Boil and skim it, and then pour it, while boiling hot, on the cucumbers. On the fourth day take the pickles from the brine. Put the alum in six quarts of boiling water and boil until the alum is dissolved. Pour this on the pickles and let them stand until the next day; then pour off the liquid, and, after scalding and skimming it, pour it on the pickles again.

Repeat this the sixth day. Should the cucumbers be not green enough on the sixth day, add a little more alum to the water. On the seventh day pour off the alum water and cover the pickles with clear boiling water. Let them stand in this water for twenty-four hours. At the end of this time take them from the water and place in the jars in which they are to be kept. Sprinkle the white mustard seed among the cucumbers.

Put the vinegar in a porcelain-lined or granite-ware kettle and set on the fire. Add the cinnamon, broken small, the nutmeg, grated, and the other spice, as well as the sugar. Boil this for five minutes; then take from the fire and partially cool. Pour this on the cucumbers. Now add to the contents of the jars the horse-radish, ginger root, and the green pepper, cut in pieces. Store the pickles in a cool, dark place. They will keep perfectly for two years if carefully made.

The quantities of sugar and spice may be varied to suit one's taste.

Tomato Pickle.

12 large ripe tomatoes.
3 onions of medium size.
4 red peppers of medium size.

2 tablespoonfuls of brown sugar.
2 tablespoonfuls of salt.
½ pint of vinegar.

Peel and slice the tomatoes. Chop the onions and peppers fine. Put all the ingredients in the preserving kettle and cook slowly for an hour and a half; then bottle and seal.

Canadian Tomato Pickle.

1 peck of green tomatoes.
6 large onions.
½ pint of salt.
3 quarts of vinegar.
1 quart of water.
1 pound of brown sugar.
2 tablespoonfuls of curry-powder.

2 tablespoonfuls of tumeric.
1 tablespoonful of ground cinnamon.
1 tablespoonful of ground clove.
1 tablespoonful of ground allspice.
1 tablespoonful of ground mustard.

Slice the tomatoes and onions and sprinkle the salt over them. Let them stand over night. In the morning drain off the liquid and put the vegetables in the preserving kettle with one quart each of water and vinegar. Let the mixture boil for five minutes, then drain well. To the drained mixture add the spice, sugar, and two quarts of vinegar. Put on the fire and boil for fifteen minutes, counting from the time it begins to bubble. Put into jars and seal.

Governor's Sauce.

1 peck of green tomatoes.
6 red or green peppers.
½ pint of grated horseradish.
½ pint of salt.
4 large onions.
½ pint of brown sugar.

1 tablespoonful of ground clove.
1 tablespoonful of ground allspice.
1 teaspoonful of white pepper.
Vinegar enough to cover the ingredients,—about two quarts.

Slice the tomatoes and sprinkle the salt over them. Let them stand over night. In the morning drain off the liquor and put the tomatoes in the preserving kettle. Add the seasonings and the peppers and onions, chopped fine. Pour over these ingredients enough vinegar to cover them well. Simmer the sauce for one hour and a half; then put up in jars and seal.

Tomato Catsup.

10 quarts of tomatoes.
1 quart of cider vinegar.
1 pound of brown sugar.
¼ pound of salt.
1 ounce of pepper corns.
1 ounce of whole allspice.

½ ounce of whole cloves.
½ ounce of whole ginger.
8 ounces of ground mustard.
3 small red peppers.
3 cloves of garlic.

Cut the tomatoes up and put them on the fire, in the preserving kettle. Add the garlic, and cook until the tomatoes are tender,—about forty-five minutes after they begin to boil. Rub them through a sieve fine enough to keep back the seeds. Put the strained mixture on the fire, in the preserving kettle. Add the sugar, salt, and pepper. Tie the whole spice and red peppers in a piece of muslin, and put them with the other ingredients. Mix the mustard smoothly with cold water, and stir into the mixture. Simmer the catsup for an hour and a half; then put up in bottles.

The catsup must be stirred often to prevent burning.

Canned Tomatoes.

Put ripe tomatoes in a large pan and cover them with boiling water. Let them stand for four or five minutes; then pour off the water and pare the tomatoes. Another way to reach the same result is to have a large kettle of boiling water on the fire, and put the tomatoes in a wire basket and plunge them into the boiling water for a minute or two.

After paring the tomatoes, cut them in small pieces. Put the sliced vegetable in the preserving kettle and heat slowly, stirring frequently. Let them boil for half an hour, or longer, after they begin to boil. Fill heated jars, and seal them. When cold, put in a cool, dark place.

Spiced Currants.

3 generous quarts of currants.	1 tablespoonful of cloves.
1 quart of sugar.	1 tablespoonful of cinnamon.
½ pint of vinegar.	

Measure the currants after they have been picked. Put all the ingredients into the preserving kettle and place on the stove. Stir the mixture frequently, and when it begins to boil skim carefully. Cook for half an hour, counting from the time it begins to boil. Put it up in small jars or tumblers. This is to be served with meat.

Spiced Crab Apple.

3 pounds of crab apple.
1¼ pounds of brown sugar.
1 teaspoonful of clove.

1 teaspoonful of pepper.
1 teaspoonful of salt.

Cover the crab apples with boiling water and cook them until tender; then rub them through a sieve, pressing all the liquid through also. Put the strained fruit into a preserving kettle, and add the sugar and seasoning. Cook gently for an hour and a half; then put in tumblers. When cold, cover with paper, the same as jelly. This is to be served with cold meat.

Piccalilli.

1 peck of green tomatoes.
2 red peppers.
12 onions.
½ pint of salt.
½ pint of grated horseradish.

1 tablespoonful of ground clove.
1 tablespoonful of ground allspice.
1 tablespoonful of ground cinnamon.
3 quarts of vinegar.

Slice the tomatoes, peppers, and onions. Add the salt to the sliced vegetables, and mix well. Let this mixture stand over night. In the morning drain off the liquid; then add the other ingredients, and, putting the mixture in a preserving kettle, cook for four hours, stirring often. Put the piccalilli in glass jars while hot, and it will keep for a year or more.

CHAPTER XXII.

FOR THOSE WHO LIVE ON FARMS.

LIFE on a farm has its bright and dark sides, as does life elsewhere. If all other things were equal, the pure air, abundance of sunshine, plentiful supply of good milk, butter, eggs, vegetables, and fruit should make the farmer's family the healthiest and happiest of any class in the land. But to counterbalance all these advantages there are the monotony of life and food, and often unwholesome water, where one would expect to find only the purest. The farmer's wife or daughter need not feel that she is buried; that she is nobody; that she has no mission in life; that she is largely a drudge. Every honest man or woman, unless we exclude some of the very rich, must do some work. Now, this work, whether it be in the kitchen, shop, on the farm, in the counting-room, store, or any of the professions, may become drudgery or may be made in some degree a pleasure. Everything depends upon the home life. The mission of the farmer's wife and daughter is one of great responsibility. It means the physical, mental, and moral health of the entire family. I know of no class of women whose mission means more to humanity.

Have the home sweet and healthful. Remember that pure air and sunshine in the house are the greatest purifiers. Do not exclude them. Impure water carries poison through the system more effectually than if it were in solid food. Water may look clear and sparkling, yet be filled with the germs of disease. A well never should be placed where the sewage from the house or barn can filter into it. If the well be near the house, do not allow slops, suds, etc., to be thrown on the ground near it. If there be a drain to carry off the household slops and suds it should be laid as far as possible from the well and so constructed that there shall be no leakage. Whatever else you may lack, be firm in your efforts to have pure water, and pure air and sunshine in plenty in the house.

Try to get as much variety in your food as possible, especially in the matter of the more substantial things, such as vegetables, meats, fish, soups, and breads. Try to educate your family and yourself up to the point where pies, cake, doughnuts, etc. need not be a daily dish on your table. Instead of these, have plenty of fresh stewed fruits when in season, and canned fruits at other periods. These fruits, with good bread, rolls, rusk, buns, etc., are healthful, and so simple that one does not tire of them.

Learn to make simple puddings and other desserts for the noonday meal. If you follow these suggestions you will reap a rich reward in a healthy, clear-headed family. You must think for yourself, too. Keep up, as much as possible, with the outside world. Take a part of a day at least once a week to meet other people, and manage to get in a visit to town now and then. Read some bright new books. Do not devote all your spare moments to fancy work or the trimming of underclothing for yourself and your children; you would be wasting your energies and making extra work for ironing day. Keep yourself, as much as is in your power, a bright, happy, thinking woman, and you will be an inspiration and tower of strength to your family and neighborhood. This, perhaps, seems a little like a sermon, but I mean every word of it.

To Prepare Meat for Corning.

All meats should be kept until free from animal heat before being put into brine. This will take at least forty-eight hours. Have the meat cut into suitable pieces and sprinkled lightly with fine salt and saltpetre in the proportion of one tablespoonful of saltpetre to four of salt. Lay the meat on a board that is slightly inclined, so that the surface blood which is drawn from the meat can run off. At the end of forty-eight or more hours put it in the brine.

All meats should be completely covered with brine. If there be any tendency to float, lay pieces of board on the meat and put weights on these. Large stones will answer.

Pickle for any Kind of Meat.

12 gallons of water.	3 pounds of brown sugar.
3 gallons of salt.	2 ounces of potash or washing soda.
¾ pound of saltpetre.	

Put all the ingredients in a large kettle and set on the fire. Stir frequently, and skim until clear; then pour into a large tub, being careful not to turn in the sediment. Any kind of meat may be put into this pickle when cold. Beef should remain in the pickle from one to four or five weeks, as one may desire it slightly or thoroughly salted.

Pickle for Tongues.

6 gallons of water.	¾ of a pound of saltpetre.
9 quarts of salt.	2 ounces of washing soda.
2 quarts of brown sugar.	

Prepare this pickle the same as directed for meat pickle It will require ten or twelve days' time to pickle the tongues. If the flavor of juniper berries be liked, simmer half a pound in one quart of water for one hour; then strain the liquid into the brine.

Corned Shoulder of Mutton.

Rub two tablespoonfuls of salt into a shoulder of mutton and let it stand for one day; then put it into a pickle for five or six days.

To Cure Hams.

8 hams of good size.
8 quarts of fine salt.
4 quarts of brown sugar.
4 ounces of saltpetre.

1 ounce of washing soda.
½ ounce of ground mace.
½ ounce of ground clove.

Mix all the ingredients together and rub thoroughly into the hams. Pack the meat in a cask or tub having the skin side down. After three weeks change the top layer to the bottom. Let the hams lie in pickle for six or seven weeks; then wash them, and wipe them dry, and finally hang them up to smoke. It will take from one to two weeks to smoke them. They are often smoked three months.

Hams may be pickled in a brine such as is prepared for tongues. They should remain in it from four to six weeks, if they are to be kept through the year.

If you have no smoke-house, six or eight hams can be smoked in a hogshead. Fasten a strong piece of board or joist across the top of the hogshead and suspend the hams from this. Have an old tin or iron pan in which to make the fire. For fuel use corn cobs, green hickory, or oak chips. About twenty corn cobs are enough to use at a time. Have some ashes in the bottom of the pan. Put some live wood coals on this, and then pile on the corn cobs or chips, and place all under the hogshead. Cover the hogshead with several thicknesses of old quilts and carpets. This is to keep in the smoke and also to check the fire, which should just smoulder, making a great deal of smoke and little heat. The fire must be renewed every day. You must be careful not to get so much fire that the meat will be heated.

When thoroughly cured, sew each ham in a thick cotton bag and hang all in a cool dry place, or pack them.

To Cure Breakfast Bacon.

Select the flank pieces and the thin end of the ribs of the pork, and treat the same as the hams. It is not necessary to pickle or smoke these thin pieces quite so long a time as the thick hams.

Sausage Meat.

15 pounds of pork.
2 ounces of white pepper.
4 ounces of salt.
1 ounce of sage.
½ an ounce of coriander.

Have the pork about one third fat and two thirds lean. Chop it fine, and free from all bits of gristle. Mix the seasoning thoroughly with it. Fill cases with this, or pack in stone jars and keep in a cool, dry place.

English Sausage Meat.

16 pounds of pork.
2 ounces of white pepper.
6 ounces of salt.
1 ounce of sage.
1 ounce of summer savory.
½ ounce of thyme.
1 nutmeg.

Prepare the sausage meat as directed in the preceding rule.

To Cure Jowl and Chines.

When a hog is being cut up, take out the backbone and remove the greater part of the fat; then cut the chine in pieces about a foot long.

Split open the head and take out the brains. Next cut off the snout. Cut the head in two, and cut off the upper bone to give the cheeks a good shape. Mix three teaspoonfuls of saltpetre and one cupful of salt. Rub this over the jowl and chines. Now pack them closely in a small butter-tub, and place a piece of board and a heavy weight on top of them. Put two quarts of coarse salt in a large kettle, and, after setting the kettle on the stove, put in seven quarts of hot water. When this begins to boil, skim it carefully, and set it away to cool. When this brine is cold, pour it over the meat. Keep in a cold place. The jowl and chines will be ready for use in about three weeks; they will keep for a year.

When all the meat has been used, the brine may be scalded, skimmed, and cooled, and used again for the same purpose.

To Cook Jowl.

Wash the jowl, put it in a stewpan and set on the fire. Cover it with cold water and heat it slowly to the boiling point. Skim, and set back where it will simmer for three hours. The water should not more than bubble. Serve with sliced and boiled turnips and boiled potatoes.

Spinach or cabbage boiled in salted water, then drained and chopped, and seasoned with salt and butter, should be served with the jowl when possible. Later in the season substitute beet and other greens for the spinach and cabbage. In families where economy has to be practised it is customary to cook the cabbage or greens and the turnips with the jowl. No butter is then required for seasoning.

Chine Pillau.

3 gills of boiling water.
½ pint of rice, scant measure.
3 pounds of chine, fresh or salt.
½ teaspoonful of powdered sage.

1 tablespoonful chopped onions.
½ tablespoonful of flour.
¼ teaspoonful of pepper.
1 teaspoonful of salt.

This is a cheap and savory dish. Wash and wipe the pieces of chine carefully, and lay them in a small dripping pan. Sprinkle the powdered sage over them and then cook for an hour in a moderate oven, being careful not to let the gravy burn. It is a good plan to set the pan on the grate, to prevent the bottom from becoming very hot. At the end of the hour take the meat from the oven and place it in a large stewpan. Into the pan in which the meat was cooked put the chopped onion. Set the pan on top of the stove and stir the contents until the onion begins to turn a golden brown; then add the flour, and stir the mixture until it froths. Gradually add the boiling water, stirring all the time. Season with salt and pepper. Let this simmer for five minutes.

Wash the rice in three waters, and put it in the stewpan with the chine. Strain the gravy over this. Cover the stewpan closely, and set it back where its contents will hardly simmer for an hour and a half. Serve very hot.

Should the chine be very salt, be scant in the measurement of salt, but if it be fresh, heap the teaspoon as full as it will hold, and also rub two scant teaspoonfuls of salt into the chine when it is put in the oven. The onion may be omitted.

How to Render Lard.

The best lard is that made from the fat which lies around the kidneys, and is termed leaf lard. Remove all the skin, and cut the lard in small pieces. Put it in an iron pot, and heat slowly, stirring it frequently. Cook it in this manner until the pieces of fat look shrivelled and straw-colored. On no account let it get so hot that it will smoke. Draw the pot back where the lard will partially cool; then strain it through a piece of cheese-cloth. Tin pails are satisfactory vessels in which to keep lard. Do not put on the covers until the lard is cold. Keep in a cool, dry place.

Hogs' Head Cheese.

Have the head split, scraped, and thoroughly cleaned. Put it in a stewpan, with enough boiling water to cover it generously, and simmer for five hours, skimming the liquid several times during the first hour. Place the head on a platter and remove the bones. When the meat is cold, chop it fine, and season each solid quart with two tablespoonfuls of salt, a level teaspoonful of pepper, and a teaspoonful of powdered and sifted sage. Add to this mixture half a pint of the water in which the head was boiled. Cook the mixture slowly for half an hour, and then turn into deep earthen dishes. Place a plate with a weight on top of each dish, and put away in a cool place. This cheese will cut in smooth slices.

If spice and other kinds of herbs be liked, they may be added with the other seasonings.

Should a part of the cheese be kept so long that there is danger of its spoiling, heat it slowly to the boiling point; then let it simmer for half an hour, and cool as before.

Scrapple.

½ of a pig's head.
2 quarts of water.
½ pint of corn meal, — generous measure.

2 teaspoonfuls of salt.
⅓ teaspoonful of pepper.
2 leaves of sage.

Clean the pig's head and put it in a stewpan with the hot water. Let it simmer for three hours; then take it from the fire and cool it. When cold, remove the bones and chop the meat fine. Add this and the seasonings to the liquor in which it was boiled, and return to the fire. When the contents of the stewpan begin to boil, sprinkle in the meal, stirring all the time. Cook for two hours, stirring frequently. Rinse a deep bread pan in cold water, and pour the hot mixture into it. Set away in a cold place.

When the scrapple is perfectly cold, cut it into slices about half an inch thick, and after rolling these in flour, or breading them, fry until brown.

Tripe.

Lay the tripe on a table and scrape it with a broad-bladed knife; then wash it thoroughly in several waters. Soak it for five or six days in salt and water, changing the water every other day, and using a quart of salt to three gallons of water. At the end of this time boil it gently for ten hours, turning it frequently, that it may not stick to the bottom of the boiler and burn. When the tripe has been boiling for eight hours, add half a pint of salt.

The boiled tripe may be used plain, with a butter sauce, or it may be broiled, fried in batter, soused, etc. When soused it will keep for several weeks.

Soused Tripe.

8 pounds of boiled tripe.
3 pints of vinegar.
1 stick of cinnamon.
6 whole cloves.
1 small blade of mace.

Cut the tripe in pieces and place it in a stone pot. Heat the vinegar and spice to the boiling point and pour over the tripe. Set away in a cool place and it will keep for several weeks. It will be ready for use in twelve hours, and it may be broiled or fried.

Pigs' Feet.

Pigs' feet should be treated in every particular the same as tripe. After being boiled they may, when cold, be broiled, or be fried in batter or crumbs. They may be soused, and then be broiled or fried.

To Preserve Rennet.

Rennet is the lining membrane of one of the stomachs of the calf. Select the stomach of a healthy calf, and empty it.

Remove the outer skin and the fat. Wipe the rennet, and then salt it well, using about half a pint of salt, and putting the greater part of it in the sack. Let the rennet lie on a dish for five or six hours, then stretch it on a forked stick. Cover it with netting, to protect it from flies, and hang it up in a cool, dry place. When the rennet is dry (which will be in about a week) put it in a paper bag or a glass jar, and keep it in a cool, dry place. This rennet may be used in making cheese or rennet wine.

Rennet Wine.

Wash the rennet, and cut it into small pieces. Put this in a wide-mouthed bottle, with one quart of sherry. This will be ready for use in four or five days. Rennet wine is used with fresh milk to make delicate desserts, such as slip, rennet custard, etc.

When the quart of wine has been used, a second quart may be poured on the rennet in the bottle.

If salted rennet be used, soak it for several hours in cold water to remove the salt.

Essence of Rennet.

Clean a rennet and cut it into small bits. Put these in a glass jar with three ounces of salt. Work the salt into the rennet with a spoon. Now cover the jar, and put in a cool place for six weeks. At the end of this time add a gill of rum and a pint of water. Let this stand for two days; then filter through paper, and bottle for use. This essence may be employed the same as rennet wine, using with it any flavor one wishes.

THE DAIRY.

The suggestions given for the work in the dairy are for the guidance of the woman who has only the simplest appliances to work with, and only a small amount of milk or cream to handle. In the large dairies, with such modern apparatus as the separator, and other fine machinery, the process of making butter differs from that outlined in this chapter. The essentials are always the same, whether it be in the smallest and most primitive dairy, or in the largest and most modern. There must be perfect cleanliness and freedom from odors. Wood floors and racks on shelves and in refrigerators must be watched carefully; for wood absorbs the moisture from milk and water, and will taint milk, butter, and cheese very quickly. The greatest care is therefore needed, that all the woodwork shall be washed clean, and dried thoroughly. Guard against letting any of the wood about the dairy become milk- or water-soaked.

Care of Milk and Cream.

Milk and all the products of milk require the most careful attention. Thorough cleanliness and good ventilation are absolutely necessary. Milk, butter, and cream quickly absorb any odors that there may be near by. If possible, one room or pantry should be kept exclusively for the dairy products. If this be impossible keep one side of the room — that nearest the window — for this purpose. Never put strong-odored or warm food in this room. Keep the room scrupulously clean and *dry*. Every utensil that is used about milk in any form must be first washed in cold water, then in hot suds, and finally scalded in clear, boiling water. Wipe perfectly dry with towels that are kept for this purpose, and that are washed and scalded every day. Now put the utensils out in the sun. If the day be wet, put them by an open window to air. The milk, cream, butter, etc., that come from such a dairy cannot fail to be of a superior quality.

When the milk is brought in, pour it through a fine strainer into the pans, and then set the pans in place. If at any time it be necessary to mix the night and morning milk, cool the fresh milk before it is added to the older milk. Adding warm milk to cold milk will cause the whole mass to spoil quickly.

When the cream is being collected for butter making, it must not be kept so long that it becomes very sour, or in winter until it becomes bitter. Have a stone jar in which the cream can be kept. In summer keep it in the coldest place you have, but in winter it must be kept where it will become slightly sour, without becoming bitter. Old butter-makers advise skimming the cream as free as possible from milk. Every time a batch of cream is added to that in the jar, stir the contents of the jar, in order to mix thoroughly the new and old cream.

The cream should not be allowed to remain on the milk until sour. Skim it while both milk and cream are sweet.

Butter Making.

The quality of the butter will depend largely upon the care of the milk and cream. It will help the butter-maker to use a thermometer. One suitable for dairy work can be purchased for twenty-five cents at any store where they keep such goods, or where they keep dairy supplies. The cream should be slightly sour, and when put into the churn the temperature should be from 58° to 60°. In cold weather place the cream jar in a pan of hot water, and stir frequently until the cream is raised to the desired temperature; in hot weather use ice water, if necessary.

In churning it is important that the stroke shall be slow and steady. Rapid churning causes the cream to froth, and spoils the texture of the butter. It should take at least from thirty to forty minutes' churning to bring the butter.

As soon as the butter begins to form into small masses, draw off the buttermilk and pour cold water into the churn. After a few strokes of the dasher, draw off the water and pour in fresh cold water, adding a teaspoonful of salt to every quart of water. Work the butter for a few minutes, then draw off the water. Put the butter in a wooden bowl and salt it, allowing one ounce of salt to each pound of butter. Many butter-makers allow four extra ounces of salt to every ten pounds of butter. If the butter is to be packed for future use, this is necessary.

Let the salted butter stand in the bowl over night. In the morning work all the buttermilk and water out of the butter, and then shape into any form you please. Wet pieces of thin cotton in salt and water, and wrap the rolls in them.

The less milk there is in the cream, the sooner the butter will come. The amount of butter to a quart of cream will depend upon the quality of the cream. A quart of thick cream will give a pound of butter, whereas it may take more than two quarts of thin cream to produce the same amount.

If only one cow be kept for family use, a small stone churn will be found valuable for churning the small quantities of cream which one will have. Of course, a patent churn is better for large quantities, as the work can be done more easily with it.

Too much working makes the butter tough and waxy. Work it only enough to free it from water and buttermilk. Never have the hands touch the butter; use wooden paddles for the work.

If the cream be very cold it will froth, and the butter will be a long time in coming. When it does come, it will be light and spongy, instead of being smooth and firm. Most winter butter lacks color. If you wish to impart a yellow tinge to it, grate the dark orange part of the carrot, and simmer it in sweet milk for twenty minutes. Strain the milk, and, when cool, add to the cream in the churn. Use half a pint of grated carrot and a pint of milk for every eight quarts of cream.

Cottage Cheese.

Put a pan of thick sour milk over a stewpan of hot water, and heat almost to the boiling point. When the pan has been over the water for about six minutes, turn the thick milk gently with a large spoon, getting the hot part on top. When the whey becomes so hot that it cannot be touched by the finger, turn the mass into a strainer and let the whey drain off. When the curd is free from whey, season it with salt and butter, allowing one teaspoonful of salt and one tablespoonful of butter to every four quarts of sour milk. A gill of thick, sweet cream, also, may be stirred into the curd. Press the cheese into a bowl, or shape it into balls. This cheese is good only while it is fresh.

Be careful not to have the milk too sour, or to get the curd too hot.

CHAPTER XXIII.

CARE OF THE SICK.

IN every household the time comes when a knowledge of the proper care of the sick is desirable. One should not wait for the necessity to arise before acquiring this knowledge. The physician will do his part, but the care and food are as important as are his medicines. In a book of this kind there is not space completely to cover the subject of preparation of food for the sick, much less the care of the sick. It is hoped, however, that the simple instructions given in this chapter may help the inexperienced to bring comfort and health to their suffering ones. In the body of the book there will be found directions for preparing many kinds of simple dishes that are suitable for the invalid, such as simple soups, broiled meat, fish, and birds, vegetables, toasts, jellies, and simple desserts.

All the food prepared for the sick should be of the best quality, and cooked in the simplest and most careful manner. The service should be the daintiest the house affords. Let the tray be covered with a clean, well-ironed napkin, and the china, glass, and silver be clean and bright. Tea, coffee, or chocolate should be taken to the sick-room in a small pot and poured in the presence of the patient. Have the cream and sugar in a small pitcher and bowl. Serve broth or soup in a dainty bouillon cup or a pretty little bowl. Put cream or milk toast in a small dish and serve small portions on a pretty plate. Serve dry toast in a fresh napkin, and butter portions as the patient requires. Broiled meat or fish should be put on a warm plate, and another

CARE OF THE SICK. 339

warm plate be placed over this to keep the food hot while it is being carried to the patient's room.

A patient should not have to wait for food beyond the regular time. No one, unless he has been ill, can understand the terrible sinking feeling that comes to a weak patient if the time for his taking food is forgotten.

In caring for the sick an infinite amount of patience, sympathy, and cheerfulness is required. If one be harsh or neglectful, even once, it may mean a whole life of regret.

Cleanliness and Ventilation.

The bedding, the clothes of the patient, and the rooms must be kept absolutely sweet and clean. If it be impossible to sweep the room, all dust may be wiped from the floor with a dry cloth. If the room be carpeted, — which is a pity when one is sick, — brush it with a soft hair brush, and then wipe the carpet with a cloth wrung out of warm water. If possible, ventilate the room two or three times a day by having the wind sweep through it. Protect the patient by extra blankets, and then spread a sheet or blanket over the head board, letting it come down over the head and shoulders of the patient. One cannot realize what a restful tonic this pure air is for the patient.

Bathing.

Few things are more refreshing to a sick person than a sponge bath. It should be given morning and night. A little alcohol in the water is invigorating, and prevents the patient from taking cold. Have but little water in the sponge, and begin with the face and neck. Keep the body covered, and wash only a small part at one time. Wipe with a soft towel. At night the patient may be rubbed with alcohol, using the hand. This rubbing often insures a good night's rest. Rubbing is beneficial at almost any time.

Turpentine Applications.

Refined turpentine is often very valuable in the sick-room. In cases of inflammation of the bowels, kidneys, or bladder, and of congestion of the lungs, a turpentine application often will relieve the most intense pain. Indeed, this remedy is good and safe for almost any pain that can be reached by external applications.

There are two ways of using the applications. When the turpentine is to remain on the patient for a long time, mix it with lard, and spread the mixture on flannel. Lay this on the seat of pain. It may be kept on for several hours. Use a tablespoonful of spirits of turpentine to half a pint of lard. If the pain be intense, two or three tablespoonfuls of turpentine may be used.

Another method is to wring flannel out of hot water, sprinkle the turpentine on this, and lay the flannel on the seat of pain. Cover with a dry flannel, and upon this lay a soft towel. Use a teaspoonful of turpentine for a surface about a foot square. In case of great pain even more turpentine may be required. Few patients can endure this hot application more than twenty minutes or half an hour. When the flannel is removed cover the inflamed part with a piece of soft linen.

If the pain come from gas in the stomach or bowels, put eight or ten drops of spirits of turpentine on a lump of sugar and let the patient eat this. Turpentine is very good to give in this way whenever there is bloating of the bowels from an accumulation of gas.

To Relieve Neuralgia.

When one is suffering from neuralgia in the head, put him in a warm bed. Make a brick very hot and cover it with several thicknesses of flannel. Fold a coarse, thick cloth and place it on the pillow. Lay the brick on this and wet thoroughly with rum. Rest the most painful part of the head or face on the brick, and throw a blanket over the patient, covering the head. Keep covered in this way until the pain ceases. When the blanket is removed, wipe the moisture from the head, face, and neck; then bathe in alcohol or rum, to prevent taking cold.

Another remedy is to make salt very hot by stirring it over the fire in a frying-pan; then pour it into a bag, which should be securely tied. Have the patient lie down, and cover him well. Place the bag of hot salt on that part of the head or face where the pain is located. The salt will retain the heat a long time. This method is much easier than the first, but it will not relieve one so quickly nor so thoroughly.

To Keep Cracked Ice.

It often happens that a patient is obliged to take a great deal of cracked ice. In such a case make a bag of rather thin flannel, and cut a small hole in the bottom. Have a long tape run in the hem at the top. Hang this bag in a large pitcher, fastening it at the top with the tape. Fill the bag with cracked ice, and cover the pitcher with several thicknesses of flannel.

To Break Ice in a Sick Room.

Place the piece of ice on a napkin and press a large pin or needle firmly into it. It will break off smoothly at this point. If ice be scarce, it is best to put it in the flannel bag in one large piece and chip it off as required.

Mutton Broth.

1 pound of the scraggy end of the neck of mutton.
1½ pints of cold water.
1 tablespoonful of barley.
¼ teaspoonful of salt.

See that the meat is perfectly sweet. Cut off all the fat; then cut the lean meat in pieces and put it in a stewpan with the bones and cold water. Place the stewpan on the stove; and when the broth begins to boil, skim it and set back where it will just bubble. Put the barley in another stewpan with a pint of cold water, and place on the fire. Cook for one hour; then pour off the water, and, after putting the barley with the broth, cook for three hours longer. Add the salt, and strain the broth; or, if the patient can bear it, remove the bones and serve the meat and barley in the broth.

Chicken Broth.

½ of a fowl.
1 quart of water.
½ teaspoonful of salt.

Free the fowl from fat and skin, and cut in small pieces, breaking the bones. Wash the meat, and, putting it in a stewpan with the cold water, place it on the fire. When the broth begins to boil, skim it carefully. Draw the stewpan back to a cooler part of the range, where the broth will only bubble for three hours. Add the salt, and strain.

A tablespoonful of rice, tapioca, or sago may be cooked in this broth, if it be thought best for the patient.

Clam Broth.

Get a dozen clams in the shell, and wash them in several waters; then soak them for an hour in a pan of cold water. On taking them from the water, put them in a stewpan and set on the fire. Add a gill of water, and, covering the stewpan, cook for fifteen minutes. Pour the liquor through a fine strainer. Taste to see if salt enough. It may be too salt; in which case add a little boiling water to the broth.

Mutton Custard.

1 quart of milk.	1 tablespoonful of flour.
2 ounces of mutton suet.	½ teaspoonful of salt.
Stick of cinnamon, 5 inches long.	

The suet must be from the kidneys; sweet, and free from all tough membrane. Shred it very fine, and put it in the double-boiler with the cinnamon and milk; reserving, however, one gill of the milk. Cook for one hour, then strain. Return the strained liquid to the double-boiler, and place on the fire. Mix the flour and cold milk to a smooth paste, and stir into the hot mixture. Add the salt, and cook for ten minutes. Give the patient as much of this as he will willingly take; say, half a pint every four or five hours. Keep the patient warm and quiet. This is a particularly good remedy in severe cases of bowel and stomach trouble, being nourishing and soothing.

Oysters Roasted in the Shell.

Get ten or a dozen good oysters in the shell. Wash the shells, and place them in an old baking-pan. Put the pan into a hot oven, keeping it there until the shells begin to open. Remove the upper shells and place the under ones, containing the oysters, on a large plate. Serve at once. The oysters should be seasoned with butter, salt, and pepper.

Steamed Oysters.

Put eight or ten large oysters in a little fancy dish or saucer, and place in the steamer. Cook for about five minutes. Season with salt, pepper, and butter, and serve at once with hot toast.

Oyster Roast.

Have a slice of crisp toast in a little dish. Put half a pint of oysters in a saucepan, and set on the fire. When they boil, skim them, and season with salt, pepper, and butter. Pour the oysters and liquor on the toast and serve at once.

Beef Tea.

Put in a large-mouthed bottle one pound of beef, free of fat, and chopped fine. Add to it half a pint of cold water, and let the mixture stand for an hour. At the end of that time place the bottle in a saucepan of cold water. Place the pan on the fire, and heat the water slowly almost to the boiling point, without letting it boil. Cook the beef for two hours; then strain, and season with salt.

The thick sediment which falls to the bottom when the tea has stood awhile is the most nutritious part, yet many people serve only the clear and poorer part to the patient. It is to keep this sediment (the albuminoids) in a soft, digestible condition, that care is taken not to let the water which surrounds the bottle boil. Great heat hardens the albuminoids.

If a patient take a great deal of beef tea, the flavor may be changed occasionally by putting a piece of stick cinnamon about an inch square into the bottle with the meat and water.

Beef Tea, No. 2.

Put into a bowl a pound of beef, free of fat, and chopped fine. Add half a pint of cold water, and stir well. Place the bowl in the refrigerator for four hours. When the tea is to be given to the patient, strain into a saucepan the quantity required. Season it with salt, and place the saucepan on the fire. Stir constantly until the tea becomes hot, but do not let it boil.

This tea has a peculiarly bright flavor, and affords a pleasant change from that made by long steeping in hot water.

Beef Juice.

Use a piece of round or flank steak about an inch thick. Broil it for eight minutes; then put it on a warm plate and, after cutting it in small pieces, press in the lemon squeezer. Season with a little salt. This may be fed to the patient; or a little bread may be soaked in it; or add a little hot water, and you have beef tea.

Round Steak.

When you cannot get a tender, juicy steak, or when the patient's power of mastication is not good, a nutritious and digestible steak can be prepared from the round of beef. Lay a thin slice of round steak on a board. Scrape one surface with a sharp knife until there is nothing left on that side but the tough fibres; then turn the meat over, and scrape the other side in like manner. When the tender meat is scraped off, put it in a small dish. Press this into a square, having it about half an inch thick. Rub the bars of a double-broiler with a little butter, and lay the steak between them. Broil over clear coals for five minutes; then place on a warm dish, spread a little butter on the steak, season with salt, and serve at once.

Raw Beef Sandwiches.

Scrape some beef in the manner described for preparing round steak. Season it generously with salt. After cutting four slices of stale bread as thin as a wafer, spread the beef on two of the slices, and lay the other slices on top, pressing them down carefully. Cut them into pieces about an inch square. Arrange these tastefully on a fringed napkin or in a pretty little dish.

Flour Gruel.

1 pint of milk.
1 tablespoonful of flour.
⅓ teaspoonful of salt.

After reserving half a gill of the milk, put the remainder in the double-boiler and set on the fire. Mix the flour with the cold milk, and stir into the boiling milk. Cook for half an hour. Add the salt; then strain and serve.

Oatmeal Gruel.

1 quart of water.
2 tablespoonfuls of oatmeal.
½ teaspoonful of salt.

Have the water boiling in a stewpan. Stir rapidly, and sprinkle the oatmeal into it, stirring all the while. Cover, and set back where it will cook gently for two hours. At the end of that time add the salt, and serve. This gruel may be strained or not, as may be best for the patient. A part of the gruel may be poured into a cup and a few spoonfuls of milk or cream be added to it.

If the gruel be liked thick, use four tablespoonfuls of oatmeal.

Indian Meal Gruel.

1 quart of boiling water.
3 tablespoonfuls of Indian meal.
1 tablespoonful of flour.
1 gill of cold water.
½ teaspoonful of salt.

Put the boiling water in a saucepan and set on the fire. Mix the flour and meal with the cold water, and stir into the boiling water. Boil gently for two hours. Add the salt, and strain; then serve. A little cream may be added to the gruel when it is served.

Arrowroot Gruel.

½ pint of milk.
1 teaspoonful of arrowroot.
⅓ saltspoonful of salt.

Reserve four tablespoonfuls of milk and put the remainder on to boil. Mix the arrowroot with the cold milk, and stir into the boiling milk. Add the salt, and cook for ten minutes.

Cracker Gruel.

2 tablespoonfuls cracker crumbs. | 1 gill of boiling water.
1 gill of milk. | ¼ teaspoonful of salt.

Put the cracker crumbs in a saucepan and pour the boiling water upon them, stirring all the time. Place the saucepan on the fire and stir the mixture until it boils. Add the milk and salt, and continue stirring until the gruel boils again. Serve at once.

For some tastes half a teaspoonful of butter is an agreeable addition.

Milk Punch.

½ pint of milk.
1 heaped tablespoonful of sugar.
1 tablespoonful of rum.

Mix these ingredients and serve at once; or give the punch a froth by pouring the mixture from one bowl to another, holding the bowl high as the liquid is poured from it.

Egg Tea.

1 gill of hot water or milk.
1 tablespoonful of powdered sugar.
1 egg.

Beat the white of the egg to a stiff dry froth, and beat the sugar into it. Next add the yolk of the egg, and beat well. Pour the hot milk or water on this, and serve. If you choose, a little nutmeg or wine may be added to the mixture.

Eggnog.

Eggnog is made the same as egg tea, using cold milk and a tablespoonful of brandy, wine, or rum.

Rice Water.

½ gill of rice.
1½ pints of cold water.
½ teaspoonful of salt.

Wash the rice and put with the water in a saucepan. Place on the fire and cook for thirty-five minutes. Strain the liquid, and season with the salt.

Half water and half milk may be used in this drink, if you prefer.

Apple Water.

Bake three tart apples in rather a quick oven until they are tender. Sprinkle one tablespoonful of sugar over them, and return to the oven until the sugar becomes browned. Crush the apples, and pour a pint of boiling water upon them. Let them stand for fifty minutes; then strain and cool the water.

Barley Water.

½ gill of barley.
1½ pints of water.
¼ teaspoonful of salt.

Wash the barley, and put it on the fire in a stewpan, with one pint of cold water. Cook for one hour. Pour off the water and rinse the barley. Add the pint and a half of cold water, and cook for two hours longer. Season with the salt, and strain. If lemon be good for the patient, add a tablespoonful of juice to the strained liquid, and sweeten with two lumps of sugar.

Crust Coffee.

Dry some crusts of bread in the oven; then toast them until dark brown. Break up these crusts, and measure out half a pint. Put these in a bowl, and pour a pint and a half of boiling water upon them. Cover the bowl for ten minutes, then strain the coffee. This may be served hot or cold.

Wine Whey.

Put half a pint of sweet milk into a double-boiler, and when it boils add a gill of sherry. Stir well, and let it cook until the curd and whey separate. If the wine be quite sour, the milk will separate at once; sometimes it is so sweet that an extra quantity is required to curdle the milk. If there be any objection to the use of more wine in a case like this, add a teaspoonful of vinegar. Pour the liquid through a fine strainer.

Moss Lemonade.

1 tablespoonful of sea-moss farina.
1 quart of boiling water.
3 tablespoonfuls of sugar.
3 lemons.
$\frac{1}{16}$ teaspoonful of salt.

Put the farina in a bowl or pitcher, and pour the boiling water on it. Stir well, and steep for an hour. Add the salt, sugar, and lemon, and strain. This is an excellent drink when a cold has settled on the lungs. Serve hot or cold.

Should there be any reason why the patient cannot take lemon, use some other flavor.

Restorative Jelly.

½ box of gelatine.
1 tablespoonful of granulated gum arabic.
3 tablespoonfuls of sugar.

2 tablespoonfuls of lemon juice.
2 cloves.
½ pint of port.

Put all the ingredients in a bowl for two hours. At the end of that time place the bowl in a saucepan of boiling water, and cook, stirring frequently, until all the ingredients are dissolved. Strain, and set away to harden. The bowl must be kept covered all the time the jelly is soaking and cooking.

This jelly is to be used when the patient finds it difficult to swallow either liquid or solid food. A small piece of it, placed in the mouth, melts slowly, and is swallowed unconsciously. The sugar may be omitted, and a gill of port and a gill of beef juice be used; the beef juice to be added when the jelly is taken from the fire. Other stimulants may be substituted for port.

Senna Prunes.

24 prunes.
2 tablespoonfuls of senna leaves.
1 pint of boiling water.

Steep the senna in the water, where it will keep hot for two hours; then strain the water. Wash the stewpan, and put into it the senna water and the prunes, well washed. Cover, and place the stewpan on a part of the range where the contents will just simmer. Cook until the prunes have absorbed all the water; then put them in a jar, and use as required. This is a mild and pleasant remedy for constipation. The prunes are delicious, and will keep for months. They are convenient to take when travelling.

A Gargle for a Sore Throat.

Put into a goblet of cold water one teaspoonful of tincture of muriate of iron, and one heaped teaspoonful of chlorate of potash. Gargle the throat with this. It will do no harm if a small quantity of the liquid be unintentionally swallowed.

Camphorated Oil.

Put into a large bottle four ounces of olive oil and four of spirits of camphor, and shake well. When there is pain in the chest or lungs rub with the camphorated oil. This is excellent to use in case of sprains or bruises.

For a Cold in the Head.

Mix together in a large bottle four ounces of ammonia and four of camphor. A cologne bottle with a glass stopper is the best for this preparation. When there are symptoms of a cold in the head inhale this mixture frequently.

Lime Water.

Put about four ounces of quicklime in a bowl, and pour upon it two quarts of cold water. Stir the mixture well, and cover. Let this stand for four or five hours. At the end of that time pour off the clear liquid and bottle it. Throw away the sediment.

CHAPTER XXIV.

WHEN CLEANING HOUSE.

THE season of house-cleaning is greeted with different degrees of welcome, or horror, by the several members of the family. Some people appear to think there is no good reason for this annual thorough cleaning of the house; others, however, are really glad when the time comes round again, because it furnishes an opportunity to take account of stock, as it were, discarding the worthless, and renewing wherever it is necessary. When the cleaning is finished, pride and content come with the feeling that rest and comfort can be taken with a clear conscience in a house that one knows is in good condition from top to bottom.

System Absolutely Necessary.

Every house certainly should have a thorough cleaning every year, that there may be a check put upon the accumulation of dust or dirt which might breed disease, even if no other reason influenced the housekeeper. This yearly cleaning need not be a season of discomfort to the family. If possible, a little extra help should be engaged; but even if this be out of the question, the work can be done in such a way that every one shall not be worn out by the time the cleaning is finished. Too much should not be attempted at once. If one room be taken at a time, and be finished before work is begun in another, the whole house can be cleaned without any great difficulty. It is always wise, if possible, to wait until the necessity for furnace or stove fires is past. If the house be heated by stoves, and there be some rooms in which a fire is needed only in the coldest weather, such rooms may be cleaned first, the stoves in the other rooms being removed later. There should be a perfect system in doing this work. Housekeepers differ in regard to the part of the house where the cleaning should begin, some starting with the attic and others with the cellar. Since the furnace must be cleaned some time, and dust may escape through the pipes into the various rooms above, it seems to me that the proper place to begin is down-stairs.

Cleaning the Cellar.

In no part of the house is it so important that the cleaning be thoroughly done as in the cellar. Not a corner should be slighted. Begin with the furnace. Have the registers closed in every room. Remove all the cinders and ashes, and clean out all the flues and pipes. Many housekeepers have the pipes removed, but the smoke-pipe is really the only one that it is necessary to take down. This pipe is liable to rust, because of the moisture it gathers from the chimney; nevertheless, if there be no way of heating and drying the house during a cold, damp period in summer except by building a fire in the furnace, it would be cheaper to renew this smoke-pipe every few years than run the risk of having the family made ill from receiving a chill. While the men are in the house to clean the furnace, it would be economy to have them clean the flues in the range, and also the chimneys. Open the cellar windows to bring everything into the light. Have the coal bins cleaned. Brush everything free from dust. Now sweep the ceiling and walls as well as the floor. Brush the walls once more. Wash the windows and any closets, shelves, or tables there may be in the cellar.

Do not Omit Whitewashing.

Now have the walls whitewashed. Before the various articles stored in the cellar are put back in place, brush them again. Sweep the floor once more. Paint with black enamel varnish the iron parts of the furnace, and also any iron pipes that may be exposed to moisture. An excellent whitewash may be made by putting eight quarts of unslaked lime into a large tub, and pouring over it enough boiling water to make a paste. Stir well, and cover until cold, stirring occasionally, that the wash may be smooth. Dissolve one quart of salt in two quarts of hot water. Dissolve also half an ounce of indigo in about a pint of hot water. Add these substances to the slaked and cooled lime. Now beat well, and add enough cold water to make the mixture the consistency of thin cream. The wash will then be ready to use.

A tub of charcoal and another of lime are excellent things to keep in the cellar. They make it sweeter and dryer, and the charcoal is, of course, very convenient to have on hand for fuel. The unslaked lime should be put in a tub or barrel, with space for it to expand to twice its bulk. It slakes in the air and expands rapidly during the process.

From Cellar to Attic.

After the cellar is cleaned, the next move is to begin at the top of the house and work down. It is not safe in these days, when houses are kept almost as warm in winter as they become in summer, to take it for granted that anything is perfectly free from carpet-bugs, moths, and other insects. Every article in the storeroom should be examined, brushed, and shaken. All the boxes, drawers, and closets should be brushed, wiped, and lined with new paper. As a measure of safety all receptacles should be saturated with naphtha just before their contents are replaced. Woollen goods, furs, and feathers should be wet with naphtha and folded in old cotton or linen sheets. They will be perfectly safe for a year or more, provided they have been thoroughly shaken and brushed, so that no insects' eggs remain in them. Pieces of carpets and other large articles should be hung out of doors, on lines, before being put away.

Having taken care of the closets, drawers, boxes, and stored goods, the next thing will be to clean the room. Brush the articles of furniture and set them outside the room. Brush the walls, ceiling, and windows. After sweeping the floor wash the windows and woodwork, and also the floor, wiping very dry. Let the room air for an hour or more; then return all the articles to their places.

Taking up and Cleaning Carpets.

Have two strong sheets made of unbleached cotton. Remove the carpet tacks with a tack-lifter, being careful to put every one of them in a box or bowl. It is not only extremely painful, but also dangerous, to step on a rusty tack, and the housekeeper should make it a matter of conscience to see to it that none are left lying about. When all the tacks have been removed fold the carpet carefully, lengthwise; then roll it up and put it in one of the sheets, tying this. Put the linings in the other sheet. Take both sheets into the yard or some field near by, and after spreading the linings, sweep them on both sides, pile them up, and cover with the sheet. Spread the carpet and beat with a rattan or long switch. Sweep it, and then turn it over and beat again. Let it lie on the grass, wrong side up, until the room is ready.

The small yards in city houses are not the proper places for cleaning carpets, as the dust rises and enters all the surrounding houses. There is in some cities a law against beating carpets in such narrow quarters.

Sweeping and Dusting.

When the carpet and linings have been removed from the room, sprinkle the floor with either moistened sawdust, fine sand, or bits of damp paper; then sweep up the dust. Go over the floor a second time. Brush the ceiling and walls of the room and closets, being careful to get every crack free from dust. Clean, with a small brush, the tops of the doors and windows, the window sashes, the ledges and blinds, and all the grooves in the woodwork. For the walls and ceiling use a broom covered with Canton flannel, or any old flannel. Let the strokes on the walls be straight downward. If there be a fireplace in the room spread thick papers on the hearth and clean both the grate and fireplace. Take the bedstead apart and lay each piece on the floor, grooved side up. Be careful that there is not a particle of dust left in it. Pour naphtha into every groove. Be generous, for it is not expensive and will hurt nothing. Have near by a bowl of naphtha, into which dip the ends of the slats. If there have been any indications of insect life in the bed or room, spray all the cracks in the floor, walls, and woodwork. Now sweep the floor for the third time and wash it with hot diluted lime water, which is made by pouring four quarts of boiling water upon one quart of quicklime, and letting the mixture stand covered for several hours; then pouring into another pail the clear water. Put one quart of this water to two gallons of hot. The boards will be made whiter and sweeter by the use of the lime water.

Washing Painted Surfaces.

Next wash the paint. If it be white do not use ordinary soap. Wring a flannel cloth out of hot water and dip it lightly in whiting. Rub with this, and then wash off all the whiting; next wipe with the cloth wrung out of hot water, and finally rub with a dry flannel until the surface is perfectly dry. Have a pointed stick for all the grooves and corners. If the woodwork be grooved a great deal, as is now the fashion, a small scrubbing brush, such as is sold for cleaning kitchen boards, will be found helpful, as a few strokes the length of a long grooved panel will clean it perfectly. If soap be preferred to whiting, use the white castile, as this will not turn the paint yellow, nor will it soften it, as is apt to be the case with soaps in which the alkali is strong. Now wash the blinds, then the window casings and ledges, and finally the glass of the windows.

When cleaning paint it is well not to have the cloth so wet that the water will run on the paint, as it will leave streaks. Wash only a small place at a time. Wash the blinds with clear water. When you come to the window ledges do not use so much water that it will run down on the outside of the house, marring the appearance of the walls. Always rub with the grain of the wood.

Take the covers from the furniture, and dust again, washing the mirror in the dressing-case. Clean and polish the furniture.

Laying the Carpet.

Lay the carpet linings on the floor, putting a small tack here and there to keep them in place. Put the carpet on the floor, unrolling it in the direction in which it is to be laid. Begin to tack it at the end of the room which is the most irregular. If there be a fireplace or bay-window in the room, fit the carpet around these places first. Use large tacks to hold the carpet temporarily in place; they can be withdrawn when the work is finished. When the carpet is fitted to a place, use small tacks to keep it down. Tack one end of the carpet, stretching it well; then a side, then the other end, and finally the other side. Be careful to keep the lines straight, and to have the carpet fit tightly; for if it be loose, it will not only look bad, but will not wear well.

When the carpet is laid, pour a little naphtha on any soiled places, and rub with a piece of flannel until the spots disappear. Always have a window open at such times, to allow the gas to escape. Put about six quarts of warm water in a pail and add four tablespoonfuls of household ammonia. Wring a woollen cloth out of this, and wipe the carpet.

Put the furniture and other articles in place. When all the chambers are finished, clean the hall and stairs. All the chambers and upper halls are to be cleaned in the same manner, one room at a time. If the stairs be carpeted, take up the carpets and have them cleaned and put away until all the front part of the house has been cleaned.

Rooms on the First Floor.

The rooms on this floor nowadays are generally shut off by portières, over and under which the dust sifts into the adjoining rooms when one of the series is being cleaned, unless the housekeeper provide the proper screens. Have for this purpose sheets of strong, unbleached cotton, a yard longer and wider than the height and width of the openings. If you take down your portières and tack these sheets on the top and at the bottom of the casings, the other rooms will be well protected. Now dust and remove the small ornaments. Beat and brush the upholstered furniture. Remove from the room as much of the furniture as possible. Take down the window draperies and shake the dust from them in the yard. Have the dining-room table made its full length, and lay an old sheet over it Spread the draperies on this, one at a time, and wipe them with a clean piece of cheese-cloth; then fold them carefully, if they are not to be hung again until fall, and, pinning them in clean sheets, put them away in boxes or drawers. Next take down the shades, and after wiping them with a clean cloth roll them up and put them aside until the room is cleaned. Cover the large pieces of furniture, and if there be carpets to be taken up proceed in these rooms as directed for the bedrooms. If there be brasses, take them to the laundry or kitchen to be cleaned. Take down the shades of the chandeliers and wash them. If the carpets are to be taken up, they should be removed at once, and if they are not, brush the ceiling, walls, woodwork, windows, blinds, and ledges, and then sweep the carpet. When the dust settles sweep a second time; be careful to brush the corners and edges thoroughly with a small broom. After the carpet is thoroughly swept, saturate the edges and corners with naphtha, leaving the doors and windows open, of course. Now clean the paint and windows. When the room is clean put three tablespoonfuls of household ammonia in about six quarts of water, and, wringing a clean cloth out of this, wipe the carpet. Change the water as soon as it becomes dark. Replace the furnishings. Of course, if the floors be of polished hard wood, half the burden of house-cleaning is removed.

Kitchen, Pantry, and Closets.

Last, but not least, on the programme comes the back part of the house. Beginning with the china closet, remove and wipe all the dishes. Brush the walls, ceiling, and shelves. Take the drawers to the kitchen and wash and wipe them, afterward drying them in the sun or before the fire. Wash all the woodwork and the floors before replacing the dishes. Clean the kitchen closets and pantry in the same manner. Wash and scour all the wooden, tin, and iron utensils, getting them perfectly dry and sweet in the sunlight, if possible. Line the shelves and floor of the pot closet with thick brown paper, and put the utensils in place. Take down the kitchen shades and wipe them with a clean cloth. Brush the ceiling and walls. If the walls be painted, wash them in warm ammonia water, — four tablespoonfuls of ammonia to six quarts of water. Have ready a second pail of clear hot water and a clean cloth. Go over the washed space with the clean cloth and water; then wipe dry. If the woodwork be hard or grained, wash it in the same manner; using, however, only half as much ammonia. Wash the windows, scour the tables and sink, clean the pipes and faucets, black the stove, and wash the floor. When all this is done go over the woodwork with a flannel dampened with linseed oil and turpentine, — half of each; then rub with a dry flannel. The laundry and back halls should receive the same attention. Then the piazza and yard should be put in order.

CHAPTER XXV.

ODD BITS OF USEFUL KNOWLEDGE.

Points of Difference in Various Brands of Flour.

MUCH trouble in cooking arises from the difference in various brands of flour. There are often, indeed, variations in the same brand. All are caused by the different modes of making the flour, and changes in the kind of wheat used.

When flour is made by the roller process, two cupfuls will make a much stiffer batter than flour made by the old process of grinding between stones, or produced by first crushing by rollers and then grinding between stones. Millers all over the country are always looking for, and frequently making, improvements in the processes which they are accustomed to follow. This necessarily results in changes in the texture and quality of their products. Then, too, it makes a difference whether the wheat used is spring or winter wheat. In the Eastern States, where mills are few, the flour comes largely from Minnesota and other Western States. This flour has in the last fifteen or twenty years been made almost wholly by the roller process, and chiefly of spring wheat. The distinguishing quality of this flour is this: if rubbed between the fingers it feels rough and granular, and if pressed in the hand it will not hold its shape, but fall apart as granulated sugar would. When using this flour by measure, allow one eighth more wetting than for flour made by grinding between stones.

Recently a number of millers have modified the new process by using the rollers for cleansing, separating, and grinding until the last stages of the work, when the flour is put between stones and ground smooth and fine. When this is done the distinguishing features between the old and new processes are lost. This flour is smooth to the touch, will keep its shape if pressed in the hand, and will not absorb as much moisture as the more granular kind. It can be used equally well for bread, cake, and pastry. Some of the mills in New York, Pennsylvania, Ohio, and Michigan make this flour in perfection.

Flour that is made of new spring wheat will not give so good bread when first made as it will after it has been kept for a month or more. A great deal of the trouble with bread comes from this condition of the flour. A barrel of flour that will not make good bread to-day, simply because the wheat was too new when ground, will, if kept for two months, make perfect bread, if the yeast be good; for, after all, the yeast is more frequently than the flour the cause of failure to make satisfactory bread.

When one buys flour in small quantities there will always be an uncertainty as to how it will work until after the first time it is used. Even in small families it is better to get flour by the barrel, as it improves with age. Another thing for the housekeeper to remember is that the whitest flour is not the most nutritious. What is called first-quality flour does not contain nearly so large a quantity of the best elements of the wheat as the second quality, which is much darker, but gives a sweeter and more nutritious loaf.

It is wonderful to see the various processes through which the wheat goes before it comes out of the mill. There is no question that flour which is made by the roller process in the first stages and finally ground between the stones will give the most satisfaction. The wheat is more thoroughly cleaned than when the flour is made wholly by the old process, and the separation of the hard substance and the dust from the wheat is more thorough than by the old mode, and therefore when the flour comes from the millstones it is free from undesirable substances.

When and Why Soda, Cream of Tartar, and Baking Powders are Used.

Soda may be used in all kinds of bread, cake, pudding, and griddle cakes where an acid also is used. The acid may be cream of tartar, vinegar, lemon juice, sour milk or cream, molasses, or something else. If two teaspoonfuls of cream of tartar be used, there must be one teaspoonful of soda, save in cases where the cream of tartar is used only to give tone and firmness of texture to a pudding or cake in which only the whites of the eggs are employed, — such as many of the meringue puddings, and angel cake.

In puddings and cakes where molasses, lemon juice, or vinegar is used, soda should be used instead of baking powder, because the baking powder is a combination of an acid and alkali, and the proportions are so carefully adjusted that the two ingredients neutralize each other.

Sometimes a rule for cake or gingerbread calls for one teaspoonful of soda and one of cream of tartar. In such cases allowance is made for the acid in the molasses, or in the sour milk or cream that is used. Again, in making cake in which a good many eggs and wine or brandy are used, a small quantity of soda, but no cream of tartar, is called for. This is because there is enough acid in the wine and butter to neutralize the small quantity of soda and produce the required amount of carbonic acid gas.

It will be seen, by these statements, that the housekeeper who uses baking powder can do without cream of tartar, but she must be provided with soda when using molasses and sour milk and cream.

Soda should never be dissolved in hot water, because some of the gases would be liberated and wasted, and a greater amount of soda would be needed to make good this waste than if the soda were dissolved in cold water.

Housekeepers should remember, when making biscuit and dumplings with baking powder, that three teaspoonfuls of the powder will be required to make one quart of flour light. The manufacturers' directions often call for only two, and the result is unsatisfactory.

About Whipping Cream.

Have the cream very cold. Put it in a bowl or pail, and set this dish in a pan of cold water, — ice water if possible. Have a large bowl or pan set in another pan of ice water. Place the whip-churn in the cream, tipping a little to one side, that the air and cream may be forced through the holes in the bottom of the churn. Draw the dasher up about one third the length of the cylinder; then press down. Let the upward stroke be light, and the downward stroke hard. If you will count time in this way: *one*, two ; *one*, two, — it will insure a regular stroke, which is important.

When the bowl is full of froth, skim it off into the larger bowl, being careful not to skim too near the liquid cream. A little of the froth will become liquid, but this can be poured back into the bowl and whipped again.

WHIP-CHURN.

The cream must be neither too thick nor too thin. If too thick, thin it with milk. When cream is too thick for whipping, the bubbles will be very small and the cream will hardly double in volume. This kind of cream makes most desserts too rich. When the cream is too thin, the bubbles will be large and clear, and will break when touched. Such cream as is sold at creameries as thick or heavy cream, and costs from fifty to eighty cents a quart, — depending on the locality, — will require a pint of milk to a pint of cream. The thin cream sold at the creameries is often too poor to be whipped.

The whip-churn is a tin cylinder, perforated on the bottom and sides, in which a dasher of tin, also perforated, can be easily moved up and down. When this churn is placed in a bowl of cream and the dasher is worked, air is forced through the cream, causing it to froth.

Good cream may be frothed with a whisk, or with an egg-beater, but the whip-churn described above is, to my mind, the most satisfactory for this work.

How to Prepare Bread Crumbs.

There are two methods of preparing bread crumbs. Such as are to be used for escaloped dishes or dishes prepared *au gratin*, etc., should always be grated. That means, of course, that stale bread — not dried bread — should be used. This gives light, fluffy crumbs.

For breading, pieces of bread should be dried in a slow oven until not a particle of moisture is left. The dried bread should then be put in a bag and pounded fine with a wooden mallet. Now rub the crumbs through a common flour sieve, and put them away in glass jars. There should always be kept on hand a good supply of these dry crumbs.

Breading Articles for Frying.

The albumen of the egg hardens so quickly when exposed to a high temperature that it is used as a protection for articles of food that lack albuminous matter enough on the surface instantly to form a hard coating. The egg does not take a fine, brown color ; therefore, bread or cracker crumbs are used with it to give the food crispness and a rich color. Covering an article of food with egg and bread crumbs is called breading. Put the egg in a deep plate, and beat it thoroughly with a spoon, but not enough to make it light. Have the crumbs in another plate, or they may be spread in a thick bed on a board. Have the article that is to be breaded seasoned well with salt, and slightly with pepper, if the latter be used at all. Put the article in the egg, and with a tablespoon dip up and pour the egg over every part of it. Not a spot should escape the coating. With a broad-bladed knife lift the article from the egg, and roll it in the dried crumbs, being careful that every part is covered. Lay the breaded food on a flat dish or on the board until dry.

Never place one breaded article on another when drying or frying. When ready to fry, shake off the loose crumbs. Place in the wire basket, being careful not to crowd. Fish, meat, croquettes, etc., when dry after breading, may be placed in the refrigerator until the time for frying. They will keep for twelve hours or longer.

Sometimes a very thick crust is desired on some kinds of food. In that case bread all the articles, and when they are dry, give them a second coat of egg and crumbs.

Ways to Get Onion Juice.

Pare a fresh onion and bruise the side by striking with the dull edge of a knife; then press the flat side of the blade of the knife against the bruised place. The juice will fall in drops. If a large quantity be required, cut the onion fine, put it in a piece of cheese-cloth, and press in a lemon squeezer kept solely for this purpose.

Getting Rid of the Odor of Onions.

If the hands and the utensils which were used in preparing raw onions be thoroughly washed in cold water before soap or hot water touches them, the odor of the vegetable will disappear.

Stoning Raisins in an Easy Manner.

Stem the raisins, and, putting them in a bowl, cover with boiling water. Immediately pour off the water. This softens the skins and makes the raisins puff up so that the stones are removed with ease.

To Freshen Bread and Cake.

If you wish to freshen a stale loaf of bread or cake, put it in a deep pan, cover it closely and set it in rather a cool oven for about twenty minutes. The loaf will be almost as fresh as when first baked, but it must be used the same day, as it dries quickly when reheated in this manner.

Making a Bouquet of Sweet Herbs.

Tie together one spray of parsley, one sprig each of thyme and summer savory, one small leaf of sage, and one large bay leaf. This bouquet will flavor a gallon of soup. It must not cook in it for more than an hour. When only a small amount of soup or sauce is to be flavored, the bouquet should be cooked in the liquid but a short time, — perhaps from ten to twenty minutes.

Preventing a Meringue from Falling.

The means of preventing a meringue from falling when it is taken from the oven are simple. Usually the trouble arises from baking the meringue in too high a temperature. If you beat the whites of the eggs to a stiff, dry froth, then gradually beat in the powdered sugar (a generous tablespoonful for each white of an egg), put the meringue on the pie or pudding when partially cooled, and bake in a moderate oven, with the door open, for eighteen to twenty minutes, the annoyance may be avoided.

To Temper Iron and Earthen Ware.

Heat the iron slowly and then cool slowly. It is best, when it can be done, to grease the inside of the iron utensil and fill it with cold water; then heat the water gradually to the boiling point, and cool slowly. Earthenware is to be put in a kettle of cold water, which is then to be heated slowly to the boiling point, and cooled slowly. If convenient, put a little bran in the water.

Flour Paste.

Mix one heaped tablespoonful of flour with five of cold water. Pour on this a scant gill of boiling water, stirring all the time. Stir the mixture on the fire until it boils up, then strain.

What to do When Burning Accidents Occur.

There are many simple remedies which, in case of burning accidents, can be applied before the physician comes. So much immediate and future suffering can be averted by the prompt use of some remedy, that everybody should have fixed in mind some of the proper things to do. Slight burns, such as one often gets in the kitchen or laundry, can be relieved, and blistering be prevented, by coating the burned part with oil, lard, or butter, then covering with baking soda, and finally with a piece of linen. In a short time the pain will cease, and, unless the burn be very deep or the remedies be applied too late, there will be no blister. Lime water also is good for burns.

Children are often scalded by falling into hot water left within their reach, or by overturning some hot liquid upon themselves. In a case of scalding it must be remembered that the clothes clinging to the body are saturated with the hot liquid, and that as long as they are allowed to remain in this condition the heat will be kept in, and the burn become deeper. The first thing to do in a case of this kind is to pour cold water over the sufferer. This at once cools the clothing, which should afterward be taken off as gently but quickly as possible. Next pour sweet oil over the burns and cover them with soda, if you have it; if not,

ODD BITS OF USEFUL KNOWLEDGE. 369

cover with soft linen cloths, and then wet with lime water. If there be no oil at hand, lard will do. The things at which to aim are, to cover the burn at once with some pure oily substance and then with soda or lime water, to take out the fire; to have the place covered with linen, which will not stick to the wound; and, finally, to cover closely from the air. Nothing is better for this purpose than a thin roll of cotton batting spread over the linen. Sometimes the cotton batting is saturated with oil and laid directly on the wound; but it is apt to cling to the flesh, and cause much trouble and suffering. A fine quality of cotton batting may be obtained at any druggist's.

In every house there should be a closet or drawer on the first floor where a few simple remedies are kept. Here is a list for burns: a roll of old linen, such as handkerchiefs, napkins, pieces of table-cloths, sheets, and pillow-cases; a roll of cotton batting, a bottle of sweet oil, with the stopple drawn and gently put back, so that it can be quickly removed; a bottle of lime water; a box of powdered baking soda; a ball of soft darning cotton; and a needle, thread, thimble, and scissors. One may have no use for these things in many years; but the trouble of keeping them is trifling, and should there be need of them the advantage of having them ready for use is beyond estimation.

To make lime water, put about half a pound of unslaked lime in an earthen bowl, and pour over it three pints of boiling water. Stir with a stick, and put away in a cool place for eight or ten hours. At the end of that time pour off the clear lime water, letting the sediment remain in the bowl. Bottle the water, and put the stopple in, but not so far that it cannot be easily drawn.

Use of Naphtha in the Household.

Naphtha has come to be a power in cleaning establishments, and to some extent in the household. Before giving any directions for its use, I want to state that this fluid is extremely dangerous unless ample precautions be taken; but with proper care there is not the slightest danger. Naphtha is very volatile, giving off a highly inflammable gas. It is dangerous even to have an uncorked bottle of it in a room where there is a light or fire. If, however, when naphtha is being used, the windows in the room be open and there be neither light nor fire, there will not be a particle of danger.

Soiled carpets and garments may be cleaned by sponging with naphtha. Buffalo bugs and moths can be destroyed with it. For stuffed furniture use naphtha freely. Put the article on the piazza and pour the fluid into it, being sure that every part is saturated. After a day or two, repeat the process, and I think you will find that both worms and eggs are destroyed. Still, it will be necessary to keep a close watch; for it is more difficult to destroy the eggs than the worms, and they may be hatched out after days, or even weeks, have passed. I know that if the naphtha be used again at this time the trouble will be at an end. Furs and woollen garments should be well beaten, and then saturated with naphtha. There is no danger in this generous use of the fluid out of doors; but in the house great care must be exercised. Windows should be opened, and there should be no light or fire in the room for several days, if naphtha has been used in large quantities.

When rugs or carpets are attacked, have two hot flat-irons ready. Wet with hot water the parts that are affected. Place several thicknesses of wet cloth over this, and apply the hot iron, which should stand there for at least ten minutes, that the steam may penetrate every part. When all is done, pour on naphtha; also, pour it about the edges of the carpet. Remember that wiping with naphtha has no effect; it must be a generous bath. Let me say again, that the danger from the fluid comes from the gas, and that the windows are to be opened, and no fire or light allowed in the room during the work, or for a few hours after it is done.

Bedbugs can be banished from a room with two or three applications of naphtha. Take the bed apart and dust it. Let the parts lie flat on the floor with the grooved sides up. Saturate the bed with naphtha, filling the grooves. Pour the fluid into the pillows and mattresses, wetting the seams and tuftings thoroughly. Spray any cracks there may be in the walls. If there be a carpet on the floor it will be well to give it a naphtha bath, to clean and brighten it. When all this is done, close the room, leaving the windows open. It should stand in this way for at least eight hours, that the gas may pass off. Should any bugs appear after this, repeat the operation. The second time will not fail.

When putting away furs, flannels, rugs, etc., have the articles well beaten. Put them in sheets, and wet with naphtha; then pin the sheets and put the articles away in boxes or drawers.

A Word Regarding Stains.

Stains of all kinds are constantly getting on all sorts of articles and fabrics. Great care must be used in removing them, as the treatment that is good for one kind will produce the most disastrous results with another. A few simple remedies are given for the most common stains that trouble the housekeeper.

To Remove Grease Spots.

Where soap and hot water can be used, wash the spots in very hot water, using plenty of soap; then rinse well. French chalk or fuller's earth may be powdered and mixed with cold water, to make a thick paste. Spread this on the grease spot and let it remain for several days; then brush off. If the stain has not fully disappeared, apply the mixture a second time.

Oxgall may be used on dark colors; if purified, it may be used on any color. It can sometimes be bought at a druggist's in a purified state. Chemists also combine oxgall with turpentine and other cleaning agents. This preparation is effective and safe in removing grease.

In the case of delicate fabrics that can be washed, the spots may be rubbed with yolk of egg before the washing. Naphtha is usually effective in removing grease.

Here is still another way. Put a piece of blotting paper under the grease spot and another over it. Place a warm iron on the upper one. After a while remove the iron and paper, and, if the grease has not entirely disappeared, repeat the process with fresh paper.

If a large amount of oil or grease be spilled on a flat surface, immediately cover the place thickly with whiting, wheat flour, or meal of any kind. This will absorb some of the oily substance, and prevent it from spreading. After an hour or two brush off this substance and apply the usual remedies.

Grease spots on carpets may be taken out by covering the spots with fuller's earth, wet with spirits of turpentine. Let it stand until the earth is a fine dry powder.

Delicate fabrics, like silk, crêpe, ribbons, scarfs, etc., may be spread on a clean cloth and then be covered with powdered French chalk or fuller's earth. Roll up the article and put away for a few weeks and it will become clean.

To Take Grease from Wood and Stone.

Put one gill of washing soda and one quart of boiling water in a stewpan and place on the fire. When the soda is dissolved, pour the boiling liquid on the grease spot. Rub with an old broom. An hour or two later rub with a mop. Rinse out the mop; then wash with clean hot water. Be careful not to get the soda water on your hands, clothing, or boots.

Removing Stains from Marble.

If the stains were made by grease, spread wet whiting or chloride of lime on them and let it remain for several hours; then wash off. Washing soda, dissolved in hot water, mixed with enough whiting to form a thick paste, and kept on the stains for several hours, will remove grease spots.

Sometimes the marble has a discolored appearance from scratches. If it be rubbed hard with wet whiting and then washed and wiped dry, the mark will disappear. Ink and iron rust are usually removed with an acid, but if that be employed on marble, it will dissolve the stone. The remedies given for grease spots can, however, be used. Should an acid be used on marble, pour ammonia water on the spot and it will neutralize the acid, thus saving the marble.

Treatment of Fruit Stains.

One of the simplest methods is to place the stained part of the cloth over a bowl and continue pouring boiling water through until the stain disappears. If this be done soon after the article is stained, there will be no trouble in most cases.

Oxalic acid will remove fruit stains. As it is useful for many purposes, it is well to keep a bottle of it in some safe place. Put three ounces of the crystals in a bottle with half a pint of water. Mark the bottle plainly.

When stains are to be removed have a large pail of water and a bottle of household ammonia at hand. Wet the stained parts with the acid and then rub. When the stains have disappeared, put the article in the water. Wash thoroughly in several waters, and then wet the parts with the ammonia, that all trace of the acid may be removed. Finally, rinse again.

Coffee, Tea, and Wine Stains on Table Linen.

If treated at once such stains seldom give much trouble. Place the stained part over a large bowl and pour boiling water upon it until the stain disappears. If, however, the stains be of long standing, and have been washed with soap, it will be difficult to get rid of them. Javelle water (which can be made at home or bought of a druggist) will do it. Put about half a pint of Javelle water and a quart of clear water into an earthen bowl; let the stained article soak in this for several hours; then rinse thoroughly in three waters. It is only white goods that can be treated in this manner, as the Javelle water bleaches out the color. Another way to do is to put a little of the Javelle water in a saucer or small bowl, and soak the spot in this until it disappears. Rinse thoroughly.

When Cloths become Mildewed.

Put about a tablespoonful of chloride of lime in a wooden pail, or earthen bowl, and add four quarts of cold water. Stir until all the lime is dissolved, using a wooden spoon or paddle. Now put the mildewed article into the water and work it about, using the spoon or paddle. Let the article stay in the water until all the mildew has disappeared; then throw it into a tub of cold water. Wash well in this, and then rinse in a second tub of cold water; finally, wring out and dry. If the rinsing be thorough the fabric will be uninjured. It is only white goods that can be treated in this way, because chloride of lime removes colors as well as mildew.

The Best Way to remove Iron Rust.

Buy four ounces of muriatic acid at a druggist's. It is useful for various purposes. Have it marked plainly. It should, moreover, be labelled as poisonous.

ODD BITS OF USEFUL KNOWLEDGE.

Fill a large bowl with boiling water. Have another bowl or pan full of hot water. A bottle of household ammonia also is necessary. Place the spotted part of the garment over the bowl of hot water. Wet a cork in the muriatic acid and touch the iron rust with it. Immediately the spot will turn a bright yellow. Dip at once in the hot water, and the stain will disappear. When all the spots have been removed, rinse the article thoroughly in several clear waters, then in ammonia water (a tablespoonful of household ammonia to a quart of water), and finally in clear water. The acid is very powerful, and will destroy the fabric if allowed to remain upon it. Ammonia neutralizes it. If the directions be followed carefully, the most delicate fabric can be successfully treated in this way.

As muriatic acid is very destructive of tin, do not keep the bottle in the same closet with articles made of that metal.

Removing Blood Stains.

Wash the stain in blood-warm water until the greater part has been removed; then rub on some soap, and wash until the stain disappears. When the stain is on white cotton or linen goods, scald the article after it has been washed. Never use hot water until the stain is nearly removed.

Removing Sewing-machine Oil Stains.

Rub the stain with sweet oil or lard, and let it stand for several hours; then wash in soap and cold water.

To Remove Pitch and Tar.

Rub lard on the stain and let it stand for a few hours; then sponge with spirits of turpentine until the stain is removed. If the color of the fabric be affected, sponge it with chloroform and the color will be restored.

Alcohol for Grass Stains.

Rub the stain with alcohol; then wash in clean water.

Muriatic Acid for Stains on Porcelain.

When there is a great deal of iron in the water, the porcelain or china bowls in the bath-room become badly stained. Rub a little muriatic acid on the stained parts, and rinse thoroughly with cold water, adding a little ammonia to the rinsing water toward the end.

To Remove Paint.

Wet the paint with turpentine and rub with a woollen cloth. If the paint spot can be kept wet with the turpentine for a little while, it will not require so much rubbing.

Removing Ink Stains.

Tear blotting paper in pieces and hold the rough edges on the ink when it is freshly spilled. If you have no blotting paper at hand, cover the spot with Indian meal; or, the liquid ink may be absorbed by cotton batting. The first care should be to prevent the ink from spreading. If ink be spilled upon a carpet, cut a lemon in two, remove a part of the rind, and rub the lemon on the stain. As the lemon becomes stained with the ink, slice it off, and rub with the clean part. Continue this until the stain is removed.

If the stained article be washed immediately in several waters and then in milk, letting it soak in the milk for several hours, the stain will disappear.

Washing the article immediately in vinegar and water, and then in soap and water, will remove all ordinary ink stains.

Washing at once in water and then in liquid citric acid or oxalic acid is another mode. Oxalic acid is very corro-

ODD BITS OF USEFUL KNOWLEDGE. 377

sive, and should be removed from the article by a thorough washing in water. If, after the washing, the article be wet with household ammonia, any acid remaining will be neutralized.

No matter what substance be used to remove ink, the stain must be rubbed well. If the article stained be a carpet on the floor, use a brush. As the acids often affect the colors in a fabric, it is wise to try the water and milk or the water and vinegar method before resorting to the acids. Chemicals should always be the last resort, unless one be rather familiar with their action.

My own experience is that it is a most difficult matter to remove the stains of some kinds of black ink if they have stood for a few hours; whereas, other kinds, notably stylographic ink spots, can be removed easily with soap and water.

When Acids are Spilled.

A bottle of household ammonia should be kept where it can be reached conveniently at any time; then, when an acid is accidentally spilled, pour ammonia over the spot at once.

Restoring Colors.

When an acid has been spilled on a fabric its effect may be neutralized by sponging with ammonia. If an alkali, such as ammonia, soda, potash, etc., be spilled on a garment, its effect may be neutralized by sponging with weak vinegar.

If the color be not fully restored, sponge with chloroform.

To make Javelle Water.

Into a large saucepan, porcelain-lined if possible, put four pounds of bicarbonate of soda and four quarts of hot water. Stir frequently with a wooden stick until the soda is dissolved; then add one pound of chloride of lime, and stir occasionally until nearly all the solids are dissolved. Let the liquid cool in the kettle; then strain the clear part through a piece of cheese-cloth into wide-mouthed bottles. Put in the stoppers and set away for use. The part that is not clear can be put into separate bottles and used for cleaning white floors and tables; also for cleaning the sink.

In making this preparation be careful not to spatter it on your clothing or on the paint. Half a pint of this water can be put into a tub with about a dozen pails of warm suds, and the soiled white clothes be soaked in them. Much of the dirt can be removed by this method. The French laundresses use this preparation for white clothes.

A Good Cleaning Fluid.

Put into a large saucepan two quarts of water, half an ounce of borax, and four ounces of white castile soap shaved fine, and stir frequently until the soap and borax are dissolved; then take from the fire and add two quarts of cold water. When the mixture is cold, add one ounce of glycerine, one of ether, and four of ammonia crystals. Bottle and put away for use: it will keep for years.

To clean an article, first brush thoroughly, and then spread on a table. Sponge with the cleaning fluid and rub hard until the stains disappear. Then press if necessary.

This fluid will remove grease spots and stains of various kinds. It can be used on silks, cottons, and woollens. It is almost invaluable for cleaning men's clothing, dresses, carpets, etc. When a colored garment is to be sponged, try the fluid on a small piece of the goods, as it affects some colors.

Treatment of Grease Spots on Wall Paper.

If you find grease spots on wall paper, put powdered French chalk, wet with cold water, over the places, and let it remain for twelve hours or more. When you brush off the chalk, if the grease spots have not disappeared, put on more chalk, place a piece of coarse brown paper or blotting paper on this, and press for a few minutes with a warm flat-iron.

Stale Bread for Cleaning Soiled Paper.

Wipe the paper with a clean cloth. Cut a loaf of stale bread in two, lengthwise, and rub the bread over the paper, making long strokes straight up and down. When the bread becomes soiled, cut off a thin slice, and continue the work with the clean surface. A large room may require the use of two or three loaves.

Edges of books, margins of pictures, and other things may be cleaned in the same way.

Two Ways to Repair Wall Paper.

Have a set of children's paints, selecting those that have creams, browns, yellows, and perhaps green, blue, and red. Mix the colors until you get the shade of the foundation color of the paper, then lightly touch up the broken places. If the breaks be small this will be all that is necessary; but if large, it will be well when the first color is dry to touch up the place with the other colors. This is a much easier and more satisfactory method than patching the paper. If, however, the broken place be too large to be repaired with the paint, match the paper if you can and stick it on with flour paste. Never use mucilage, as it discolors the paper.

Brightening Leather Furniture.

Housekeepers often wonder if it is possible to restore the color to leather furniture which has become rusty in appearance. Furniture dealers say that real leather should not fade as long as it holds together. However, it does fade; so try this method of brightening it. Wash the leather with a sponge that has been wrung out of hot soap suds; then rub as dry as possible. Now place the furniture in the sun and wind, that it may get thoroughly dry as quickly as possible. Next, rub hard with a cloth that has been wet with kerosene. Let the furniture stand in the air until the odor of the oil has passed off.

Preventing Silks and Woollens from Turning Yellow.

Whenever you have occasion to pack away silk or woollen goods which you are afraid may turn yellow, break up a few cakes of white beeswax and fold the pieces loosely in old handkerchiefs that are worn thin. Place these among the goods. If possible, pin the silks or woollens in some old white linen sheets or garments. If it be inconvenient to use linen, take cotton sheets. Of course, it is important that the clothing shall be perfectly clean when put away.

Cleaning Dress Silks and Ribbons.

There are several methods of cleaning silks. They may be spread on a clean table and sponged with naphtha, alcohol, soap and water, etc.; or the silk may be washed in soap suds, gasoline or naphtha. As the gasoline or naphtha does not affect the colors, it is more desirable for colored silks.

If the silks be washed in suds, use the best white castile soap. Wash the silk in the suds; then rinse in clear water and hang on a clothes-horse in the shade. Do not wring it. When the silk is nearly dry lay it on a soft ironing cloth, and, after spreading either coarse brown paper or a newspaper over it, press with rather a cool iron. If naphtha or gasoline be used, have the liquid in a large bowl near an open window, and in a room where there is neither fire nor light. Wash the silk in this and hang in the air. It will dry quickly.

Black silk may be washed in ammonia water and rinsed in clear water to which has been added strong bluing and dissolved gelatine, — one quarter of an ounce of gelatine to one gallon of water.

Never iron silk unless it is absolutely necessary.

Cleaning Chamois Skins.

Chamois skins that have been used for cleaning silver, brass, etc., can be made as soft and clean as new by following these directions. Put six tablespoonfuls of household ammonia into a bowl with a quart of tepid water. Let the chamois skin soak in this water for an hour. Work it about with a spoon, pressing out as much of the dirt as possible; then lift it into a large basin of tepid water, and rub well with the hands. Rinse in fresh waters until clean, then dry in the shade. When dry, rub between the hands. Chamois jackets can be washed in the same manner, except that there should be two quarts of water to the six tablespoonfuls of ammonia. Pull into shape before drying.

To Clean Brushes.

Put enough warm water in a flat bowl or pan to cover the bristles, but not to come over the back of the brush. To each quart of water put three tablespoonfuls of household ammonia. Lay the brushes in this for about five minutes, then work them gently in the water. Rinse thoroughly in cold water, and rest them on the edge where a current of air will strike them.

Care of Straw Matting.

This floor covering should not be washed often. Boil together for one hour two quarts of bran and four of water. Strain this, pressing all moisture out of the bran.

Add two quarts of cold water and two tablespoonfuls of salt to the strained mixture. Wash the matting with this and rub dry with a clean cloth.

To Clean Woods in Natural Finish.

To clean woodwork in your halls and rooms do not wash it. Soap destroys the looks of woodwork that is finished in natural colors. Wring a flannel cloth out of hot water and wipe off the dust. When all the woodwork has been dusted in this manner go over it with a woollen cloth made damp with cotton-seed or sweet oil and alcohol or turpentine; two parts oil and one alcohol or turpentine. Rub hard, and with the grain of the wood; then rub with clean flannel. It will revive the color and gloss. Light woods must be wiped with a damp flannel and polished with a dry piece of flannel. Do not use oil on light woods.

To clean the railing of banisters, wash off all the dirt with soap and water, and when dry rub with two parts of linseed oil and one of turpentine.

All dark woods that have become soiled and dingy may be washed with soap and water, using, if possible, a piece of flannel. Dry with a soft cloth. Mix together two parts of linseed oil and one of turpentine. Moisten an old piece of flannel in this and rub the furniture with it. Finish by rubbing hard, and with the grain, with a dry old piece of flannel. If there be any white stains rub them with kerosene, using a good deal of oil and much pressure.

The soiled wood may be cleaned with turpentine instead of soap and water.

To Remove White Stains from Furniture.

Wet a woollen cloth with kerosene and rub the spot until the stain disappears. It may take a good deal of hard rubbing if the stain be deep or of long standing, but perseverance will accomplish the object.

Cleaning Brass.

There are many good preparations which come for cleaning brass. The most of them do the work quickly, leaving a brilliant polish, but the metal does not keep clean so long as when cleaned by the old method. Pound fine and then sift half a pint of rotten-stone. Add to this half a gill of turpentine and enough sweet oil to make a thick paste. Wash the brasses in soap and water, wipe dry, and then rub with the paste. Rub with a soft clean rag, and polish with a piece of chamois skin.

Conveniences when Sweeping.

If one have proper covers for the pictures and heavy pieces of furniture in the room, a great amount of trouble can be saved on the sweeping day. Buy cheap print cloth for the furniture. Have three breadths in the cover, and have it three yards and a half long. It should be hemmed, and the work can be done quickly on a sewing-machine. I find six cloths a convenient number, although we do not always need so many. Get cheap unbleached cotton, and cut it into lengths suitable for covering pictures, heavy ornaments, clocks, etc. These need not be hemmed. Always remove any coverings gently; then take them out of doors to be shaken. Fold them and put them away. They will last a long time, and pay for themselves in a year, because they save so much extra dusting, and the moving of heavy articles.

Mending Breaks in Plaster.

Mix together half a pint of powdered lime, one gill of plaster of Paris, and cold water enough to make a thick paste. Fill the holes with this and smooth the surface with a knife. Work quickly. If there be many breaks mix only as much plaster as can be used in ten minutes, as it hardens quickly.

Another method is to fill the breaks with putty. When the plaster or putty is dry, the places can be touched with water colors to correspond with the rest of the wall.

Cement for Stoves and Iron Ware.

Mix together enough water glass and iron filings to make a thick paste. Apply this to the cracks or holes, and heat gradually almost to a red heat. This substance will bear a white heat, although of course one would rarely have occasion to test it to this degree. The water glass and iron filings can be bought at a druggist's.

Cement for China.

Dissolve one ounce of powdered gum-arabic in a gill of boiling water. Stir enough plaster of Paris into the liquid to make it the consistency of thick cream. Use immediately.

ANOTHER RULE. — Powder quick-lime and stir it into the white of an egg, making rather a thick paste. Coat the broken edges lightly with this, and tie the pieces together.

How to Fasten Handles of Knives and Forks.

Mix together two ounces of powdered rosin, one ounce of powdered sulphur, and one ounce of iron filings. Keep these in a box, and, when a knife or fork becomes loosened from the handle, fill the opening in the handle with the powdered mixture. Heat the tang of the instrument and press it into the handle. Should it not go in to the hilt, heat again, and the second attempt will be successful.

Do not pack the powder into the opening. Should the powder blaze up when the heated metal is inserted, blow out the flame. Be careful to turn the fork-tines or knife-blade around until in the right position, before the filling becomes hard.

Value of a Drop of Oil.

Every housekeeper knows how annoying it is to have the hinges of the doors squeak, and the locks and bolts refuse to move unless great force be used. Many do not realize that a few drops of oil will, as a rule, remedy these annoyances. First spread a newspaper on that part of the floor over which the hinges swing. Now, with the sewing-machine oil can, oil the hinges thoroughly, and then swing the door back and forth until it moves without noise. Wipe the hinges, but let the paper remain for a few hours, to guard against the possible dripping of oil. For locks and bolts, protect the floor in the same manner. Oil them thoroughly, working them until they will move with ease. The egg-beater and the ice-cream freezer should be oiled frequently in the same manner.

What to do when the Chimney is Cold.

When lighting a fire where the chimney has not been used for some time, start the current of air upward by burning a paper in the stove pipe, or by holding it in the chimney, if it be a grate fire.

If the heat has been turned off from a room for some time it occasionally happens that the heated air will not come through the pipe when it is turned on again. In that case close for a few minutes nearly all the registers which serve as outlets for the other pipes, and the heat will be forced into the cold pipe. After this it will go that way naturally.

To Prevent Kid from Cracking.

When kid boots require a dressing, rub a little castor oil into the kid before the dressing is put on. This will keep the leather soft.

Testing the Oven Heat with Paper.

Have white paper for testing the heat of the oven. Put a piece on the bottom of the oven and close the door. For pastry, the oven should be hot enough to turn the paper dark brown in five minutes; for bread, the heat should turn it in six minutes. All kinds of muffins can be baked at this heat. Cup cakes should be put into an oven that will turn a piece of white paper dark yellow in five minutes. Sponge and pound cakes require heat that will turn white paper light yellow in five minutes. Bread requires great heat at first; later, the heat is to be reduced. Cake should have rather a cool oven. The heat can be increased later.

Oven Thermometers.

Many efforts have been made to produce a thermometer which will indicate the temperature of the oven, but, so far as I know, none made with mercury have been satisfactory. There is made in this country, however, an "oven clock," which can be set into the door of the oven. This is based on the principle of the contraction and expansion of the metals. To get the greatest benefit from these clocks the housekeeper must make her tests herself; that is, she must learn that when the hand points to a certain number the oven is right for roasting; when at another point, that the heat is right for baking bread, cake, etc. After she has established these facts, she may write out a table which will serve as a safe guide in the future.

Ridding the House of Water Bugs.

Strew powdered borax about the pipes and in any cracks in the walls or woodwork where water bugs appear. If this be persisted in, and everything be kept perfectly clean, you can rid the house of the insects.

Keeping Flies from Chandeliers.

Wipe the chandeliers with a soft cloth that has been wet in kerosene oil. This should be done several times during the summer. Fly specks can be wiped off in the same manner, even when on gilt picture frames; but the cloth must be only slightly moistened in the latter case, and used lightly, else the gilt itself may come off.

Driving away Ants.

Put green walnuts around the places where the ants come and they will disappear; or, strew fresh pennyroyal around. If it is impossible to get the fresh herb, use the oil. Tar mixed with hot water, and placed in bowls or jars in the room or closet, will often drive away these pests.

Care of the Hands.

Doing housework is apt to make the hands become rough. Have thick gloves to wear when making fires and cleaning stoves and grates. Wear, when sweeping and dusting, old gloves that fit loosely. As much as possible use one kind of soap; changes of soap and water irritate the hands. Have soft hand-towels in the kitchen, and always wipe the hands perfectly dry. When the work is done rub the hands with bran and vinegar diluted with water. Rinse them in tepid water and wipe perfectly dry. Rub a little cold cream into the hands at night, and also, if convenient, after the coarse work has been done for the day.

Cold Cream.

2 ounces of cocoa butter.
2 ounces of spermaceti.
2 ounces of white wax.

2 ounces of rose water.
4 ounces of sweet almond oil.

Break up the wax, spermaceti, and cocoa butter. Put all the ingredients into a bowl, and place this in a pan of boiling water. Stir the mixture until it becomes a soft, smooth mass; then put it in little jars, and keep in a cool dry place. This is excellent for the hands and face. In winter use only one ounce of spermaceti.

Cupfuls, Half-pints, and Gills.

The ordinary kitchen cup is supposed to hold half a pint, and nearly all writers of cook-books base their measurements on this understanding. Nearly all first-class kitchen furnishing stores keep what are known as measuring cups. They are made of tin, and hold half a pint, old measure. One cup is divided into four parts, and one into three. A set of these cups will be found of the greatest value in the kitchen, as they insure accurate measurements.

QUART MEASURE.

Here is a table which will be helpful to those who do not have such cups to work with : —

1 cupful = ½ pint.
½ cupful = 1 gill.
¼ cupful = ½ gill.

ODD BITS OF USEFUL KNOWLEDGE.   389

Equivalents of Measures in Weight.

New-process flour, 1 quart less 1 gill	1 pound.
Pastry flour, 1 quart, sifted	1 "
Granulated sugar, 1 heaped pint	1 "
Butter, 1 pint	1 "
Powdered sugar, 5 gills	1 "
Chopped meat, 1 pint, packed solid	1 "
Liquids, 1 pint	1 "
Eggs, 10 of average size	1 "
Corn meal, ½ pint	6 ounces.
Rice, ½ pint	8 "
Raisins, stemmed, ½ pint	6 "
English currants, cleaned, ½ pint	6 "
Bread crumbs, grated, 1 pint	4 "
Granulated sugar, 1 heaped tablespoonful	1 "
Powdered sugar, 1 slightly rounded tablespoonful	½ "
Butter, 1 rounded tablespoonful	1 "
Flour, 1 rounded tablespoonful	½ "
Baking powder, 1 heaped teaspoonful	¼ "
Soda, 1 slightly rounded teaspoonful	¼ "
Cream of tartar, 2 slightly rounded teaspoonfuls	¼ "
Ginger, 1 heaped teaspoonful	¼ "
Cinnamon, 1 heaped teaspoonful	¼ "
Allspice, 1 generously heaped teaspoonful	¼ "
Clove, 1 slightly heaped teaspoonful	¼ "
Mace, 1 heaped teaspoonful	¼ "
Pepper, 1 heaped teaspoonful	¼ "
Salt, 1 teaspoonful	¼ "
Mustard, 1 rounded teaspoonful	¼ "
Nutmegs, 5	1 "
Tea, 3 scant teaspoonfuls	¼ "
Coffee, roasted berry, 1 tablespoonful	½ "
Liquids, 2 tablespoonfuls	1 "

INDEX.

A WORD WITH THE YOUNG HOUSEWIFE.

	Page		Page
Difference between mere housekeeping and home-making	1	My idea of good housekeeping	2
Folly of "keeping up appearances"	3	Some things a good housekeeper will do	2

ABOUT FURNISHING THE HOUSE.

	Page		Page
INTRODUCTION	4	LINEN CLOSET, FURNISHING	13
Carpets and rugs, selecting	6	Bed spreads and blankets	18
Chambers, what to buy for the	5	Doilies	16
Cutlery, fashions in	9	Linen, imported	14
Dainty things for the table	9	Napkins, size and quality of	16
Dining-room furniture	5	Sheets and pillow cases	18
Dinner and tea set, choosing a	7	Table-cloths and napkins	14
KITCHEN, WHAT IS NEEDED IN THE	11	Tea, carving, and tray cloths	17
List of articles most in use	12	Towels, bath and bedroom	20
Range, the	11	Towels, kitchen and pantry	21
		Sitting-room, comfort in the	0

DIVISION OF THE HOUSEHOLD WORK

	Page		Page
INTRODUCTION	22	Morning, what to do in the	23
Cleaning a room by system	26	Servant, where one is kept	26
Day of rest, a	28	Servants, two or more in the family	29
Every-day duties	23		
Last half of the week, duties in the	27	Special work for special days	24

INDEX.

SOME THINGS TO BE LEARNED EARLY.

	Page		Page
Bath-room, about the	36	Washing Dishes	38
Fires, proper management of	31	Cautions, some special	40
Furnace fire, points about the	32	China, tins, and iron-ware	39
Garbage barrel, do not neglect the	37	Glassware, proper care of	38
Lamps, getting the greatest good out of	34	Knife blades, do not slight the	41
		Rust and other annoyances	42
Plumbing, taking care of	35	Silver, care of	40
Refrigerator, the, keeping sweet	33		

WORK ON WASHING DAY.

	Page		Page
Introduction	44	Silk undergarments, the right way to wash	46
Curtains, lace, cleaning	47		
Curtains, washable, how to launder	47	Soap, borax	50
		Soap, hard, rule for	49
Flannels, how to wash	45	Soap, soft	50
Ironing	48	Starching	48
Satines, ginghams, and prints	44		

IN THE DINING-ROOM.

	Page		Page
Introduction	52	Refinement not exclusively for the rich	53
Breakfast table, at the	54		
Dinner table, how to set the	55	Serving meals without a servant	58
Duties of the waitress	57	Table, setting the	52
Luncheon and tea table	56	Waitress, duties of the	57

BUYING FOOD AND CARING FOR IT.

	Page		Page
Beef, fore quarter of	64	Hind quarter of beef	62
Beef, hind quarter of	62	Leg of mutton	72
Beef, loin of	70	Loin of beef	70
Beef, rump of	71	Market, going to	60
Beef, sirloin, second cut	66	Milk	73
Butter	73	Mutton, carcass of	67
Buying for a small family	70	Mutton, leg of	72
Chops, rib	69	Odds and ends, care of	77
Chuck ribs	61	Rib chops	69
Clarifying fat	76	Ribs, chuck	61
Eggs	73	Ribs, first five	61
First five ribs	61	Rump of beef	71
Food, care of	75	Sirloin of beef, second cut	66
Fore quarter of beef	64	Sirloin roast	68
Going to market	60	Small family, buying for a	70
Groceries	74		

INDEX.

SOUPS.

	Page		Page
Bean	92	Lima bean	90
Bean, cream of	92	Macaroni	82
Bean, Lima	90	Macaroni and tomato	88
Beef	82	Mock bisque	87
Bisque, mock	87	Oxtail	83
Chicken	86	Oyster	92
Chowder, clam	73	Pea, dried	91
Chowder, fish	94	Plain stock	80
Chowder, salt codfish	95	Potato	89
Clam chowder	93	Rice	82
Clam	93	Rice, cream of	86
Codfish chowder, salt	95	Salt codfish chowder	95
Corn	89	Scotch broth	84
Cream of bean	92	Stock, a good plain	80
Cream of dried peas	91	Stock, second	81
Cream of rice	86	Tomato	87
Dried pea	91	Tomato, No. 2	88
Dried pea, cream of	91	Tomato and macaroni	88
Fish chowder	94	Veal broth	84
Hub	90	Vegetable soup	85

FISH.

	Page		Page
Introduction	96	Fish cakes, fresh	104
Baked fish	98	Fricassee of lobster	109
Baked salt mackerel	99	Fried fish	100
Boiling fish	97	Fried oysters	107
Breaded fish	101	Fried scallops	105
Breaded lobster	109	Halibut, broiled	100
Broiling fish	99	How fish should be broiled	99
Broiled halibut	100	How to boil fish	97
Clams, roast	111	Lobster	108
Clams, steamed	111	Lobster, breaded	109
Clams, stewed	110	Lobster, curry of	108
Codfish, salt, in cream	102	Lobster, escaloped	109
Crabs, escaloped	110	Lobster, fricassee of	109
Creamed oysters	107	Mackerel, baked salt	99
Curry of lobster	108	Oysters au gratin	106
Escaloped crabs	110	Oysters, creamed	107
Escaloped fish	101	Oysters, escaloped	106
Escaloped lobster	109	Oysters, fried	107
Escaloped oysters	106	Oysters on toast	105
Escaloped shrimp	110	Oyster stew	105
Fish balls	103	Roast clams	111
Fish cakes	103	Salt codfish in cream	102

FISH (continued).

	Page		Page
Scallops, fried	105	Stewed clams	110
Shrimp, escaloped	110	Stewed oysters	105
Steamed clams	111		

HOW TO COOK MEAT.

	Page		Page
Baked hash	147	Chops, pork	139
Beef, braised	131	Cold lamb stew	135
Beef, shin, stewed	129	Cold meat, blanquette of	138
Beefsteak and onions	124	Cold mutton stew	135
Beefsteak roll	132	Cold roast, beef stew from	134
Beef stew from cold roast	134	Corned beef, boiled	113
Beef olives	133	Corned beef hash	146
Blanquette of cold meat	138	Corned beef, spiced	114
Boiling	112	Creamed chicken	158
Boiled corned beef	113	Creamed dried beef	135
Boiled fowl	154	Creamed turkey	159
Boiled ham	115	Croquettes, breading	151
Boiled leg of mutton	112	Croquettes, meat and potato	152
Boiled tongue	115	Croquettes, mutton	150
Braised beef	131	Curried rabbit	163
Breaded chicken	157	Cutlets, mutton, sauté	128
Breaded chops	127	Cutlets, veal, breaded	128
Breaded sausages	129	Dried beef, creamed	135
Breaded veal cutlets	128	Duck, roast	160
Breading croquettes	151	Fat, how to keep	126
Broiling	122	Fat, the kind to use	126
Broiling in a frying-pan	123	Fresh meat hash	146
Broiled chops with bacon	123	Fresh tongue	115
Broiled kidneys	142	Fricassee of rabbit	162
Broiled small birds	162	Fricassee of veal	137
Broiled tripe	144	Fried chicken	158
Broiled venison	163	Fried liver and bacon	143
Calf's liver sauté	143	Fried salt pork	139
Chicken, breaded	157	Fried tripe	145
Chicken, creamed	158	Frizzled smoked beef	135
Chicken dressing	157	Frying	124
Chicken, fried	158	Frying basket, the way to lower it	127
Chicken gravy	156	Frying-pan, to broil in	123
Chicken livers en brochette	144	Gravy, chicken	156
Chicken pie	160	Grouse, roast	161
Chicken, roast	155	Ham, boiled	115
Chicken, stewed	159	Ham, roast	121
Chicken, white fricassee	160	Hamburg steaks	133
Chops, breaded	127	Hash, baked	147
Chops, broiled, with bacon	123	Hash, corned beef	146

HOW TO COOK MEAT (*continued*).

	Page		Page
Hash of fresh meat	146	Roast pork	121
How to clean and truss poultry	153	Roast ptarmigan	161
How to keep fat	126	Roast rib of beef	118
How to roast meat in the oven	117	Roast turkey	156
Kidneys, broiled	142	Roast veal	120
Kidneys sauté	141	Salt pork, fried	139
Kidneys, stewed	141	Salt pork in batter	140
Lamb, roast	119	Sanders	149
Leg of mutton, boiled	112	Sausages, breaded	129
Liver, fried, with bacon	143	Sausage cakes	140
Livers, chicken, en brochette	144	Sausage hash	147
Meat and potato croquettes	152	Science in roasting meat	116
Meat cakes	148	Sheep's hearts, stewed	142
Meat, how to roast in the oven	117	Shin of beef, stewed	129
Meat, minced, on toast	148	Small birds, broiled	162
Minced meat on toast	148	Small timbales	149
Miscellaneous modes	129	Smoked beef, frizzled	135
Mutton, boiled leg of	112	Smoked tongue	115
Mutton croquettes	150	Spiced corned beef	114
Mutton cutlets sauté	128	Steak, Hamburg	133
Mutton, ragout of	137	Steamed mutton	113
Mutton, roast	120	Stew from cold lamb or mutton	135
Mutton, steamed	113	Stewed chicken	159
Mutton, stuffed	120	Stewed kidneys	141
Olives, beef	133	Stewed sheep's hearts	142
Partridge, roast	161	Stewed shin of beef	129
Pickled tongue	115	Stuffed mutton	120
Pie, chicken	160	Tongue, boiled	115
Pork chops	139	Tongue, pickled	115
Pork, roast	121	Tongue, smoked	115
Pot roast	130	Tongue toast	148
Poultry, to clean and truss	153	Tripe, broiled	144
Ptarmigan, roast	161	Tripe, fried	145
Rabbit, curried	163	Tripe fried in batter	145
Rabbit, fricassee of	162	Turkey, creamed	159
Ragout of mutton	137	Turkey or chicken dressing	157
Rib of beef, roast	118	Turkey, roast	156
Roast chicken	155	Veal cutlets, breaded	128
Roast duck	160	Veal cutlets, sauté	136
Roast grouse	161	Veal, fricassee of	137
Roast ham	121	Veal olives	136
Roasting meat, science in	116	Veal, roast	120
Roast lamb	119	Venison, broiled	163
Roast mutton	120	Venison steak sauté	163
Roast partridge	161	White fricassee of chicken	160

SAUCES FOR MEAT AND FISH.

	Page		Page
Bechamel	165	Egg	167
Bisque	168	Hollandaise	168
Bread	171	Maître d'hôtel butter	170
Brown	164	Mint	170
Brown, No. 2	164	Mushroom	165
Butter	167	Mustard	166
Butter, maître d'hôtel	170	Parsley	166
Caper	167	Tartar	169
Cream	166	Tomato	169
Currant jelly	170	White	165
Curry	167		

SALADS.

	Page		Page
INTRODUCTION	172	Lobster	174
Beet	175	Mayonnaise dressing	172
Chicken	174	Potato	176
Cooked salad dressing	173	Potato, No. 2	176
Fish	174	Salad dressing, cooked	173
French dressing	173	Tomato and lettuce	175
Lettuce and tomato	175	Vegetable	175

VEGETABLES.

	Page		Page
INTRODUCTION	177	Cabbage, baked	195
Asparagus on toast	192	Cabbage, creamed	194
Asparagus with cream sauce	192	Cabbage, fried	195
Baked beans	190	Cabbage, hashed	194
Baked cabbage	195	Canned corn	188
Baked hominy	197	Canned peas	191
Baked rice	198	Carrots, boiled	186
Baked sweet potatoes	182	Cauliflower au gratin	187
Beans, baked	190	Cauliflower, boiled	187
Beans, butter	189	Celery	199
Beans, shelled kidney	190	Corn, canned	188
Beets	185	Corn, green	188
Boiled carrots	186	Corn oysters	188
Boiled cauliflower	187	Creamed cabbage	194
Boiled macaroni	196	Creamed onions	184
Boiled onions	183	Croquettes, potato	182
Boiled potatoes	178	Croquettes, rice	198
Boiled rice	197	Dried Lima beans	189
Boiled sweet potatoes	182	Dried Lima beans, No. 2	189
Boiled turnips	185	Egg plant, fried	196
Browned sweet potatoes	183	Fresh Lima beans	189

INDEX. 397

VEGETABLES (continued).

	Page		Page
Fried cabbage	195	Potatoes, stewed	179
Fried egg plant	196	Potatoes, stewed, No. 2	179
Green corn	188	Potatoes, sweet, baked	182
Green peas	191	Potatoes, sweet, boiled	182
Greens	193	Potatoes, sweet, browned	183
Hash, vegetable	198	Potatoes, sweet, warming over	183
Hashed cabbage	194	Rice, baked	198
Hashed potatoes	180	Rice, boiled	197
Hominy, baked	197	Rice croquettes	198
Lettuce, how to keep crisp	199	Salsify	187
Lima beans, dried	189	Shelled kidney beans	190
Lima beans, dried, No. 2	189	Sliced tomatoes	184
Lima beans, fresh	189	Spinach	193
Lyonnaise potatoes	181	Squash	195
Macaroni, boiled	196	Squash, summer	196
Macaroni with cheese	197	Stewed potatoes	179
Mashed turnips	186	Stewed potatoes, No. 2	179
Nichewaug potatoes	181	Stewed tomatoes	184
Onions au gratin	184	String beans	188
Onions, boiled	183	Succotash of dried Lima beans and canned corn	190
Onions, creamed	184	Summer squash	196
Parsnips	186	Tomatoes au gratin	185
Peas, canned	191	Tomatoes, sliced	184
Peas, green	191	Tomatoes, stewed	184
Potato cakes	182	Turnips, boiled	185
Potato croquettes	182	Turnips, mashed	186
Potatoes au gratin	180	Vegetable hash	198
Potatoes, boiled	178	Warming over sweet potatoes	188
Potatoes, hashed	180		

MISCELLANEOUS DISHES.

Apple fritters	207	Bread, fried	206
Apple sauce, evaporated	213	Bread omelet	205
Apple sauce, green	213	Breaded eggs	202
Apples, broiled	213	Broiled apples	213
Apples, fried	213	Corn meal mush	210
Apricots, evaporated	214	Cracker cream toast	209
Baked eggs	202	Cranberry jelly	213
Baked omelet	205	Cranberry sauce	215
Baked pears	214	Creamed eggs	202
Baked sweet apples	212	Dumplings	215
Baked toast	208	Eggs au gratin	201
Batter for fruit fritters	207	Eggs, baked	202
Boiled eggs	200	Eggs, boiled	200
Boiled hominy	211	Eggs, breaded	202

MISCELLANEOUS DISHES (*continued.*)

	Page		Page
Eggs, creamed	202	Mush, fried	210
Egg cutlets	203	Oatmeal mush	210
Eggs, fried	201	Omelet, baked	205
Eggs, poached	200	Omelet, plain	203
Eggs scrambled	201	Oyster crackers, roasted	206
Evaporated apple sauce	213	Peaches, evaporated	214
Evaporated apricots	214	Pears, baked	214
Evaporated peaches	214	Plain omelet	203
Fried apples	213	Poached eggs	200
Fried bread	206	Prunes, stewed	214
Fried eggs	201	Rarebit, Welsh	206
Fried hominy	211	Rhubarb sauce	215
Fried mush	210	Roasted oyster crackers	206
Fritters, apple	207	Scrambled eggs	201
Fruit fritters, batter for	207	Soft butter toast	208
Fruit sauces	212	Stewed prunes	214
Green apple sauce	213	Sweet apples, baked	212
Hominy, boiled	211	Syrup, maple, from sugar	207
Hominy cakes	211	Toast, baked	208
Hominy, fried	211	Toast, cracker cream	209
Maple syrup from sugar	207	Toast, milk	208
Milk toast	208	Toast, soft butter	208
Mush	209	Welsh rarebit	206
Mush, corn meal	210		

BREAD IN VARIOUS FORMS.

	Page		Page
INTRODUCTION	217	Buckwheat cakes	235
Baking powder biscuit	226	Buttermilk or sour milk muffins	230
Baking powder griddle cakes	236	Cakes, baking powder griddle	236
Baltimore hominy bread	234	Cakes, blueberry griddle	237
Biscuit, baking powder	226	Cakes, bread griddle	236
Blueberry griddle cakes	237	Cakes, buckwheat	235
Blueberry muffins	232	Cakes, sour milk graham griddle	236
Boston brown bread	222	Cakes, ground rice griddle	237
Bread, Baltimore hominy	234	Cakes, hominy griddle	236
Bread, corn	233	Cakes, hominy, with sour milk, griddle	237
Bread dough, rolls from	223		
Bread, entire-wheat	221	Cakes, raised flannel	238
Bread, graham	221	Cakes, sour milk griddle	235
Bread griddle cakes	238	Cakes, sour milk Indian griddle	236
Bread made with dry yeast	219	Corn bread	233
Bread, pulled	223	Corn cake, spider	233
Bread, rye	222	Corn dodgers	234
Bread, steamed Indian	223	Cream of tartar muffins	232
Bread, water	220	Crumpets	227

INDEX. 399

BREAD IN VARIOUS FORMS (continued)

	Page		Page
Dry yeast, bread made with	219	Parker House rolls	224
Entire-wheat bread	221	Pin wheels	227
Flour pop-overs	228	Pop-overs, flour	228
Gems, wheat	229	Pop-overs, graham	229
Graham bread	221	Pulled bread	223
Graham muffins	231	Quick luncheon rolls	227
Graham muffins with sour milk	231	Raised flannel cakes	238
Graham pop-overs	229	Raised wheat muffins	230
Griddle cakes, bread	238	Raised wheat waffles	240
Griddle cakes, baking powder	236	Rolls from bread dough	223
Griddle cakes, blueberry	237	Rolls, luncheon	226
Griddle cakes, ground rice	237	Rolls, quick luncheon	227
Griddle cakes, hominy	236	Rolls, milk	225
Griddle cakes, hominy, with sour milk	237	Rolls, Parker House	224
		Rolls, sponge	224
Griddle cakes, sour milk	235	Rye bread	222
Griddle cakes, sour milk graham	236	Rye muffins	231
Griddle cakes, sour milk Indian	236	Rye muffins, with sour milk	231
Ground rice griddle cakes	237	Rye pop-overs	229
Hominy griddle cakes	236	Sally Lunn	228
Hominy griddle cakes with sour milk	237	Sour milk graham griddle cakes	236
		Sour milk griddle cakes	255
Hominy waffles	240	Sour milk Indian griddle cakes	236
Hop yeast	218	Sour milk or buttermilk muffins	230
Luncheon rolls	226	Spider corn cake	233
Milk rolls	225	Sponge rolls	224
Muffins, blueberry	232	Steamed Indian bread	223
Muffins, buttermilk or sour milk	230	Waffles	238
Muffins, cream of tartar	232	Waffles, hominy	240
Muffins, graham	231	Waffles, raised wheat	240
Muffins, graham with sour milk	231	Water bread	220
Muffins, raised wheat	230	Wheat gems	229
Muffins, rye	231	White corn meal muffins	233
Muffins, rye, with sour milk	231	Yeast, hop	218
Muffins, white corn meal	233	Yellow corn meal muffins	232
Muffins, yellow corn meal	232		

CAKE.

	Page		Page
Angel	244	Dropped doughnuts	250
Blackberry jam	242	Gingerbread, maple sugar	248
Blueberry	247	Gingerbread, soft molasses	248
Chocolate icing	252	Gingerbread, soft molasses, No. 2	249
Clinton doughnuts	249	Gingerbread, soft molasses, No. 3	249
Cold water	245	Hermits	247
Corn starch	244	Icing	252

CAKE (continued).

	Page		Page
Maple sugar gingerbread	240	Soft molasses gingerbread	248
Plain cup	245	Spice	241
Plain sponge	243	Strawberry shortcake	251
Raised fruit	241	Strawberry shortcake, No. 2	251
Rich cup	245	Swiss	246
Rich sponge	242	Tea	246

PASTRY.

Apple pie, sliced	254	Mince meat	254
Apple pie, stewed	255	Mince pies	255
Apple turnovers	259	Peach pie	255
Berry pies	256	Plain paste	253
Berry tarts	258	Sliced apple pie	254
Chocolate pie	258	Squash pie	256
Cream pie	257	Stewed apple pie	255
Delicate paste	253	Sweet potato pie	257
Lemon pie	256	Washington pie	258

PUDDINGS.

Apple and Indian	262	Dumplings, steamed apple	262
Apple sponge	263	English rice	280
Apple tapioca	262	Farina, cold	280
Baked apple	261	Farina fruit	281
Baked apple dumplings	261	Farina, hot	280
Baked Indian	271	Graham	270
Baked rice	280	Hot farina	280
Berry	266	Indian and apple	262
Blackberry	267	Jam	268
Blueberry	265	Lemon	273
Blueberry, No. 2	266	Little fruit	265
Boiled rice	278	Mock Indian	272
Bread	272	Oatmeal	278
Caramel	276	Orange snow	283
Chester	269	Peach tapioca	263
Chocolate	275	Plum	269
Chocolate, No. 2	275	Prune	263
Cocoanut	277	Prune tapioca	264
Cold farina	280	Quick steamed apple	261
Cold rice	279	Quiver	268
Corn starch	276	Raspberry tapioca	264
Cottage	273	Rhubarb	267
Cream	274	Rice balls	279
Custard	277	Rose	281
Dumplings, baked apple	262	Snow	282

PUDDINGS (continued).

	Page		Page
Snow, No. 2	282	Steamed Indian	271
Snow blancmange	283	Steamed Indian and apple	271
Sponge	273	Steamed Indian berry	271
Sponge apple	263	Tapioca	278
Steamed apple	260	Tapioca prune	264
Steamed apple dumplings	262	Tapioca raspberry	264
Steamed batter	268	Turkish	270
Steamed black	267	Wayne	270

PUDDING SAUCES.

Cinnamon	286	Golden	287
Clear	286	Hot cream	288
Clear lemon	286	Italian	287
Creamy	284	Molasses	285
Egg	285	Nutmeg	286
Foaming	284	Vinegar	285
Fruit	285	Wine	284

SWEETS.

Apricot ice	299	Orange jelly	294
Baked cup custards	290	Orange sherbet	298
Blackberry jelly	294	Peach ice	299
Blancmange, chocolate	292	Peach ice cream	297
Blancmange, moss	292	Pistachio ice cream	297
Blancmange, sea moss farina	292	Raspberry jelly	294
Chocolate ice cream	297	Rennet custard	290
Cider jelly	293	Sea moss farina blancmange	292
Coffee jelly	294	Slip	291
Cup custards, baked	290	Soft custard	289
Cup custards, steamed	290	Steamed cup custards	290
Custard, soft	289	Strawberry Bavarian cream	291
Directions for freezing	295	Strawberry ice cream	297
Lemon jelly	293	Strawberry jelly	294
Lemon sherbet	298	Tapioca custard	290
Milk sherbet	298	Vanilla ice cream	296
Moss blancmange	292	Wine jelly	293

BEVERAGES.

Boiled coffee	302	Cocoa shells and nibs	306
Breakfast cocoa	304	Coffee	301
Broma	304	Filtered coffee	302
Chocolate	304	Lemonade	306
Cocoa	304	Tea	300

PRESERVES AND PICKLES.

	Page		Page
Blackberry jam	314	Pear marmalade	315
Canadian tomato pickle	320	Pears, preserved	308
Canned rhubarb	314	Piccalilli	323
Canned tomatoes	322	Pickle, tomato	320
Canning fruits	311	Pickles, cucumber	318
Catsup, tomato	321	Pineapple, preserved	310
Covering jellies	316	Pineapple, uncooked, preserved	310
Crab apples	308	Preserved peaches	307
Crab apple jelly	318	Preserved pears	308
Crab apple, spiced	323	Preserved pineapple	310
Cucumber pickles	318	Preserved uncooked pineapple	310
Currant and raisin jam	315	Preserved plums	309
Currant jelly	316	Preserved quinces	309
Currant jelly, No. 2	317	Pulp of fruit, what to do with it	307
Currants, spiced	322	Quality of the fruit	307
Different fruits need different treatment	312	Raspberry jam	314
		Rhubarb, canned	314
Filling the jars	312	Small fruits, how to can	313
Governor's sauce	321	Spiced crab apple	323
Grape preserve	309	Spiced currants	322
Jam, blackberry	314	Sun cooked strawberries	311
Jam, raisin and currant	315	Sweet cucumber pickles	319
Jam, raspberry	314	Tomatoes, canned	322
Jellies	315	Tomato catsup	321
Jelly, currant	316	Tomato pickle	320
Other jellies	318	What to do with fruit pulp	307
Peaches, preserved	307		

FOR THOSE WHO LIVE ON FARMS.

	Page		Page
INTRODUCTION	324	Jowl, to cook	329
Bacon, to cure breakfast	328	Lard, how to render	320
Butter making	335	Milk, care of	334
Cheese, cottage	335	Mutton, corned shoulder of	326
Cheese, hogs' head	330	Pickle for any kind of meat	326
Chine and jowl, to cure	328	Pickle for tongues	326
Chine pillau	329	Pigs' feet	332
Corned shoulder of mutton	326	Pillau, chine	329
Corning, how to prepare meat for	325	Rennet, essence of	333
		Rennet, to preserve	332
Cottage cheese	335	Rennet wine	333
Cream, care of	334	Sausage meat	328
Dairy, the	334	Sausage meat, English	328
English sausage meat	328	Scrapple	331
Essence of rennet	333	Soused tripe	332
Hams, to cure	327	Tongues, pickle for	326
Hogs' head cheese	330	Tripe	332
Jowl and chine, to cure	328	Wine, rennet	333

INDEX. 403

CARE OF THE SICK.

	Page		Page
Introduction	338	Lemonade, moss	349
Apple water	348	Lime water	351
Arrowroot gruel	347	Milk punch	347
Barley water	348	Moss lemonade	349
Bathing	339	Mutton broth	341
Beef juice	345	Mutton custard	343
Beef tea	344	Neuralgia, to relieve	340
Broth, mutton	341	Oatmeal gruel	346
Camphorated oil	351	Oyster roast	343
Cleanliness and ventilation	329	Oysters roasted in the shell	343
Cold in the head, remedy for	351	Oysters, steamed	343
Cracked ice, to keep	341	Prunes, senna	350
Cracker gruel	347	Punch, milk	347
Crust coffee	349	Raw beef sandwiches	345
Custard, mutton	343	Restorative jelly	350
Eggnog	348	Rice water	348
Egg tea	349	Roast oysters	343
Flour gruel	346	Roasted oysters, in the shell	343
For a cold in the head	351	Round steak	345
Gargle for a sore throat	351	Sandwiches, raw beef	345
Gruel, arrowroot	347	Senna prunes	350
Gruel, cracker	347	Sore throat, a gargle for	351
Gruel, flour	346	Steak, round	345
Gruel, Indian meal	346	Steamed oysters	343
Gruel, oatmeal	346	Tea, beef	344
Ice, cracked, to keep	341	Tea, egg	349
Ice, to break in a sick room	341	Turpentine applications	340
Indian meal gruel	346	Ventilation and cleanliness	339
Jelly, restorative	350	Wine whey	349

WHEN CLEANING HOUSE.

	Page		Page
Introduction	352	Kitchen, pantry, and closets	359
Carpets, laying the	357	Rooms on the first floor	358
Carpets, taking up and cleaning	355	Sweeping	356
Cleaning the cellar	353	System absolutely necessary	352
Dusting	356	Washing painted surfaces	356
From cellar to attic	354	Whitewashing, importance of	354

ODD BITS OF USEFUL KNOWLEDGE.

	Page		Page
A word regarding stains	371	Ants, how to drive away	387
About whipping cream	364	Bouquet of sweet herbs, how to make	367
Acids, what to do if they are spilled	377	Brass, how to clean	383
Alcohol for grass stains	376	Bread, to freshen	367

ODD BITS OF USEFUL KNOWLEDGE (*continued*).

	Page		Page
Bread crumbs, how to prepare	365	Hands, the care of	387
Breading articles for frying	365	Heat of the oven, how to test	386
Brightening leather furniture	379	Herbs, sweet, making a bouquet of	367
Brushes, to clean	381		
Burning accidents, what to do in case of	368	How to prepare bread crumbs	365
		Iron and earthen ware, to temper	367
Cake, to freshen	367		
Care of straw matting	381	Iron rust, the best way to remove	374
Care of the hands	387		
Cement for china	384	Javelle water, how to make	377
Chandeliers, keeping flies from	387	Kid, to prevent from cracking	385
Chimney, what to do when it is cold	385	Leather furniture, to brighten	379
		Marble, removing stains from	373
Cleaning brass	383	Matting, care of	381
Cleaning chamois skins	381	Measures, equivalents of, in weight	389
Cleaning dress silks and ribbons	380		
Cleaning fluid, a good	378	Mending breaks in plaster	383
Coffee, tea, or wine stains on linen	374	Meringue, to prevent from falling	367
Cold cream	388	Mildewed clothes, treatment of	374
Colors, restoring	377	Muriatic acid for stains on porcelain	376
Conveniences when sweeping	383		
Cream, about whipping	364	Naphtha, use of, in the household	369
Crumbs, how to prepare	365		
Cupfuls, half-pints, and gills	388	Oil, value of a drop of	385
Driving away ants	387	Onions, getting rid of the odor of	366
Equivalents of measures in weight	389		
		Onion juice, ways to get	366
Flies, to keep away from chandeliers	387	Oven heat, testing with paper	386
		Oven thermometers	386
Flour, difference in various brands	361	Paint, to remove	376
		Paper, soiled, how to clean	378, 379
Flour paste	368	Paste, flour	368
Fruit stains, treatment of	373	Pitch and tar, to remove	375
Frying, breading articles for	365	Plaster, mending breaks in	383
Furniture, to remove stains from	382	Points of difference in various brands of flour	361
Getting rid of the odor of onions	366	Porcelain, stains on, how to remove	376
Grass stains, alcohol for	376		
Grease spots on wall paper, treatment of	378	Preventing a meringue from falling	367
Grease spots, to remove	371	Preventing silks and woollens from turning yellow	380
Grease, to take from wood and stone	372		
		Raisins, how to stone	366
Handles of knives and forks, how to fasten	384	Removing blood stains	375
		Removing ink stains	376

INDEX. 405

ODD BITS OF USEFUL KNOWLEDGE (*continued*).

	Page		Page
Removing iron rust	374	To make Javelle water	377
Removing sewing-machine oil stains	375	To prevent kid from cracking	385
		To remove grease spots	371
Removing stains from marble	373	To remove paint	376
Restoring colors	377	To remove pitch and tar	375
Ridding the house of water bugs	386	To remove white stains from furniture	382
Silk goods, to keep from turning yellow	380	To take grease from wood and stone	372
Soiled paper, stale bread for cleaning	379	To temper iron and earthen ware	367
Stains, a word regarding	371	Use of naphtha in the household	369
Stains, fruit, treatment of	373		
Stains on linen, — coffee, tea, or wine	374	Value of a drop of oil	385
		Various brands of flour, points of difference in	361
Stains on porcelain, muriatic acid for	376	Wall paper, treatment of grease spots on	378
Stains, removing ink	376		
Stale bread for cleaning soiled paper	379	Wall paper, two ways to repair	379
		Water bugs, ridding the house of	386
Stoning raisins in an easy manner	366	Ways to get onion juice	366
Straw matting, care of	381	What to do when burning accidents occur	368
Sweeping, conveniences to use when	383	What to do when the chimney is cold	385
Sweet herbs, making a bouquet of	367		
Tar, how to remove	375	When and why soda, cream of tartar, and baking powders are used	363
Testing the oven heat with paper	386		
Thermometers, oven	386	When acids are spilled	377
To clean brushes	381	When clothes become mildewed	374
To clean woods in natural finish	382	Woollen goods, to keep from turning yellow	380
To freshen bread and cake	367		

www.ingramcontent.com/pod-product-compliance
Lightning Source LLC
Chambersburg PA
CBHW022115290426
44112CB00008B/676